P.O.W.

WARTIME LOG

OF

F/SGT T.D.GLENN

Lovingly compiled and recreated
by
Rosamund Glenn

A Wild Wolf Publication

Published by Wild Wolf Publishing in 2010

Copyright © 2010 T.P.Glenn

All rights reserved. No part of this book may be reproduced, stored in a retrieval system or transmitted in any form or by any means without the prior written permission of the publishers, except by a reviewer who may quote brief passages in a review to be printed by a newspaper, magazine or journal.

First print

This journal is a recreation of the wartime diary of F/Sgt T.D.Glenn. It has been recreated to look as close to the original text as possible, including layout and grammatical and other errors. The views in this publication do not necessarily reflect the views of Wild Wolf Publishing.

ISBN: 978-0-9563733-7-3

www.wildwolfpublishing.com

Introduction

Thomas Duke Glenn died in Feb 2000, leaving behind not only family and friends, but two very special books. They contain his daily writings, poems, sports results, songs and thoughts that were his life from the day he was shot down to the day he returned home to Newcastle upon Tyne.

They are written in pencil and, after typing them up, I am in awe that they and he survived. I have laughed and cried, and am privileged to have had this opportunity to share in this very special time with Tom. I hope you feel the same after reading it.

Special thanks go to Ryan Dudley (nephew of the pilot, Allan Hockley) for sharing his research (used on the back cover) and for his hard work in tracing the crew and their families. Thanks also to Rod (Tom's grandson) for his time, his input, but mostly for publishing the book.

The following, found in the front cover of the diary in Tom's handwriting on a piece of scrap paper, seems appropriate to add here.

```
        This is my scrap book, here I keep,
      My treasured thoughts come take a peep
      These things I've treasured, odds and ends
           To share them with my friends.
        Come sit beside me and we'll look
           And turn the pages of my book
          And dream a dream of happy things
     Of trees, and flowers, and stars, and wings
         And when the twilight shadows fall
           This is the sweetest thing of all
             To turn the pages of the years
             Remembering with happy tears
       The faithful love - the perfect friend
           The things we treasure to the end.
```

This book is dedicated to Tom Glenn, his pilot Allan Hockley and their mid upper gunner Ray Simpson. We salute you all.

Roz Glenn

Tom, left, front row. Allan Hockley, middle, front row.
The crew of BU-A "Able"

Fortress II, SR384, BU-A "Able" 24 May 1944

Introduction

Thomas Duke Glenn died in Feb 2000, leaving behind not only family and friends, but two very special books. They contain his daily writings, poems, sports results, songs and thoughts that were his life from the day he was shot down to the day he returned home to Newcastle upon Tyne.

They are written in pencil and, after typing them up, I am in awe that they and he survived. I have laughed and cried, and am privileged to have had this opportunity to share in this very special time with Tom. I hope you feel the same after reading it.

Special thanks go to Ryan Dudley (nephew of the pilot, Allan Hockley) for sharing his research (used on the back cover) and for his hard work in tracing the crew and their families. Thanks also to Rod (Tom's grandson) for his time, his input, but mostly for publishing the book.

The following, found in the front cover of the diary in Tom's handwriting on a piece of scrap paper, seems appropriate to add here.

```
        This is my scrap book, here I keep,
        My treasured thoughts come take a peep
     These things I've treasured, odds and ends
            To share them with my friends.
          Come sit beside me and we'll look
              And turn the pages of my book
            And dream a dream of happy things
      Of trees, and flowers, and stars, and wings
           And when the twilight shadows fall
              This is the sweetest thing of all
               To turn the pages of the years
                Remembering with happy tears
        The faithful love - the perfect friend
             The things we treasure to the end.
```

This book is dedicated to Tom Glenn, his pilot Allan Hockley and their mid upper gunner Ray Simpson. We salute you all.

Roz Glenn

Tom, left, front row. Allan Hockley, middle, front row.
The crew of BU-A "Able"

Fortress II, SR384, BU-A "Able" 24 May 1944

Foreword

The POW diary of Flight Sergeant Thomas Duke "Tommy" Glenn is the written record of one man's experiences and observations; however it is also the collective memory of more than 232,000 allied prisoners of war who were detained in German camps between 1939 and 1945. It serves as a tribute to those young men who lost their lives flying over the skies of Europe and also to those who were fortunate enough to return home after years of captivity.

Ryan Dudley,
nephew of pilot, Allan Hockley.

We Will Remember Them

I HAD NO SHOES AND I MURMURED

UNTIL I SAW A MAN WHO HAD NO FEET

"TIME"

"WE TAKE NO NOTE OF TIME, BUT FROM ITS LOSS"
YOUNG

P. of W.

No. 18

KRIEGSGEFANGENLAGER DER LUFTWAFFE No 7.

Sagan/Schles

GERMANY

In Memoriam

P/o. Hockley, Alan James Noel.

> Our "Skipper" and Pilot, who gave his life, so that we may live, remaining at the control of the aircraft, thus allowing all but one of us to parachute to safety.
> He was a native of Sydney Australia, aged 26, who was always tolerant, generous, sporting and certainly one of the best pilots in the R.A.F. or R.A.A.F.

Sgt. Simpson, Raymond. "Ray" to us.

> Our mid-upper gunner, a native of Kings Lynn, Norfolk, age 20. He was always very keen, happy and generous and a good-hearted lad to get along with.

R.I.P

A Letter to Saint Peter

Let them in Peter, they are very tired
Give them the couches where the angels sleep.
Let them wake whole again to new dawns fired with sun not war.
And may their peace be deep
Remember where their broken bodies lie….
And give them things they like. Let them make noise
God knows how young they were to have to die
Give swing bands, not gold harps to these our boys.
Give them love, Peter – they have had no time –
Girls sweet as meadow wind, with flowering hair.
They should have trees and bird song, hills to climb –
The taste of summer in a ripened pear.
Tell them how they are missed, say not to fear,
It's going to be all right with us done here.

                              Believed original from "American Mercury"

Scanned from the diary

HONI SOIT QUI MAL Y PENSE

THIS BOOK BELONGS TO

1516970 F/SGT GLENN. T.D

KRIEGSGEFANGENENLAGER DER LUFTWAFFE NR.7.

——————— X ———————

HOME: 2, LANSDOWNE GARDENS

NEWCASTLE-ON-TYNE.2.

NIL DESPERANDUM

FORWARD

WHAT TIME I AM AFRAID, I WILL TRUST IN THEE. IN GOD I
WILL PRAISE HIS WORD, IN GOD I HAVE PUT MY TRUST; I
WILL NOT FEAR WHAT FLESH CAN DO UNTO ME.
PSALM 56.

"BEYOND THIS PLACE OF WRATH AND TEARS
LOOMS BUT THE HORRORS OF THE SHADE,
AND YET THE MENACE OF THE YEARS
FINDS AND SMALL FIND ME UNAFRAID.

IT MATTERS NOT HOW STRAIGHT THE GATE,
HOW CHARGED WITH PUNISHMENT WITH SCROLL,
I AM THE MASTER OF MY FATE;
I AM THE CAPTAIN OF MY SOLE."

THIS ABOVE ALL; TO THINE OWN SELF BE TRUE,
AND IT MUST FOLLOW AS THE NIGHT THE DAY,
THOU CANST NOT THEN BE FALSE TO ANY MAN, FAREWELL;
MY BLESSING SEASON THIS IN THEE!
HAMLET

HONESTY IS THE BEST POLICY

CONTENTS

FRONT PORTION	PAGE
MISCELLANEOUS	1 - 16
PERSONAL – ADDRESSES AND DATES OF OUTGOING MAIL	1
CAMP SONG	2
DATES OF INCOMING MAIL	3
OUR VERSION OF "BLESS EM ALL"	4
OCCUPANTS OF HUT 53	5
MY CREW	6
PAY DETAILS AND A NOTE OF BOOKS I'VE READ	7
PARCEL CONTENTS	8 – 9
CONTENTS OF AMERICAN GIFT CASE	10
CAMP OFFICIALS	12
CAMP EXCHANGE MARKET PRICES	14
INDEX TO DIARY PROPER	15

ADDRESSES

MISS JEAN COOPER
42, HINTON ROAD
GLOUCESTER.

H.A. GRIFFIN,
17, PRIORY AVE.,
CHINGFORD, ESSEX

MISS JEAN TAYLOR
475 LOBLEY HILL
GATESHEAD -ON-TYNE. 11.

MRS CADMAN
"ST AMI"
45 ORCHARD CLOSE
THORPE
NORWICH

R A HOLLINGWORTH
TUDOR LODGE   (NEW)
WESTFIELD (OLD)
GOSFORTH
NEWCASTLE UPON TYNE 3

R A . HOLLINGSWORTH
23 NORTHFIELD ROAD
GOSFORTH
N/C-ON-TYNE 3

MRS ASKEW
42 CASTLE DRIVE
PENRITH
CUMBERLAND

COLIN RICKABY
HARPER ADAMS COLLEGE
NEWPORT
SALOP

MRS COWIN
27 WORDSWORTH STREET
PENRITH
CUMBERLAND

B BALFOUR
30 RIPON GDNS
JESMOND
N/C-ON-TYNE 2

MRS SMART
197 BIRCHFIELD ROAD EAST
NORTHAMPTON

MISS JOAN PICKUP
9 GREENLEACH LANE
WORSLEY
MANCHESTER

Birthdays	
Father	16th September
Mother	11th April
Peter	14th April
Micky	30th April
Joan	12th May
Jean C	10th October
Jean T	22nd January
Jean K	14th November

DATES OF OUTGOING MAIL

B.B.C 16/11/44 P.C.//
MRS ASKEN 17/9/44P.C.// MRS SMART 16/10/44 XMAS P.C//PC.C 15/1/45
GRIFF 17/9/44 P.C // MRS COWIN 16/10/44 XMAS P.PC//
BOB 11/9/44 P.C.// MRS CAPMAN 11/10/44 XAMS LETTER//
21/2/45 P.C.//18/11/44P.C.//21/12/44P.C.//

HOME 3/6/44 P.C.//18/6/44 LETTER//2/7/44 LETTER//11/7/44 P.C. 25/7/44
DAD'S BIRTHDAY LETTER//3/8/44 P.C.//6/8/44 LETTER//18/8/44
LETTER//30/8/44 P.C.//11/9/44 LETTER//21/9/44 P.C.//1/10/44
LETTER//16/10/44 XMAS LETTER// 20/10/44 P.C. 30/10/44 LETTER//9/11/44
P.C.//16/11/44 LETTER//25/1/44 LETTER//5/12/44 LETTER//12/12/44
LETTER//23/12/44 P.C.//1/1/45 LETTER//10/1/45 P.CP//15/2/45
P.CP//17/2/45/LETTER//24/2/45 LETTER//6/3/45 LETTER//19/3/45
LETTER//4/4/45 LETTER//20/4/45 P.CP//3/5/45P.C.//
J. TAYLOR 3/1/45//17/2/45//P.CP3/4/45//3/5/45 P.CP//
J. PICKUP 1/1/45P.CP//
J.COOPER 11/12/44 P.CP//12/1/45P.CP//22/2/45//20/4/45P.CP
B.BALFOUR 11/12/44/P.C.//
C RICKABY 5/12/44P.CP//
EVENING CHRONICLE 11/9/44 LETTER//
CATERPILLAR CLUB 19/8/44 P.C.
JEAN K. 3/8/44 P.C (BIRTHDAY)//
MICKY 7/3/45P.CP//
JEAN T. 18/6/44 P.C.11/7/44 P.CP//3/8/44 P.C.//27/8/44 P.C.//1/10/44 P.C.//
16/10/44 P.C XMAS//8/11/44 P.C.//2/12/44 P.C. BIRTHDAY//
JEAN C. 18/6/44P.C.//12/7/44 P.C.//3/8/44 P.C. BIRTHDAY) // 30/8/44P.C.
//1/10/44 P.C.//17/10/44 P.C. XMAS//16/11/44 P.C.

2   Camp Song
<u>(to the tune of "You are My Sunshine")</u>

THE OTHER NIGHT, BOYS, WHILE WE WERE FLYING
THE NIGHT WAS DARK AND BLACK AS PITCH;
UP CAME THE FLAK BURSTS AND THEN THE FIGHTERS
AND OUR POOR KITE WE HAD TO DITCH.
THEN CAME THE "JERRIES" AND WE WERE CAPTURED
AND TAKEN TO THE LOCAL JAIL.
WE HAD A FEED THERE AND I ASSURE YOU
THE BREAD WAS SCARCE AND BLACK AND STALE –
EARLY NEXT MORNING WHEN WE AWOKE, BOYS,
THEY TOOK US TO THE GESTAPO.
WE GOT NO FOOD OR CIGARETTES, BOYS –
FOR TO THEIR QUERIES WE ANSWERED NO!
AFTER THIS COURSE OF HUMAN KINDNESS,
WE WENT TO DULAGLUFT HOTEL,
THE ROOMS WERE SINGLE THE FOOD WAS LOUSY
AND THERE WAS A 'NASTY' SMELL.
INTERROGATION HAS UNSUCCESSFULLY, THEY ONLY KEPT
US FOR A WEEK.
NAME, RANK AND NUMBER WAS ALL WE GAVE THEM,
AFTER THAT WE WOULD NOT SPEAK;
AND THE CLOUDS TURNED INTO SUNSHINE
THE RED CROSS PARCELS CAME OUR WAY.

SO IN THE CAMP WE LIVE IN COMFORT!
WAITING FOR THE FREEDOM DAY
THE OTHER NIGHT, DEAR, AS I LAY DREAMING,
I DREAMT OF YOU SO FAR WAY;

BUT WHEN THE DAY COMES AND WE ARE FREE, DEAR,
I'LL COME BACK HOME, WITH YOU, TO STAY.

FREEDOM IS SUNSHINE, THE ONLY SUNSHINE,
IT MAKES US HAPPY, IT MAKES US GAY,
DESPITE THE HARDSHIPS, THERE'S CONSOLATION
THAT OUR MATES WILL WIN THE DAY.

––––––––––––––– X –––––––––––––––

DATES OF INCOMING MAIL

MRS CADMAN 16/10/44 LETTER//
D RICKERBY 19/10/44 LETTER//
HOME. 19/10/44 (2) LETTERS //2/11/44//11/12/44 (3) //30/12/44 (3)//
KEN HETHERINGOTN 31/12/44//
MR & MRS RIDE 28/10/44//
HELEN SMITH 28/10/44//
BOB HOLINGSWORTH 2/11/44//11/12/44//
JEAN TAYLOR 2/11/44//
MICKY GLENN 31/12/44 (2)//
COLIN RICKERBY 10/11/44//
JEAN COOPER 11/12/44//2/1/45//
BETTY BALFOUR 11/12/44//
JEAN PICKUP 31/12/44//
MRS SMART 30/12/44 (2)//

4   OUR VERSION OF "BLESS 'EM ALL"

THERE'S A FOUR ENGINED BOMBER
JUST LEAVING ITS BASE
BOUND FOR ALIEN SHORE;
HEAVILY LADEN WITH 'COOKIES' AND SUCH
PRESENTS TO EVEN THE SCORE;
THERE'S MANY A FLAK BATTERY THROWING UP HELL
THERE'S MANY A FIGHTER AS WELL.
BUT THE UNLUCKY 'BOD' THAT GETS
CAUGHT THE POOR SOD
SHOUTS 'REACH FOR YOUR PARACHUTES ALL'

BLESS 'EM ALL, BLESS 'EM ALL,
THE FLAK BATTERIES, FIGHTERS AND ALL
BLESS ALL THE AGs AND BOMB AIMERS TOO
BLESS ALL THE PILOTS AND THE REST OF THE CREW
FOR WE'RE SAYING GOOD-BYE TO THEM ALL
AS BACK TO THE ESCAPE HATCH WE CRAWL
WE HAVEN'T A NOTION
IF WE'RE ON THE OCEAN
SO CHEER UP ME LADS
LET US FALL!

OCCUPANTS OF HUT 53

DIVISION II

P.O.W NO		
18	F/SGT. GLENN, NAVIGATOR, 21 (1939-43 STAR)	NEWCASTLE-ON-TYNE
36	F/SGT. LYALL, WIRELESS OPERATOR, 21 (1939-43 STAR)	AUSTRALIA
23	F/SGT. GUNDY, BOMB-AIMER, 23 (1939-43 STAR)	NEW ZEALAND
49	F/SGT RODGERS, WIRELESS OPERATOR, 24 (D.F.M 1939-43 STAR)	CASTLEFORD
24	SGT HALLETT, ENGINEER, 21 (1939-43 STAR)	ANDOVER
35	SGT LOVATT, REAR GUNNER, 20 (1939-43 STAR)	SOUTH SHIELDS

——————— X ———————

TOMMY LYALL, MARRIED ONLY 18 DAYS AND 21 ONLY TWO DAYS WHEN WE WERE SHOT DOWN. BILL HALLETT 24 DAYS OVER 21 WHEN WE WERE SHOT DOWN. "RODG" (F/SGT RODGERS) MARRIED ONE YEAR ON JULY 31ST THIS YEAR. BILL HALLETT AND NICK LOVATT WERE TO HAVE BEEN MARRIED ON THEIR NEXT LEAVE. BOB GUNDY AND I HAD NO SUCH 'TIES' -------ONLY WORRIES!!

6 MY CREW

P/O HOCKLEY PILOT "SKIPPER" FROM SYDNEY, AUSTRALIA

F/SGT GLENN NAVIGATOR "TOMMY" FROM NEWCASTLE-ON-TYNE

F/SGT GUNDY BOMB-AIMER "BOB" FROM AUCKLAND. N Z

F/SGT LYALL W/OPERATOR "TOM" FROM NEWCASTLE, AUSTRALIA

SGT. HALLETT ENGINEER "BILL" FROM ANDOVER, HANTS

SGT LOVATT REAR GUNNER "NICK" FROM SOUTH SHIELDS CO DURHAM

SGT SIMPSON MID-UPPER GUNNER "RAY" FROM KINGS LYNN NORFOLK

SGT McCUTCHAN WAIST-GUNNER "JIM" FROM EDMONTON ALBERTA CANADA

SGT LLOYD W/OPERATOR "BOB" FROM CHESTER

PAY AND ALLOTMENT (TO COME!)
F/S 16/6 PER DAY
W/O 19/= PER DAY

DATE	EXTRA (RISE)	CASH	ALLOTMENT
25/5/44	8-0-0	7-2-0	1-15-0
8/6/44	NOTIFICATION	7-2-0	1-15-0
22/6/44	TO PAY A/CS	7-2-0	1-15-0
6/7/44	TO SEND £100	7-2-0	1-15-0
20/7/44	HOME SENT	7-2-0	1-15-0
3/8/44	18/11/44	7-2-0	1-15-0
17/8/44		7-2-0	1-15-0
31/8/44		7-2-0	1-15-0
14/9/44	5=0	7-2-0	1-15-0
28/9/44	5=0	7-2-0	1-15-0
12/10/44	5=0	7-2-0	1-15-0
26/10/44	5=0	7-2-0	1-15-0
9/11/44	5=0	7-2-0	1-15-0
23/11/44	5=0	7-2-0	1-15-0
7/12/44	5=0	7-2-0	1-15-0
21/12/44	5=0	7-2-0	1-15-0
4/1/45	5=0	7-2-0	1-15-0

STATEMENT OF A/C APPLIED FOR ON 22/12/44

<u>BOOKS I'VE READ</u>

"THE VALLEY OF THE GIANTS"
"CAPTAIN PAUL JONES"
"SHORT STORIES" BY MAUPASSANTE
"MISS TIVERTIINS SHIPWRECK"
"BUSMAN'S HONEYMOON"
"WHILE ROME BURNS" BY ALEXANDER WOOLCOTT
"READ 'EM AND WEEP"
"COWBOY SONGS"
"DORIS MOORE" BY GUY THORNE
"THE THURSDAY TURKEY MURDERS"
"WINGS ON MY FEET" BY SONJA HENIE
"MAN OF PROPERTY" BY JOHN GALSWORTHY
"THIS ABOVE ALL"   "MY SHADOW AS I PASS"
"LOVE AT FIRST FLIGHT"   "LOST FIELDS"
"THE MURDER AT CROME HOUSE" "GENERAL KNOWLEDGE"
"DR. THORNE" BY TROLLOPPE   "ACCOUNTANCY AS A CAREER"
"POLITICAL ECONOMY"

PARCEL CONTENTS

<u>SCOTCH</u>
1 TIN OF MEAT (VARIED) – STEAK & KIDNEY PIE ETC
1 TIN OF BACON OR PORK SAUSAGES
2 PKTS OF BISCUITS (34)
1 TIN SYRUP
1 TIN OF CONDENSED MILK
1 TIN OF MEAT ROLL
1 TIN ROLLED OATS
1 PCKT OF SWEETS (8)
1 BAR OF CHOCOLATE (¼LB)
1 PCKT OF DRIED FRUIT (PRUNES, APRICOTS OR RAISONS)
1 PCKT OF SUGAR (¼ LB)
1 TIN OF MARGARINE OR BUTTER (½LB)
1 TIN OF CONDENSED CHEESE
1 PCKT OF TEA (¼LB)
1 TIN OF COCOA (¼LB)
1 TIN OF POWDERED EGG
1 BAR OF SOAP
1 TIN OF FISH (SALMON OR PILCHARDS)

ADDITIONAL: 50 CIGARETTES – CRAVEN 'A'

———————   ———————

<u>ENGLISH</u>
1 TIN OF MEAT (VARIED)
1 TIN OF CONDENSED MILK
1 TIN OF JAM (½LB)
1 PCKT OF BISCUITS (13)
1 PCKT OF SUGAR (¼LB)

A LITTLE OF WHAT YOU FANCY DOES YOU GOOD!!

1 TIN OF MEAT ROLL
1 TIN OF PUDDING (USUALLY APPLE OR MIXED FRUIT)
1 TIN OF ROLLED OATS
1 MIXED VEGETABLES
1 TIN OF CONDENSED CHEESE (⅛ LB)
1 TIN OF MARGARINE (½ LB)
1 BAR OF CHOCOLATE (¼ LB)
1 PCKT OF TEA (¼ LB)
1 TIN OF COCOA (¼ LB)
1 TIN OF POWDERED EGG
1 BAR OF SOAP
1 TIN OF SALT, MUSTARD OR PEPPER
1 TIN OF FISH (SALMON OR PILCHARDS)

ADDITIONAL: 50 CIGARETTES – CRAVEN A

———————————— X ————————————

AMERICAN

1 TIN OF BULLY BEEF
1 TIN OF SPAM
1 PCKT OF BISCUITS (12)
1 TIN OF KLIM (POWERED MILK)
1 BOX OF SUGAR CUBES
1 TIN OF JAM (SMALL)
1 TIN OF MEAT PASTE
100 CIGARETTES (AMERICAN)
1 TIN OF MARGARINE (1LB)
1 PCKT OF CHEESE (½ LB)
1 PCKT OF DRIED FRUIT
1 TIN OF SALMON

1 TIN OF COFFEE
1 BAR OF SOAP
2 BARS OF CHOCOLATE
   (¼ LB ea)

CONTENTS OF AMERICAN GIFT CASE RECEIVED AT WEZTLAR 2/6/44

1. 60 AMERICAN CIGARETTES (CHESTERFIELD)
2. VEST
3. 1 PR PANTS
4. PRS COTTON SOCKS
5. HANDKERCHIEFS
6. 1 PR PYJAMAS
7. 2 TOWELS
8. 1 PR SLIPPERS
9. 1 PIPE
10. 2 PACKETS OF TABACCO (VELVET & GRAINGER)
11. 1 PACKET OF PIPE CLEANERS
12. 2 PACKETS OF CIGARETTE PAPERS
13. 6 TABLETS OF SOAP
14. 1 TUBE OF TOOTHPASTE
15. 1 TOOTHBRUSH AND CASE
16. 1 COMB AND CASE
17. 1 HAIRBRUSH
18. 4 PACKETS OF RAZOR BLADES (20) GILLETTE
19. 1 RAZOR
20. 1 STICK OF SHAVING SOAP
21. 1 BOX CASCARA TABLETS
22. 1 BOX VITAMIN TABLETS (100)
23. 10 PACKETS OF CHICLETS (CHEWING GUM)
24. HOUSEWIFE
25. 1 JERSEY
26. 2 BARS OF WASHING SOAP
27. 2 PRS SHOELACES
28. 1 PACKET OF BUTTONS (CONFISCATED BY JERRY)
29. BOX OF ELASTOPLAST
30. 1 TIN OF SHOE POLISH AND RAG

RIGHTEOUSNESS EXALTETH A NATION

"BETWEEN THE IDEA
AND THE REALITY;
BETWEEN THE MOTION
AND THE ACT,
FALLS THE SHADOW"
— T.S. ELIOT

A WARTIME LOG

FOR

BRITISH PRISONERS

"SO HERE I'LL WATCH THE NIGHT AND WAIT
TO SEE THE MORNING SHINE;
WHEN HE WILL HEAR THE STROKE OF EIGHT
AND NOT THE STROKE OF NINE"
— A.E. HOUSMAN

Gift from
THE WAR PRISONERS' AID OF THE Y.M.C.A.
37, Quai Wilson
GENEVA - SWITZERLAND

12 CAMP OFFICIALS

CAMP LEADER: F/SGT THOMPSON
    (S.S.M. LLOYD TAKEN AWAY BY THE GERMANS)
ASS. CAMP-LEADER: W/O LANE
ADJUTANT: F/SGT WALKTY
    (SGT. HILL TAKEN AWAY BY THE GERMANS)
MAN-OF CONFIDENCE: F/SGT GREEN
QUARTERMASTER: W/O BISHOP
MESSING COMMITTEE: W/O BISHOP
                      F/SGT GOODALL
                      SGT STEVENSON
ENTERTAINMENTS   F/SGT STURGES
                      SGT LYNCH
RED+PARCEL DIS   F/SGT VIDDLER
DEBATING SOCIETY   SGT STEVENSON   F/SGT COPE
                      F/SGT GRIFFITHS SGT NORRIS
                      F/SGT GLENN   F/SGT BIRD

PARCEL CHIEF: SGT PEARCE
CAMP EDITOR: F/SGT SINDALL
SPORTS: SGT RAY
LIBRARIAN: F/SGT WOODWARD
CHURCH LEADER: SGT PARKER
MEDICAL ORDERLIES: F/SGT KING
                      F/SGT ELLIS
STORES: F/SGT BROWN
LAUNDRY CHIEF: SGT CROSS

LAUGH, AND THE WORLD LAUGHS WITH YOU; 13
CRY, AND YOU CRY ALONE.

THIS BOOK BELONGS TO

1516970 F/SGT GLENN, T.D. (18L7)

KRIEGSGEFANGENENLAGER DER LUFTRWAFFE
                                    NR 7

HOME: 2, LANDSDOWNE GARDENS
        JESMOND,
   NEWCASTLE-ON-TYNE, 2

BANKAU
NR KREUTZBERG,
SAGAN/SCHLES,
GERMANY

14   MARKET PRICES
(LIABLE TO FLUCTUATION!)

```
1 BAR OF CHOCOLATE            35 CIGARETTES
1 PCKT OF TABACCO             50    "
1 PCKT OF CHEWING GUM         20    "
1 TIN OF SYRUP                10    "
1 TIN OF JAM (AMERICAN)       10    "
   "    "     " (ENGLISH)     20    "
1 TIN OF BISCUITS             20    "
1 PCK SUGAR (ENGLISH)         20    "
   "    "   (AMERICAN)        20    "
1 PCK CHEESE (    "    )      20    "
   "    "     (ENGLISH)       15    "
1 PCKT DRIED FRUIT            15    "
SALT, PEPPER, MUSTARD         15    "       EA(!)
1 TIN OF CONDENSED MILK (OR KLIM) 35 "
```

---------------------X------------------------

```
RAZOR BLADES              5 CIGARETTES EACH
PIPES                     50    "       "
TOOTHPASTE                35    "       "
RAZOR                     50    "       "
WATCH (LATEST OFFER!)     800   "       "
SLIPPERS                  50    "       "
COMB                      50    "       "
TOOTHPASTE                50    "       "
```

<u>"ELEGANTES" NOT ACCEPTED!</u>

STONE WALLS DO NOT A PRISON MAKE; NOT IRON BARS A CAGE

CONTENTS

	Page
DAY TO DAY DIARY	
24-5-44 to 23-9-44	1 – 54 (o)
(CONTD) 23-9-44 to 14-11-44	84 – 93
(CONTD) 14-11-44 TO 11-12-44	54(r) - 54(s)
VIGNETTES OF PRISON LIFE	54 (p -q)
OCCUPANTS OF 42/12	54 (t)
PLAN OF NEW CAMP	54(u)
"HUT 53 AT ITS BEST"	54(v)
CAMP PERSONALITIES	54(w-x)
SOME OF THE BOYS	55-61
PALS ADDRESSES	62-63
"ODDS AND ENDS"	64-83
THE NORTH EASTERN CLUB	94-97
"THE INVASION"	98-100
SPORTS RESULTS	101-106
MISCELLANEOUS	107 – 111
LABELS, NOTES – SOUVENIRS "THOSE WE HAVE LOVED"	111 - END

16

<u>The Gift of Belief</u> – a very great gift, seeing what a man believes is and will be true for him, however false it may prove to others.

He who believes nothing, sows nothing and therefore reaps nothing – good or ill.

---x---

CLUBS FORMED ON THE CAMP	NEW CLUBS
LANCASHIRE AND DISTRICT	YORKSHIRE CLUB
LONDON	EASTERN COUNTIES CLUB
NORTH-EASTERN	BOAT CLUB
SOUTH-WESTERN	BELLEROPHON CLUB
CANADIAN	{ST. ANDREWS SOCIETY
AUSTRALIAN	{(SCOTTISH CLUB)
MIDLANDS	IRISH CLUB
WELSH	
GLIDER PILOTS	

---X---

"CHANCE"

CHANCE WILL NOT DO THE WORK – CHANCE SENDS THE BREEZE;
BUT IF THE PILOT SLUMBER AT THE HELM,
THE VERY WIND THAT WAFTS US TOWARDS THE POST
MAY DASH US ON THE SHELVES –
THE STEERMAN'S PART IS VIGILANCE
BE IT ROUGH OR SMOOTH.

DAY TO DAY DIARY

1

24/5/44 TOOK OFF FROM BASE FOR THE LAST TIME. WE FOUND A RAT IN THE DISPERSAL BEFORE GETTING IN THE KITE AND KILLED IT. FROM THEN ON IT SEEMED AS THOUGH A CLOUD ENVELOPED THE CREW!

25/5/44 SHOT DOWN EARLY MORNING. TERRIBLE FEELING OF UTTER LONELINESS AS I FLOATED DOWN IN PARACHUTE. WAS HIT UNDER CHIN AND THEN REALISED I HAD LANDED IN WATER. SWAM TO A PARTLY SUBMERGED HAYSTACK AFTER PRESSING 'CHUTE IN TO MUD UNDER WATER. AT DAWN SWAM TO SUBMERGED BUILDINGS WHERE MUCH TO MY RELIEF CAME ACROSS BOB. MADE OURSELVES AS COMFORTABLE AS POSSIBLE DRIED THE TOBACCO OF SOME CIGS. THAT I HAD WITH ME AND MADE SOME OTHER CIGARETTES. THEY WERE GOOD TO US!!

2   A JOB WORTH DOING IS WORTH DOING WELL

WE HAD A HORLICKS TABLET EACH APPROXIMATELY EVERY FOUR HOURS FOR FOOD. WE HAD NOTHING TO DRINK. IN AFTERNOON WE SLEPT (OR TRIED TO WITH OUR THOUGHTS SO "HAYWIRE") AND IN EVENING MADE A RAFT, BUT IT WAS A FAILURE.

26/4/44 MADE ANOTHER RAFT, BUT ALSO A "DUD". REMADE IT AND IT FLOATED OK. A HEAVY SHOWER DURING MORNING ENABLED US TO GET A DRINK, BY USING A JAM-JAR TO COLLECT WATER DRIPPING FROM A ROKEN DRAIN PIPE. SUN CAME OUT LATER AND I SWAM OVER TO HAYSTACK TO RECOVER SOMETHING. UNSUCCESSFUL. PREPARED SOME CLOTHING ETC. FOR CROSSING TO DYKE AT DUSK. COMMENCED ATTEMPT AT ABOUT 8.00 P.M. WHEN PATROLS HAD FINISHED. HAD TO ABANDON RAFT AFTER COVERING A SHORT DISTANCE. CARRIED A VALISE OF CLOTHING AND LEFT THE REST. WE HALF WADED AND HALF SWAM ANOTHER 20 YARDS WITH STILL ANOTHER 150 TO GO, WHEN TWO DUTCHMEN SAW US FROM THE BANK. WE HAD BEEN WATCHING

THEM AND THEY APPEARED TO US TO BE OK. WE WERE BEGINNING TO FEEL COLD AND FATIGUED WITHOUT MENTIONING HUNGER. WE FINALLY WAVED TO THEM TO WHICH

3. A WISE MAN IS HIS OWN BEST ASSISTANT.

WE RECEIVED AN IMMEDIATE RESPONSE. THEY COMMENCED TO COME TO OUR AID IN A BOAT. WE COVERED ANOTHER 50 YDS. AND THEY JUST WAITED. THEY TOOK US OFF, DRIED OUR CLOTHES AND GAVE US PLENTY OF BREAD. WE WENT TO BED.

27/5/44 AFTER A LOVELY NIGHTS SLEEP, WE HAD TWO OUT (SOME 200 INHABITANTS) TO SEE US, GIVING US MANY 'V' SIGNS. WAITED IN THE GERMAN OUTPOST FOR CELL – ONE APIECE TO STAY THE NIGHT. SOME BREAD AND BLACK COFFEE CAME IN BEFORE DARK. I LAY ON MY BUNK AND AGAIN MY THOUGHTS WANDERED TO HOME, MY LAST LEAVE, MY PALS BACK AT CAMP AND THE WAY WE HAD BEEN DECEIVED. WHAT IS THE NEXT MOVE? AN AIR RAID ALARM

4 VARIETY IS THE SPICE OF LIFE

SOUNDED AMIDST MY THOUGHTS AND I OCCUPIED SOME OF MY TIME WATCHING THE GERMANS MANNING SOME LIGHT GUNS OPPOSITE. THEN CAME THE ALL-CLEAR AND EVENTUALLY SLEEP.

28/5/44 ROSE EARLY AND HAD A PIECE OF DRY BLACK BREAD FOR BREAKFAST. ALL DAY BOB AND I TRAVELLED BY TRAIN TO VENLO UNDER ESCORT, WHERE A BIG HOUSE HAD BEEN TAKEN OVER FOR TEMPORARY QUARTERS FOR PRISONERS OF WAR PRIOR TO GOING TO DULUG. RECEIVED A PLATE OF POTATO SOUP AND OUT 5.00PM, HAVING HAD NOTHING ON THE TRAIN. GOT A GLIMPSE OF SOME OF THE OTHER BOYS. LATER AN F/O JOINED US IN OUR ROOM AND WE JUST LAY CHATTING, 'RETIRED' EARLY TO FORGET OUR HUNGER!

29/5/44 ROSE EARLY FOR SOME MORE BLACK BREAD (AND MARG!) AND COFFEE. SPENT DAY CHATTERING AND LYING AROUND ON OUR 'BUNKS'. LOOKED OUT BETWEEN BRICK PILLARS THROUGH WINDOW TO THE DUTCH PEOPLE WATCHING US BELOW. EXCHANGED 'V' SIGNS!

WE LEARNT WE WERE ONLY THREE KILOS FROM THE DUTCH – GERMAN BORDER. BOB COULD SPEAK SOME DUTCH, SO WE ALWAYS KNEW THE TIME. HAD A WIZARD CHAT TO SOME OF THE BOYS. RETIRED TO BED AGAIN EARLY AS THERE WAS NOTHING ELSE TO DO.

5. PRACTICE WHAT YOU PREACH
30/5/44 WE'RE LEAVING TO-DAY - FOR THE UNBELIEVABLE DULAGLUFT. SOME 35 OF US LEFT ABOUT 11.00 AND TRAVELLED ALL DAY THROUGH THE RHINELAND, THE SCENERY OF WHICH WAS INDEED A SIGHT. WE WENT THROUGH THE RUHR, COLOGNE AND BOHN, SEEING COMPLETE DEVASTATION IN THESE AREAS BY LOOKING UNDER THE BLIND THAT WAS SUPPOSED TO BE KEPT COMPLETELY DRAWN. WE EVENTUALLY ARRIVED AT FRANKFURT, WHERE WE HAD A LONG WAIT ON THE STATION, AND WHERE, AFTER MUCH CLAMOURING THEY EVENTUALLY LET US HAVE A DRINK OF WATER. FRANKFURT WAS A CITY OF RUIN AND THEREFORE LITTLE WONDER THE CIVIL POPULATION WERE VERY HOSTILE, WHICH MADE US GLAD TO HAVE THE PROTECTION OF THE GUARDS! WE WERE GLAD WHEN WE WERE PUSHED INTO A TRAIN FOR OBERURSEL, OUR DESTINATION. ARRIVING THERE AT 9.00PM, WE REALISED HOW WEAK WE WERE WHEN WE HAD A 5 KILOS MARCH (APPROX 3 MILES) TO DO, TO THE 'HOTEL' ITSELF. THERE NINE OR TEN OF US BUNCHED TOGETHER WERE PUSHED INTO A SMALL CELL FOR THE NIGHT TO SLEEP AS BEST WE COULD. EVERYONE HAD AT LEAST TWO HOURS SLEEP UNDER THESE CONDITIONS! SOME STALE BREAD WAS FOUND LYING ON THE FLOOR, WHICH WE VERY SOON DEVOURED.

6. MORE THINGS ARE WROUGHT BY PRAYER
31/5/44 NEXT MORNING, ON A DRINK OF TASTELESS COFFEE, WE WERE SORTED, SEARCHED AND QUESTIONED AND THEN TAKEN OVER TO ANOTHER SECTION OF THE CAMP TO MANAGE AS BEST WE COULD ON DIRTY OVER-CROWDED HUTS. NEVERTHELESS WE HAD OUR FIRST SHOWER AND WASH, DRYING OURSELVES ON OUR VESTS AND SHORTS AND THEN

RINSING THEM OUT. WE QUEUED FOR HOURS FOR A SLICE OF BREAD AND SOME COFFEE, THEN WE OCCUPIED OUR TIME LOOKING OVER THE WALLS, ALL OVER WHICH WERE NAMES OF COMRADES WHO HAD PRECEDED US. I CAME ACROSS SOME OF MY PALS WHO I KNEW OF OLD, SOME OF THEM HAVING "R.I.P." AFTER THEIR NAMES. WE PLAYED CARDS – CHIEFLY A GAME KNOWN AS '500' – WHICH WE MADE OUT OF PIECES OF CARDBOARD AND WITH A BORROWED PENCIL. THAT NIGHT WE WENT TO BED EARLY AFTER THE EXPERIENCE OF THE PREVIOUS NIGHT.

<u>1/6/44</u> MOST OF THE DAY WAS SPENT QUEUING FOR WHAT LITTLE FOOD THERE WAS. IN ONE CORNER OF THE SMALL ENCLOSURE, WE FOUND SOME SMALL SHOOTS OF RHUBARB, WHICH, WHEN ONCE DISCOVERED, DID NOT REMAIN FOR LONG. THE SAME THING HAPPENED TO SOME STRAY MINT, WHICH SOME ENDEAVOURED TO DRY AND SMOKE! WE ALL RECEIVED A CIGARETTE AFTER 'DINNER'. WHAT A LUXURY! WE IDLED THE REST OF THE DAY AWAY TALKING AND PLAYING CARDS, SOME PLAYING DRAUGHTS WITH AN IMPROVISED BOARD.

7. THAN THIS WORLD DREAMS OF

<u>2/6/44</u> AN IMPROVEMENT IN BREAKFAST TO-DAY – BREAD, JAM AND COFFEE. SOME OF THE LADS LEFT THIS MORNING FOR A 'FITTING OUT' PLACE, AS IT WAS RUMOURED. CAN IT BE TRUE THAT WE ARE NOT GOING TO GET 'SOLITARY', AS SO MANY HAD HAD – SOME AS MUCH AS 30 DAYS? WE HOPED THAT IT WOULD BE OUR TURN NEXT TO LEAVE AND WE HOPED NOT IN VAIN FOR JUST BEFORE DINNER ANOTHER LIST WENT UP AND WE WERE LEAVING AT 1.00PM. WE HAD A 2½ HOURS JOURNEY BY A GAS-OPERATED 'UTILITY' BUS TO WESTLAR, WHICH WE WERE TOLD WAS A TRANSIT CAMP. THERE WE SAW OUR PALS WHO HAD LEFT US THIS MORNING, SMOKING, CHEERFUL AND WITH CASES UNDER THEIR ARM! THE RED CROSS WAS ON THE SCENE! WHAT EXCITEMENT! THE USUAL PROCEDURE OF BEING SEARCHED ETC. AND THEN WE WERE HANDED OUR CASES FULL OF CLOTHES, SOAP, CIGARETTES AND OTHER URGENT REQUIREMENTS. A SHOWER WITH TOWEL AND SOAP CAME

NEXT AND THEN TO THE ENCLOSURE FOR A MEAL AND OUR SLEEPING QUARTERS UNDER CANVAS. NEEDLESS TO SAY WE WERE SMOKING MOST OF THE TIME HAVING RECEIVED 60 CIGARETTES (AMERICAN) IN OUR CASES. AT NIGHT WE SPENT MOST OF THE TIME GOING
THROUGH OUR GIFT CASES OVER AND OVER AGAIN WITH MANY PRAISES FOR THE RED CROSS AND MANY OF US ON

8   A FRIEND IN NEED, IS A FRIEND INDEED
THE VERGE OF TEARS OF HAPPINESS. THAT NIGHT WE WERE GIVEN A CARD TO WRITE HOME AND WITH BORROWED PENCILS WE CAREFULLY WROTE IN AS MUCH AS WE COULD IN THE SMALL SPACE AVAILABLE. THAT NIGHT WE WENT TO BED HAPPIER THAN WE HAD BEEN FOR A LONG (TIME) AND TO MOST OF US WE HAD NEVER BEEN SO HAPPY.
3/6/44 TO-DAY WAS SPENT PLAYING BASEBALL, CARDS AND TALKING ABOUT OUR EXPERIENCES. THE FOOD HERE WAS VERY GOOD AND GENERALLY ENOUGH FOR OUR SHRUNK STOMACHS! THANKS AGAIN TO THE RED CROSS. WE WERE STILL AMAZED AT THE RED CROSS GIFTS OF THE DAY BEFORE. WE DID A LOT OF JOKING ABOUT THINGS AS THOUGH WE WERE BACK AT OUR OWN STATIONS. "ARE YOU GOING TO THE DANCE JOE?" "TO HELL WITH THE DANCE, LET'S HAVE SOME BEER" AND SO ON. EARLY EVENING A LIST WENT UP OF THOSE WHO WERE LEAVING THE NEXT DAY FOR A PERMANENT CAMP - A CAMP WHICH NOBODY ELSE HAD PREVIOUSLY BEEN SENT AS FAR AS THE STAFF KNEW – THIS BROUGHT SOME GROANS. SURE ENOUGH I WAS DOWN AND SO WERE MY PALS. WE WERE SORRY IN A WAY TO BE LEAVING, BUT AT LEAST WE WERE GOING SOME WHERE TO SETTLE DOWN – WE HOPED! WE RETIRED TO OUR TENTS ON ORDERS AT 9.00 IN HIGH SPIRITS.
4/6/44 BREAKFAST WENT DOWN WELL – SALMON, BREAD AND BUTTER, JAM AND COFFEE – ALL EXCEPT THE BREAD, OUT OF TINS FROM THE

9. NEVER LOOK A GIFT HORSE IN THE MOUTH
RED CROSS PARCELS, WHICH HERE WERE POOLED, AS NO ONE WAS THERE LONG ENOUGH TO RECEIVE AN INDIVIDUAL ONE. WE HAD A GOOD SHOWER AND SHAVE AND WENT TO A SHORT CHURCH SERVICE SIMPLY CONDUCTED BY ONE OF US AND THEN FELL IN WITH OUR SMALL SET OF BELONGINGS TO MARCH TO THE STATION. WE EACH RECEIVED TEN CIGARETTES AND SAID "CHEERIO AND THE BEST OF LUCK" TO OUR AMERICAN FRIENDS AND THE STAFF. THEN ON OUR WAY DOWN THE HILL ON A TWO MILE MARCH TO THE STATION WHISTLING AND SINGING WELL-KNOWN SONGS. AS WE APPROACHED THE TOWN OUR ESCORT STOPPED THE SINGING, AN ORDER WHICH WAS NOT IMMEDIATELY CARRIED OUT MUCH TO THE ANNOYANCE OF THE GUARDS. ON THE TRAIN – A SPECIAL COACH, SPECIALLY FOR PRISONERS OF WAR WITH BARRED WINDOWS AND STRENGTHENED RACKS ETC. -ITALIAN. 75 OF US WERE CROWDED INTO THE COACH FOR A JOURNEY RUMOURED TO BE LASTING FOUR OF FIVE DAYS. ON THE TRAIN WE RECEIVED JERRY RATION OF 'POLONY' AND 'RAW SAUSAGE' (SOMETHING HARD TO STOMACH DESPITE OUR HUNGER) AND BREAD. IN ADDITION A RED CROSS FOOD PARCEL BETWEEN TWO WERE HANDED OUT TO US. WE WERE SHUNTED ABOUT AND EVENTUALLY WERE NEXT TO THE ENGINE OF A GOODS TRAIN TRAVELLING AT THE APPROPRIATE SPEED OF SUCH! FOUR DAYS TO GET THERE, BE HANGED – FOUR MONTHS!! BEFORE EVENING WE BEGAN TO FEEL THE DISCOMFORT OF

10   A BIRD IN THE HAND IS WORTH TWO IN THE BUSH
TRAVELLING SO CROWDED WITH WOODEN BENCHES FOR SEATS. WE EXCHANGED PLACES WITH THOSE STANDING IN THE CORRIDOR AT TIMES TO GIVE THEM A BREAK. NOT UNTIL WE WERE SHUNTED INTO A SIDING ABOUT MIDNIGHT DID WE EVENTUALLY GET SOME SLEEP – LYING ON THE FLOOR, ON THE LUGGAGE RACK AND IN THE CORRIDOR.
5/6/44 ALL DAY WAS SPENT SPRAWLED OUT IN THE COMPARTMENT, EVERYONE SITTING IN THE MOST COMFORTABLE POSITION AND FREQUENTLY CHANGING POSITIONS. WE PLAYED CARDS AT TIMES AND OTHER

TIMES WATCHED FOREST AFTER FOREST PASS-BY. WE MADE BETTER TIME TO-DAY AS WE WERE ATTACHED TO A PASSENGER TRAIN MOST OF THE TIME. WE PASSED THROUGH THE OUTSKIRTS OF LEIPZIG WHERE WE SAW AN AERODROME WHICH HAD BEEN WELL 'DONE OVER', PROBABLY BY THE YANKS. BILL AND I CONSUMED THE CONTENTS OF OUR RED CROSS PARCEL WITH CARE, BUT OTHERS WERE MORE RECKLESS. LATER WE PASSED THROUGH SAIGON AND THE FRINGE OF BRESLAU. AT WELL PASSED MIDNIGHT WE WERE SHUNTED INTO A SIDING, ONLY BEING TIRED WE HAD BEEN TO SLEEP BEFORE THIS OCCURRED. A WELCOME CUP OF COFFEE CAME ROUND AND THEN SILENCE PREVAILED ONCE AGAIN, BUT NOT AFTER SOME 'BITCHING' HAD TAKEN PLACE OVER POSITION OF CERTAIN FEET ETC!

<u>6/6/44</u> ON THE MOVE AGAIN AT 5.00A.M. BEHIND A PASSENGER TRAIN WE ARRIVED AT OUR DESTINATION, BANKAU, AT 8.15A.M.,

11

MUCH TO EVERYONES SURPRISE. THE JOURNEY HAD TAKEN US LESS THAN TWO DAYS. ALL THE MORNING AND UNTIL 3.00 IN THE AFTERNOON WE REMAINED IN THE COACH APPARENTLY WAITING AN ESCORT TO COME FOR US. DURING THE MORNING A PASSENGER TRAIN STOPPED OPPOSITE US WITH EVERYONE STARING AT US – SOME LOOKING "DAGGERS DRAWN". A HOSPITAL TRAIN FROM THE RUSSIAN FRONT ALSO PASSED THROUGH HEAVILY LADEN WITH WOUNDED. NOW THAT WE HAD REACHED BANKAU, BILL AND I HAD A GOOD TUCK IN FOR DINNER. WHEN THE ESCORT ARRIVED, WE WERE FORMED UP OUTSIDE THE STATION AND PROCEEDED TO WALK THE 2 OR 3 MILES TO THE CAMP ITSELF. THE WOUNDED WENT BY HORSE AND CART! THE OFFICER IN CHARGE OF THE GUARDS EVEN TRAVELLED BY THAT CONVEYANCE! THE MARCH DID NOT GO DOWN WELL FOR NOT ONLY DID WE FEEL RATHER WEAK, BUT IT DECIDED TO RAIN AND VERY SOON WE GOT SOAKED THROUGH, UNDER THESE CONDITIONS, THEN, LITTLE WONDER OUR SPIRITS WERE VERY LOW WHEN WE SAW THE CAMP WE WERE TO SETTLE IN. LITTLE WOODEN 'SHACKS' MADE OF THICK CARDBOARD

CHIEFLY, IN WHICH SIX OF US HAD TO SLEEP, EAT AND LIVE. THE HUTS WERE APPROX. 9' BY 20' AND EVEN THE SMALLEST AMONG US WAS OBLIGED TO STOOP TO GET IN THE DOOR. INSIDE YOU COULD STAND UPRIGHT IN THE CENTRE BUT AS THE ROOF SLANTED DOWN AT THE SIDE YOU WERE OBLIGED TO STOOP STANDING THERE. WE WERE INSIDE A BIG

12   WHERE IGNORANCE IS BLISS, TIS FOLLY TO BE WISE

ENCLOSURE WITH SENTRY BOXES RAISED TO A HEIGHT OF 15' ALL ROUND BUILT OVER THE BARRED-WIRE ENTANGLEMENT, AND THEN IN ADDITION WE WERE PLACED INSIDE ANOTHER SMALL ENCLOSURE, WHICH WAS ONLY FENCED OFF, BUT GUARDS PATROLLED OUTSIDE. THIS ENCLOSURE WAS SO SMALL THAT WE COULD NOT EVEN PLAY WITH A BALL WE HAD MADE UNLESS IT WAS AMONG THE HITS. HOWEVER, THIS WAS ENLARGED AS MORE CHAPS ARRIVED. (PLAN OF THE CAMP IN CENTRE OF BOOK ON BLUE PAPER). ON ARRIVAL WE WERE SEARCHED, QUESTIONED AND THEN SET TO TO ORGANISE OUR PALLYASSES ETC. WHEN THINGS WERE MORE OR LESS ORGANISED, A PLATE OF SOUP EACH WAS DISHED UP, WHICH HAD BEEN PREPARED BY A GERMAN COOK. WHAT WAS LEFT OF THE EVENING WAS SPENT IN MORE ORGANISING – KNOCKING IN NAILS FOR TO HANG CLOTHES ON AND LAYING OUT THE NUT.

7/6/44 NOT FEELING IN VERY HIGH SPIRITS TO-DAY AFTER HEARING ABOUT THE PERMANENT CAMPS BACK AT TRANSIT CAMP – THEIR SPORTS EQUIPMENT, CANTEENS, BOOKS, DINING HALL, FOOD AND OTHER OCCUPATIONS – LITTLE WONDER THEN THAT IS CAME AS A SHOCK WHEN THERE WAS NOT EVEN A BALL HERE TO PLAY WITH! HAD A MEETING OF THE CAMP AND CERTAIN PEOPLE DELEGATED TO SEE ABOUT RED CROSS PARCELS, BOOKS, SPORTS NEEDS ETC. REST OF THE DAY SPENT PLAYING CARDS WITH OUR HOME-MADE PACK AND GENERALLY POTTERING ABOUT. WENT TO SLEEP AFTER A QUESTIONNAIRE ON CAPITALS OF COUNTRIES AND FILMS.

8/6/44 RED CROSS PARCELS ARRIVED TO-DAY, WHICH WERE BORROWED FROM THE ARMY CAMP IN BANKAU. THEY ALSO SENT US SOME ARE SUPPLYING US WITH THEM UNTIL OUR CONSIGNMENT ARRIVES FROM THE OFFICERS CAMP AT SAIGON – A DEPOT.

13

THEY ALSO SENT US SOME EXTRA CIGARETTES FOR WHICH WE WERE VERY GRATEFUL. A RUMOUR IS GOING ROUND THAT THE SECOND FRONT HAS STARTED, CONSEQUENTLY MUCH EXCITEMENT. TO-NIGHT THERE WAS A LOT OF ABUSE OF THE GUARDS – "SALT MINES FOR YOU" – "JOE'S COMING" – "KEEP THE RED FLAG FLYING" SUNG EVERYWHERE AND SO ON. SINGING WENT ON UNTIL NEARLY MIDNIGHT, IN EACH HUT. WE WERE CONFINED TO OUR HUTS EVERY NIGHT AT 9.00P.M.

9/6/44 BEGINNING TO GET USED TO THE PLACE. NO CONFIRMATION OF YESTERDAY'S RUMOUR, BUT NO DENIAL, THEREFORE PLENTY OF SPECULATION. COLONEL ORDERS SILENCE ON THE CAMP AFTER 10p.m. AND THREATENS REPRISALS IF LAST NIGHTS CONDUCT CONTINUES. WE PEELED SPUDS THIS MORNING. EVERYDAY WE HAVE OUR OWN WATER TO FETCH, WHICH IS SOMETHING TO DO. CARDS AGAIN – '500', CHIEFLY.

10/6/44 HAS THE SECOND FRONT STARTED? IS STILL THE BURNING QUESTION. 'ROBBY' FROM HUT 58, OVER THE WAY FROM US, CAME IN IN THE AFTERNOON AND TOLD US ABOUT HIS EXPERIENCES. MOST INTERESTING. WE ALL PLAYED PATIENCE (EIGHT VARIETIES WE KNOW) AT VARIOUS TIMES AND THE CARDS HARDLY HAD A MINUTES PEACE!

11/6/44 ROLL CALL AT 10.00 TO-DAY INSTEAD OF 9.00, AS IT IS SUNDAY TO-DAY. WENT TO CHURCH SERVICE ORGANISED BY ONE OF THE LADS ON THE CAMP. SIMPLY, BUT VERY SINCERE. SANG HYMNS WRITTEN OUT FROM MEMORY – "ONWARD CHRISTIAN SOLDIERS" AND "LEAD KINDLY LIGHT". HAD A SING-SONG AT NIGHT FOR 90 MINUTES.

14   PROCRASTINATION IS THE THIEF OF TIME

12/6/44 THE COLONEL, CAMP COMMANDANT, CONFIRMED THE RUMOUR THAT THE SECOND FRONT HAD STARTED LAST TUESDAY ON THE SIXTH. EVERYONE'S SPIRITS AMAZINGLY HIGH AND NOW THE BURNING QUESTION IS "WHEN WILL WE BE HOME?" SOME SAY CHRISTMAS – I'M AGREEING WITH THEM – AND OTHERS SAY MARCH, AND THEN OF COURSE, THERE'S

ALWAYS THE PESSIMISTS! SOME NEW LADS COMING IN TO-MORROW – SOME NEWS PERHAPS.

13/6/44 THE NEW 'BODS' ARRIVED ALL RIGHT, BUT NONE OF THEM HAD ANY MORE NEWS THAN WE HAD. WE ALL WENT OVER TO SEE IF WE RECOGNISED ANY OF THEM, BUT NONE OF MY PALS KNEW ANY. A LITTLE EXCITEMENT IN OTHER PARTS OF THE CAMP, THOUGH, AS ONE OR TWO OLD PALS MET. TINY, IN HUT 58, HAS EATEN ALL HIS RED CROSS PARCEL, SO ONLY HAS THE GERMAN RATION TO LIVE ON. CONSEQUENTLY, HE SAYS HE MUST SLEEP TO FORGET HIS HUNGER!

14/6/44 WE ALL RECEIVED A RED CROSS PARCEL, AND FROM NOW ON WE ARE TO GET ONE EVERY TUESDAY. WE READ OUR FIRST GERMAN COMMUNIQUÉ TO-DAY, WHICH PAUL HAD TRANSLATED FOR US. HE CAN SPEAK GERMAN FLUENTLY, SO HE ACTS AS OUR INTERPRETER. "RED", THE CAMP LEADER, CAME ROUND DROPPING HINTS AND TELLING US SOME OF HIS EXPERIENCES IN ITALY.

15/6/44 ANOTHER CAMP MEETING TO-DAY AND "RED", AFTER SOME ARGUING WAS RE-ELECTED CAMP LEADER WITH ONE OF THE NEW CHAPS (WHO HAD BEEN TRANSFERRED FROM ANOTHER CAMP) AS MAN-OF-CONFIDENCE. HE CERTAINLY INSPIRED CONFIDENCE FOR HE SEEMED TO KNOW WHAT HE WAS TALKING ABOUT. DECIDED TO HAVE DUTY HUTS FOR FETCHING WATER, RATIONS AND PEELING "SPUDS" AND SUNDRIES.

15. IN THE LAP OF THE GODS

16/6/44 RECEIVED THIS MONTH'S QUOTA OF TWO LETTERS AND FOUR POSTCARDS FOR WRITING HOME. MANAGED TO BORROW A PENCIL EVENTUALLY AND WROTE HOME. CARDS STILL GOING STRONG, HAVING SPENT SOMETIME TO-DAY REPLACING THEM WITH AN INDELIBLE PENCIL (THE CARDS INCIDENTALLY, WERE MADE FROM "CAPSTAN" PACKETS). PLAYED CRICKET IN EVENING.

17/6/44 CAMP MEETING AGAIN AND A DEBATING SOCIETY WAS FORMED. I WAS PLACED ON THE COMMITTEE. ANOTHER COMPLAINT ABOUT ABUSING THE GUARDS. JERRY GOING TO 'DISH OUT' SOME SOLITARY TO THOSE RESPONSIBLE IF IT DOES NOT STOP. THE WEATHER IS LOVELY, THE SUN BROWNING EVERYONE BRONZE, HOWEVER, FREQUENT VIOLENT THUNDERSTORMS OCCUR TO VARY IT.

18/6/44 WENT TO THE SIMPLE CHURCH SERVICE AND THE

SING-SONG AT NIGHT AT WHICH THERE WAS SEVERAL GOOD INDIVIDUAL TURNS.

19/6/44 MEETING OF THE DEBATING SOCIETY COMMITTEE OF SIX, AT WHICH IT WAS DECIDED TO ORGANISE DEBATES, LECTURES, DISCUSSIONS, BRAINS TRUST AND ANY OTHER SIMILAR SUGGESTIONS BROUGHT FORWARD. A PACKAGE CAME FROM THE RED CROSS WITH SOME BASEBALL EQUIPMENT, PLAYING CARDS AND WRITING MATERIAL. EACH HUT WAS SUPPLIED WITH A PACK OF CARDS. WE IMMEDIATELY POUNCED ON THEM.

20/6/44 WE ARE DUTY HUT TO-DAY, SO SPENT MOST OF THE DAY PEELING POTATOES AND WATER CARRYING. SOME NEW LADS CAME IN AT NIGHT FROM WHOM WE RECEIVED OUR FIRST AUTHENTIC NEWS ON THE SECOND FRONT. NORMAN WILMOT OF MANCHESTER WAS ONE OF

16   NEVER PUT OFF UNTIL TO-MORROW WHAT YOU CAN DO TO-DAY

THEM, AN OLD TRAINING-DAYS PAL OF MINE.

21/6/44 PAID A CIGARETTE ENTRANCE FEE TO ENTER THE WHIST DRIVE TO BE HELD TO-NIGHT AND ALSO PAID A CIGARETTE TO ENTER THE CONTRACT BRIDGE COMPETITION WITH "ROBBY" FROM 58 AS MY PARTNER. RECEIVED OUR RED CROSS PARCELS THIS MORNING OWING TO A TRANSPORT DELAY. THOUGHT "JERRY" WAS HOLDING OUT ON US. DID NOT WIN ANYTHING AT WHIST, BUT AT ONE TIME I WAS GOING STRONG FOR THE "BOOBY"!

22/6/44 HAD TO GET DOWN TO WASHING THIS MORNING – WASHED ALL MY UNDERCLOTHING, TOWELS, SOCKS, SO WANDERED AROUND IN MY PYJAMA BOTTOMS! IT IS LOVELY TO-DAY AGAIN, THIS AFTERNOON "ROBBY" AND PLAYED THE FIRST ROUND OF THE KNOCK-OUT BRIDGE COMPETITION AND WON. SPENT THE EVENING COOKING, MAKING AND BAKING A PIE OF SORTS.

23//6/44 "ROBBY" AND I GOT SAFELY THROUGH THE SECOND ROUND OF THE BRIDGE CONTEST, THEN I SAT ALL THE AFTERNOON MAKING A SLEEPING BAG OUT OF ONE OF MY BLANKETS (WE HAD 3), BY TAKING THE WOOL FROM ROUND THE EDGES OF THE BLANKET AND USING THAT TO SEW IT UP. SHORT MEETING OF THE DEBATING SOCIETY COMMITTEE. PLAYED CRICKET IN EVENING.

24/6/44 RECEIVED THE FIRST NEWS OF THE RUSSIANS DRIVE, WHICH AS WE CALCULATE, SHOULD JUST ABOUT INCLUDE US, IF THEY GET SO FAR! MOST LADS SEEM TO LOOK TO THE EAST FOR RELEASE. DEBATING SOCIETY HAD ITS FIRST MEETING, HOLDING A DISCUSSION ON

17

"IMMIGRATION". THE BOYS FROM CANADA, AUSTRALIA, SOUTH AFRICA, NEW ZEALAND AND RHODESIA WERE REPRESENTED.
25/6/44 WENT TO THE SIMPLE CHURCH SERVICE, WHEN A CANADIAN GAVE A VERY GOOD SHORT ADDRESS. TAUGHT SOME OF THE LADS HOW TO PLAY AUCTION BRIDGE AND WHEN THEY GOT "CHEESED", "RODG" TAUGHT ME HOW TO PLAY CRIB. HAD A JOLLY SING-SONG AT NIGHT, ENDING UP WITH "LAND OF HOPE AND GLORY".
26/6/44 P.T. COMMENCED THIS MORNING AFTER 9.00 ROLL CALL, SO BOB, NICK AND I HAD A GO. IT WAS QUITE ENJOYABLE, ESPECIALLY BOB AND I TRYING TO DO SOME EXERCISES TOGETHER. "ROBBY" AND I PLAYED THE THIRD ROUND OF THE BRIDGE CONTEST AND AFTER A CLOSE GAME GOT THROUGH TO THE SEMI-FINAL. PREPARATION GOING ON FOR A BIG INTAKE OF NEW LADS.
27/6/44 P.T. AGAIN. RED CROSS PARCEL DAY, SO ALL EARS COCKED FOR THE SHOUT "PARCELS". GOT BEATEN IN THE SEMI FINAL OF THE BRIDGE CONTEST BY THE ORGANISERS AFTER A GOOD START. SOME EXTRA AMERICAN CIGARETTES ARRIVED TO-DAY TO SUPPLEMENT THE 50 ENGLISH ONES WE RECEIVED WITH OUR PARCEL. WENT TO SEE IF THERE WERE ANY LADS WE KNEW AMONGST THE NEW BATCH OF 90 THAT ARRIVED, BUT THERE WASN'T ONE. TOM MET A FELLOW AUSTRALIAN HE HAD MET BEFORE. LATER ON IN THE EVENING A "GEORDIE" CAME ROUND TO SEE NICK AND I, HAVING HEARD ABOUT US. HE COMES FROM FENHAM AND AS HE WAS A MIDDLE EAST CHAP, I GAVE HIM SOME NEWS OF NEWCASTLE.
28/6/44 DUTY HUT AGAIN TO-DAY, SO 'SPUD' PEELING IN MORNING AND WATER CARRYING WHEN REQUIRED. WHIST DRIVE AT NIGHT BUT STILL FAILED TO WIN ANY

CIGARETTES AND BILL CAME OFF JUST AS BADLY TOO.

18   FAMILIARITY BREEDS CONTEMPT

29/6/44 BIG ARGUMENT TO-DAY, WHICH WASTED MOST OF THE MORNING, ABOUT WHETHER WE SHOULD POOL OUR RED CROSS PARCELS IN THE HUT OR NOT. THE RESULT WAS NEVER MUCH IN DOUBT – ABSOLUTELY IMPRACTICABLE. TO-NIGHT AFTER DARK, WE PLAYED UP THE GUARDS. IN ONE PROCESSION EACH HUT WENT OUT IN TURN TO THE LAVATORY WITH BOXES UNDER THEIR ARMS, STAYED THERE AWHILE AND THEN RETURNED TO OUR HUTS. IMMEDIATELY THE GUARDS PANICKED – THE SEARCH LIGHTS WERE PLAYED ROUND THE CAMP CONTINUOUSLY. LATER ON THE "FERRETS" CAME UP AND BOARDED UP THE LAVATORY AND EXAMINED THE FLOOR BOARDS AND THE GUARDS ROUND THE CAMP WAS DOUBLED! THEN THE COLONEL EVEN CAME UP ABOUT 4.00A.M. WHAT FUN!

30/6/44 LOT OF CLEANING UP ETC. TO-DAY, AS THREE NEUTRAL REPRESENTATIVES CAME ROUND ON BEHALF OF THE RED CROSS TO EXAMINE THE HUTS, SITE, COOKING FACILITIES, OUR CLOTHING ETC. THEIR COMMENT WAS THAT CONDITIONS WERE RATHER CRUDE, BUT THE GERMANS WERE QUICK TO INFORM THEM THAT THIS WAS ONLY TEMPORARY. SO IT IS, BUT THE BUILDING OF THE PERMANENT ONE SEEMS TO BE A VERY SLOW PROCESS. IN THE AFTERNOON THE GERMANS CARRIED OUT A GENERAL SEARCH OF THE CAMP. SWOPPED TEN CIGARETTES FOR HALF A BLOCK OF SUGAR, AS MINE WAS VERY LOW. ALSO SWOPPED THE REMAINDER OF MY "CHICLETS" (CHEWING GUM) FOR TWENTY CIGARETTES WITH "TINY" – THE EX-COPPER FROM HUT 58.

1/7/44 GOT JULYS RATION OF LETTERS AND POSTCARDS SO WROTE A LETTER HOME AND TWO PCs. THE CANADIANS HAD A CELEBRATION FOR CANADA'S BIRTHDAY AND THEY MADE SEVERAL

19. NEITHER A BORROWER NOR A LENDER BE

LARGE CAKES FOR THE CAMPS CONSUMPTION. THEY WERE CERTAINLY VERY TASTY.

2/7/44 CHURCH SERVICE AT 11.00 AND THEN TOM, RODG, NICK AND I GOT DOWN TO A SESSION OF AUCTION BRIDGE ALL AFTERNOON. ROLL CALL AT 3.30 ON SUNDAYS INSTEAD OF 4.30. SING-SONG AT NIGHT. A SHOVEL MISSING FROM THE COOKHOUSE, SO NO COCOA TO-NIGHT.

3/7/44 STILL NO SHOVEL. GERMANS PANICKED AGAIN AND A GENERAL SEARCH IN AFTERNOON REVEALING NOTHING, SO THEY THREATEN REPRISALS. A CAMP MEETING AND "RED" AND PAUL RESIGN. SEVERAL HEATED ARGUMENTS AND EVENTUALLY "RED" AGREED TO CONTINUE, PROVIDED SHOVEL IS RETURNED. "RED" IS INFORMED WHERE IT IS BY ONE OF THE GANG RESPONSIBLE AND IT IS RECOVERED. GERMANS THREATEN JAIL FOR ANYONE WHO DOES IT AGAIN. MANY "SARCY" REMARKS MADE TO "TOJO" AS HE COMES ROUND TO COUNT US ON ROLL CALL, BUT "HOPPY" (ANOTHER GERMAN WITH A LIMP) STILL HIS USUAL SELF MAKING A CRACK OR TWO NOW AND AGAIN.

4/7/44 "RED" VISITED US AGAIN IN THE MORNING, AND BEING OFFERED NOTHING, HELPED HIMSELF TO A BISCUIT! BOB CAME OUT WITH A STREAM OF PROTESTS AS USUAL. RED CROSS PARCELS TO-DAY. SOME MORE LADS CAME IN AND AN OLD PAL OF BOB'S WHO TOM AND I ALSO KNEW, CAME ROUND TO THE HUT FOR A CHAT. HE HAVE US SOME NEWS OF SOME OF OUR PALS WHO WE HAD NOT HEARD OF SINCE PARTING WITH THEM.

5/7/44 MEETING OF THE DEBATING SOCIETY COMMITTEE. WEATHER NOT SO GOOD TO-DAY SO WHIST DRIVE WAS CANCELLED.

20. ONE SWALLOW DOES NOT MAKE A SUMMER MAKE
6/7/44 WHIST DRIVE TO-NIGHT, AGAIN ALL '53' WERE UNLUCKY. ABOUT MIDNIGHT WE WERE DISTURBED BY THE MAJOR AND 'TOJO' COMING ROUND TO INDIVIDUAL HUTS AND SHINNING A TORCH ON EACH OCCUPANT AND CHECKING HIM OFF WITH THEIR IDENTITY CARD (A PHOTOGRAPH BEING ATTACHED TO EACH ONE).

7/7/44 NOTHING OF NOTE OCCURRED TO-DAY, EXCEPT AN ISSUE OF FRENCH CIGARETTES, NAMED ELEGANTES, WERE DISTRIBUTED. NEEDLESS TO SAY HOW WICKED

THEY WERE, BUT THEY WERE AT LEAST A SMOKE WHEN THE ENGLISH CRAVEN 'A' OR AMERICAN CHESTERFIELD RAN OUT. THESE CIGARETTES WERE BOUGHT FROM 'JERRY' WITH 10,000 MARKS GIVEN TO OUR CAMP BY THE OFFICERS OF SAIGON CAMP. 75,000 WERE BOUGHT AND OTHER THINGS PURCHASED BY THE REST OF THE MONEY ARE ALSO COMING.

8/7/44 RIGGED UP A SCOREBOARD FOR THE SPELLING BEE TO-NIGHT, WHICH WAS RUN BY THE DEBATING SOCIETY. I WAS SCORER AND ALSO 'GONGER' ON TIME UP OR THE WRONG SPELLING. WE HAD FOUR TEAMS, NAMELY ENGLAND, CANADA, DESERT RATS (MIDDLE EAST) AND A COMBINED SCOTCH, WELSH AND IRISH TEAM. SIX IN EACH TEAM. THE ENGLISH TEAM WON WITH 27 POINTS AND THE DESSERT RATS WERE SECOND AFTER A RUN OFF WITH THE CANADIANS, WHO TOOK THIRD PLACE. PLENTY OF AMUSEMENT WAS HAD BY ALL. THE WINNERS RECEIVED SOME CIGARETTES AND TOBACCO.

21. PREVENTATION IS BETTER THAN CURE

9/7/44 HAD TO GET DOWN TO SOME MORE WASHING, SO DID IT IN THE AFTERNOON AFTER QUEUING UP IN THE MORNING FOR A LIBRARY BOOK AND MAKING A START ON IT. THE BOOK WAS VERY GOOD – ALL ABOUT AN AMERICAN NATIONAL HERO ENTITLED "PAUL JONES". HE LIVED IN THE TIME AMERICA WAS STRUGGLING FOR HER INDEPENDENCE. MISSED CHURCH THROUGH WAITING FOR THE CAMP LIBRARY. LOVELY DAY-SUN BLAZING. WENT TO THE SING-SONG IN EVENING.

10/7/44 DUTY HUT TO-DAY. WENT ON WATER PARTIES, PEELED A FEW SPUDS AND THE REST OF THE MORNING I FILLED PALLYASSES WITH STRAW, PUTTING THEM OUT IN THE HUTS FOR THE NEW LADS COMING IN TOMORROW. IN AFTERNOON ASSEMBLED THE TABLES AND STOOLS AND DISTRIBUTING THEM TO THE HUTS. DID SOME COOKING IN EVENING FOR A TASTY MEAL BY WAY OF A CHANGE.

11/7/44 RED CROSS PARCEL DAY AGAIN, ALWAYS A DAY TO LOOK FORWARD TO. WROTE ANOTHER LETTER HOME AND A POSTCARD. PLAYED IN THE SECOND

BRIDGE TOURNAMENT WITH "ROBBY" AND GOT BEATEN-IN THE FIRST ROUND! THE CARDS WERE NOT VERY KIND TO US. THE NEW LADS CAME IN LATE ON, BUT DID NOT SEE ANYONE I KNEW.

12/7/44 RECEIVED ANOTHER 20 'ELEGANTES' (FRENCH CIGARETTES) BUT THEY WERE FORGOTTEN (FOR THE TIME BEING) AS WE HAD JUST RECEIVED OUR 50 ENGLISH CIGARETTES YESTERDAY. WENT TO THE WHIST DRIVE (HELD IN THE OPEN) AGAIN TO-NIGHT, BUT AS USUAL NONE FROM 53 WERE LUCKY FOR APART FROM BILL AND I, TOMMY AND NICK TRIED THEIR LUCK. SPENT MOST OF THE T0-DAY READING, GETTING ANOTHER BOOK OUT – A NOVEL "LOST FIELDS".

22   PENNY WISW : PENNY FOOLISH

13/7/44 EVERYBODY HAS READING MANIA AT THE MOMENT, FORGETTING CARDS AND SPORTS. I EXPECT THIS WILL SOON WEAR OFF. WAITING IN THE QUEUE FOR A POSSIBLE SECOND HELPING OF DINNER, WHO SHOULD I MEET, BUT JOHNNY PRICE, ONE OF MY BEST PALS IN TRAINING DAYS. WE ONLY NEED 'GRIFF' HERE NOW TO COMPLETE THE PICTURE. GOOD LAD JOHNNY! HE WAS BROUGHT DOWN BY FIGHTERS ON THE 24/6/44. WE EXCHANGED NEWS FOR SOME TIME AFTER DINNER, TALKING OF THE OLD LADS AND THE OLD TIMES. BOY OH BOY WHAT A CHAT!

14/7/44 PLAYED BRIDGE WITH "BALDY" AS PARTNER AGAINST TOM AND "RODG" IN MORNING FOR 1 ELEGANTE PER HUNDRED POINTS TO BE CONTINUOUS AND PAYABLE WHEN ONE PARTY IS SHORT OF CIGARETTES. WE PILED UP A LITTLE LEAD. PLAYED SOCCER IN AFTERNOON AS GOALKEEPER. OUR TEAM LOST 2-4.

15/7/44 POURED OVER A BOOK ALL MORNING. RECEIVED OUR DIARIES (THIS BOOK), SO SPENT AFTERNOON LOOKING THROUGH IT AND MAKING NOTES. ROLL CALL WAS EARLY – AT 3.30, FOR, BEFORE TEA, A BOXING TOURNAMENT WAS STAGED! ORIGINALLY IT WAS FOR 6.00 BUT THE COLONEL WANTED TO SEE IT AND AS HE COULD NOT GET ALONG AT 6.00, WE BROUGHT IT FORWARD TO PLEASE HIM, AS HE IS ENDEAVOURING TO GET US SOME BEER, PENCILS, MATCHES AND NOTE

PAPER ETC. TEA WAS NOT UNTIL 6.00. HOWEVER, IT WAS UNTIL THE LAST ROUND OF THE LAST FIGHT THE COLONEL TURNED UP. HE IS QUITE A DECENT CHAP, SO IT WAS RATHER A PITY THAT HE

23   I GAVE HIM A ROLAND FOR HIS OLIVER

MISSED IT, AS EVERY FIGHT WAS VERY GOOD WITH PLENTY OF VARIETY RESULTS:- (ALL CONTESTS 3 TWO MIN ROUNDS)

1 HEAVY WEIGHT
W/O LANE, WESTON-SUPER-MARE BEAT F/S GREENE, CANADA ON POINTS
2. FEATHER WEIGHT
SGT CLIFF MANCHESTER BEAT SGT SMART BROMLEY BY TECHNICAL KNOCK-OUT
3. WELTER WEIGHT
SGT WILSON, LONDON BEAT SGT CAITEBRAITHE, BURNLEY ON POINTS
4. LIGHT WEIGHT
SGT SHENTON, TAMWORTH BEAT SGT WILMOT, MANCHESTER ON POINTS
5. LIGHT-HEAVY WEIGHT
SGT HENRY MONTREAL BEAT F/SGT GIBSON, SOUTHAMPTON ON POINTS
6. LIGHT WEIGHT
SGT McGRAW, CHICAGO (R.C.A.F) DREW WITH SGT RONEN, EDINBURGH
7. WELTER-WEIGHT
SGT LLOYD, COLWYN BAY BEAT SGT McBURNIE, CANDA ON POINTS

AFTER TEA "BALDY" AND I CONTINUED OUR BRIDGE CONTEST WITH TOM AND RODG.

16/7/44 WENT TO THE CHURCH SERVICE AND THEN WROTE UP PART OF MY DIARY. PLAYED CARDS IN AFTERNOON AND WENT TO THE SING-

24   ABSENCE MAKES THE HEART GROW FONDER

SONG AT NIGHT. MET ANOTHER GEORDIE AFTERWARDS AND HAD A GOOD CHAT. HE COMES FROM FENHAM. HE TOLD ME THE "DUNCOW" AT HOME HAD BEEN BURNT DOWN. DISCOVERED HE WAS LAST ON LEAVE THE SAME TIME AS I WAS – AT THE BEGINNING OF MAY.

17/7/44 A NEW LOT OF BOOKS, MUSICAL INSTRUMENTS, PLAYING CARDS ETC. ARRIVED TO-DAY. WENT TO THE DEBATE AT NIGHT ON "THAT CONSCRIPTION REMAIN IN FORCE AFTER THE CESSATION OF HOSTILITIES". THE MOTION WAS CARRIED BY 44 VOTES TO 31. QUITE INTERESTING. PLAYED BRIDGE TO-DAY WITH "BALDY" AS PARTNER AGAINST TOM AND "RODG". PILING UP A LEAD OF 5620 TO BE CARRIED FORWARD!

18/7/44 RAINED ALL DAY TO-DAY – FIRST TIME IT HAS RAINED ALL DAY SINCE WE ARRIVED. WROTE UP MOST OF MY DIARY AND BROUGHT IT UP-TO-DATE. HAD SHORT MEETING OF DEBATING SOCIETY COMMITTEE. RED CROSS PARCEL DAY – GOT MY FIRST AMERICAN PARCEL (EXCEPT THE ONE BILL AND I SHARED ON THE TRAIN). HAVE HAD SCOTCH ONES BEFORE. THEY ALL VARY SOMEWHAT. AMERICAN PARCELS HAVE 100 CIGARETTES. AT NIGHT TALKED OF DREAMS WE HAD HAD WHILE HERE AND OF OUR WIVES AND SWEETHEARTS BACK HOME. ABOUT MIDNIGHT THREE "FERRETS" AND THE "FERRET-IN-CHIEF" – A CADET OFFICER, CONDUCTED A SEARCH, THEY WENT THROUGH

25. TO SPOIL THE SHIP FOR A HA'PORTH O'TAR

OUR POCKETS, CASES, LOOKED UNDER OUR BEDS AND THROUGH MY DIARY, WHAT NEXT?

19/7/44 GOT THE GAME OF MONOPOLY FOR TO-DAY, SO HAD A GAME WHICH TOOK ALL MORNING. DEN FROM 58 AND "RODG" DISPOSED OF BOB, BILL, TOM AND MYSELF. IT WAS A MISERABLE SORT OF DAY, SO PLAYED ANOTHER TWO GAMES IN THE AFTERNOON, WITH ME MANAGING TO CLEAN THE OTHERS OUT. THE WEATHER CLEARED UP FOR THE EVENING SO WE HAD OUR USUAL WHIST DRIVE. BILL WON 10 CIGARETTES WITH THE BEST 'LADIES'(!) SCORE OF THE SECOND HALF. IT DID NOT COST A CIGARETTE ENTRANCE FEE, AS THEY NOW DEDUCT A CIGARETTE FROM EVERY MAN ON HIS WEEKLY RATION, WHICH GOES TO THE ENTERTAINMENT FUND. GOT DOWN TO ANOTHER GAME OF MONOPOLY AFTER SUPPER, BUT IT WAS REDUCED TO A FARCE AS THE LIGHT FAILED. TALKED OF OLD TIMES IN BED BEFORE GOING TO SLEEP.

20.7.44 COMMENCED A 'COOKS TOUR' OF THE CAMP FOR THE SIGNATURES OF 'SOME OF THE BOYS'. RODG AND I TOOK BOB AND TOM ON AT '500' AND MADE GOOD USE OF THE FAVOUR SHOWN TO US IN THE DEALS. WE WON 4 OUT OF 5 RUBBERS. THERE IS PLENTY OF MUSIC ISSUING FORTH FROM CERTAIN HUTS NOW THAT THE MUSICAL INSTRUMENTS HAVE BEEN GIVEN OUT. THERE IS A PICCOLO, 2 FLUTES, 2 CLARINETS AND SEVERAL MOUTH ORGANS. BILL IS ENDEAVOURING TO GET HOLD OF ONE OF THE LATTER, AS HE CAN PLAY ONE WELL. RECEIVED ANOTHER SET OF UNDERCLOTHING FOR THE PAIR I HAD ON WHEN I LANDED IN THE WATER. THEY'LL BE WARM FOR THE WINTER FOR IT IS SUPPOSED TO GET PRETTY SEVERE HERE THEN. HOPING WE WILL NOT BE

26   TO MAKE MOUNTAINS OUT OF MOLE-HILLS
HERE THEN, BUT ALL REALISE WE WILL BE HERE FOR THE BEGINNING OF IT – "HOME FOR CHRISTMAS" IS STILL THE CRY. AFTER TEA SET ABOUT ORGANISING THE DEBATING SOCIETIES "QUIZZ" FOR SATURDAY NIGHT SEEING FRANK FROM 52 AND WRITING OUT QUESTIONS. TOM AND RODG PLAYED THE FIRST ROUND OF THE BRIDGE CONTEST (NOT A KNOCK-OUT COMPETITION THIS TIME). QUIZZED IN BED AND THEN JUST BEFORE WE ARE GOING TO SLEEP BOB HAS TO DISCOVER A MOSQUITO FLOATING ABOUT AND FROM THEN ON THERE WAS A COMMOTION FOR ANOTHER 2 HOURS, WITH HEADS UNDER THE BLANKETS IMMEDIATELY THE ALARM WAS GIVEN THAT IT IS MAKING USE OF ITS WINGS. EVENTUALLY SLEEP CAME OUR WAY ONLY BECAUSE OUR EYES WOULD NOT REMAIN OPEN ANY LONGER.
21/7/44 INSPECTION BY THE MAJOR, OF HUTS ETC, BUT AS WE WERE NOT PREVIOUSLY WARNED ROLL CALL AND INSPECTION WAS PUT BACK TO 10.00 TO GIVE US MORE TIME TO PREPARE. (JUST AS WELL FOR WE WERE LATE RISING AFTER LAST NIGHTS INTRUSION!) SPENT MOST OF DAY PREPARING THE "QUIZZES" FOR TO-MORROW NIGHT AND SEEING THE TEAM LEADERS. THE CAMP BAND HAVE ASSEMBLED AGAIN TO-NIGHT TO GET SOME HARMONY! GOOD COMMUNIQUE ALONG WITH QUITE A GOOD EDITION OF THE CAMP NEWSPAPER "POW-WOW". ALSO A PHOTO OF

'V1, HITLERS WEAPON (SECRET!) ON LONDON. NO 'MOSQUITO' PANIC TO-NIGHT.
<u>22/7/44</u> DUTY HUT, PEELED 'SPUDS' MORNING AND AFTERNOON – 35 CANS BY AN AVERAGE OF TWENTY OF US. SOMEONE TALKS OF THE BEST DINNERS BACK HOME! CAME ON TO RAIN AT TEATIME, SO "QUIZ" WAS CANCELLED. ROBBY AND I PLAYED PART OF OUR FIRST ROUND BRIDGE TOURNAMENT.

27. HE IS TO FEARED WHO FEARS NOT DEATH
<u>23/7/44</u> RAINING TO-DAY, SO CHURCH SERVICE HAD TO BE CANCELLED. TOMMY GOT A GAME OUT CALLED "TARANTELLA" WITH TRANSLATED RULES DONE BY 'JERRY'. CONSEQUENTLY, AFTER WE HAD UNSUCCESSFULLY STUDIED THE RULES FOR ½ HOUR, WE PLAYED 'SHOOT' WITH THE CARDS AND THEN "TIDDLEY-WINKS" WITH THE COUNTERS. FINISHED THE MORNING OFF GETTING SOME MORE NAMES IN THE BOOK. HAD A GRAND DINNER – PLENTY OF IT FOR A CHANGE AND HAD CABBAGE IN ADDITION! AFTER 3.00 ROLL CALL 'ROBBY' AND I PLAYED THE SECOND GAME OF THE BRIDGE CONTEST – LOST BY 910 PTS AND 1 RUBBER TO 2 RUBBERS. WENT TO THE CONCERT IN THE EVENING WHEN OUR NEWLY-FORMED BAND GAVE US HALF-HOURS MUSIC – OPENING UP WITH "MUSIC WHILE YOU WORK". IT SOUNDED GRAND. I THINK EVERYONE REALLY ENJOYED THE WHOLE SHOW, ALTHOUGH THERE WERE NOT MANY INDIVIDUAL TURNS. ON THE NOTICEBOARD IS THE TEXT OF HITLER'S SPEECH MADE AFTER THE ATTEMPT ON HIS LIFE. IT APPEARS TO ME THAT INTERNAL DISSENT IS GROWING TO SERIOUS PROPORTIONS FOR GERMANY. THEN LATER ON WE FOUND OUT THAT GUARDS WERE DOUBLED DURING THE NIGHT. SINCE WE HAVE BEEN HERE ONE GOOD PIECE OF NEWS AFTER ANOTHER HAS REACHED OUR EARS – SECOND FRONT – RUSSIA'S CONTINUED PROGRESS – ALLIES DEFEATING THE GERMANS IN ITALY – THE EFFECT OF OUR CONTINUING BOMBING – THE ATTEMPT ON HITLER'S LIFE – WELL, ONE COULD HARDLY EXPECT THINGS TO MOVE FASTER, COULD WE? SPIRITS HERE ARE VERY HIGH AND CERTAINLY THERE IS NO ONE ALLOWING THIS PLACE TO GET THEM DOWN DESPITE THE FACT THAT IT IS THE BEST GUARDED CAMP IN GERMANY. 'JERRY' NEVER TAKES ANY CHANCES WITH THE RAF, KNOWING THEM OF OLD AND AT TIMES THEY HAVE BEEN 'PLAYED UP' WELL! 52 DAYS TO GO TO 13TH SEPTEMBER, WHEN THE 100 DAYS

28. TO ERR IS HUMAN

IS UP – WHEN I SAY THE WAR WILL BE OVER – I HAVE A 50 CIGARETTES BET WITH TOM AND BOB ON IT. IT REPRESENTS 100 DAYS AFTER THE OPENING OF THE SECOND FRONT. MY CHANCES STILL LOOK BRIGHT.

24/7/44 HAD A GAME OF "MONOPOLY" THIS TIME AT THE INVITATION OF '58', BUT GOT BOUGHT OUT FAIRLY SOON, TOMMY WINNING. BOB AND I THEN FELT ENERGETIC, SO DREW THE BADMINTON SET FROM THE SPORTS STORE AND PROCEEDED TO PLAY. HOWEVER, THE WIND WAS STRONG AND GUSTY SO WE DID NOT HAVE MUCH OF A CLUE OF PLAYING A PROPER GAME, SO AFTER HAVING SOME FUN WITH IT, WE GOT THE RUGBY 'PILL' OUT. ONLY BREAD AND MARG FOR DINNER TO-DAY AS THERE WAS NO COAL FOR THE OVENS AND THERE WERE NO POTATOES UNTIL LATE – HAVING A HOT MEAL TO-NIGHT INSTEAD, WE HOPE! FREQUENT VISITS BY 'TINY' FOR MILK AND SUGAR - NO WONDER ITS MONDAY TO-DAY! PLAYED 'CRIB' WITH 'BALDY' AND LOST A CIGARETTE. CALLED ROUND TO SEE FRANK ABOUT THE 'QUIZZ'. BOB DID NOT GO ON PARADE AT 4.30 AS HE HAD WASHED HIS TROUSERS. PLAYED PATIENCE UNTIL EVENTUALLY OUR PROMISED HOT MEAL TURNED UP. ORGANISED THE 'QUIZZ' AND WAS 'MASTER OF CEREMONIES'. EVERYBODY THOROUGHLY ENJOYED IT AND THERE WAS MANY A LAUGH, ESPECIALLY AT TWO REPLIES IN PARTICULAR, NAMELY:- WHAT WAS THE NAME OF THE BATTLESHIP SUNK IN SCAPA FLOW? "TIRPITZ" WAS THE REPLY! THEN, FOR AMUSEMENT; WHAT DID THE MOUSE DO WHEN THE CLOCK STRUCK ONE? "RAN UP" WAS THE IMMEDIATE REPLY!! THERE WAS PLENTY OF HOWLING DOWN AND CRACKS AMONG THE TEAMS. THE "WHYNOTS" WON WITH A TOTAL OF 28½ OUT OF A POSSIBLE 36 PTS. THERE WERE SIX ROUNDS, EACH ROUND CONSISTING OF THREE QUESTIONS TO EACH TEAM.

29. IT'S LIKE POURING WATER ON A DUCK'S BACK

TEAMS WERE:-

1 THE GEN BOYS	2 THE INK SLINGERS
MR GRIFFITHS	MR HILL
" TAYLOR	" LLOYD

" RAYMOND
" COPE   (24½)
" SCOPE
" SPRIGGS
3 <u>THE NO NOWTS</u>
   MR MATTHEWS
   " BILLING
   " CRAIG
   " BURGESS
   " BATESON (21)
   " HARRISON
5 <u>THE WHYNOTS</u>
   MR TRANTER
   " SARGENT
   " PHILIPS
   " CHAPMAN
   " BROWN   (28½)
   " HARDIE

" KING
" GREENE
" BISHOP   (20½)
" THOMSON
4 <u>DUFF GEN SEXTET</u>
   MR WALKTY
   " BETHOL
   " COMFORT
   " BELVESTONE
   " PARRY-JONES (18)
   " FEREDAY
6 <u>SEVEN AND SIX (HUT 76)</u>
   MR LYNCH
   " WOODWARD
   " VIDDLER
   " STURGESS
   " BRADLEY   (18)
   " FLETCHER

MR CHAPMAN OF THE WHY NOTS WON THE INDIVIDUAL PRIZE WITH 8 PTS. EACH TEAMS SCORE IS RINGED BEDSIDE THE TEAM. FIRST TEAM RECEIVED 30 CIGARETTES AND THE INDIVIDUAL PRIZE WAS 10 CIGARETTES. AFTER THE COMPETITION I CAME BACK TO THE HUT FOR A QUICK GAME OF MONOPOLY, WHICH WE HAD NOT TIME TO FINISH BEFORE DARKNESS SET IN. THEN I MANAGED TO GET SOME SUPPER AND WE RETIRED TO BED IN GOOD SPIRITS KNOWING JOE WAS GETTING NEARER EVERYDAY. WE DISCUSSED THE POSSIBILITY OF GOING BACK HOME VIA RUSSIA AND OF THE TIME WE WOULD HAVE IF WE DID. I WOULD LIKE THE EXPERIENCE, PERSONALLY.

30   <u>PEOPLE WHO LIVE IN GLASS HOUSES CANNOT</u>
<u>25/7/44</u> PLAYED BADMINTON WITH TOM AND BOB AND THEN WENT BACK TO THE HUT TO BRING MY DIARY UP-TO-DATE. DID SOME DRAWING AND WROTE HOME. DINNER. COMPLETED MY DRAWING, THEN WENT TO THE PUMP FOR A SHOWER. IT WAS MIGHTY COLD WHEN THE SUN WAS IN! BILL AND TOM ARE PLAYING A LEAGUE CRICKET MATCH. THERE ARE NOW A LOT MORE 'JERRIES' ABOUT THE CAMP, SO WE HAVE TO TAKE CARE. THE SHOUT "FERRETS UP" IS HEARD REGULARLY – IT SERVES TWO PURPOSES, FOR WARNING US AND ANNOYING THE

JERRIES, BECAUSE THEY DO NOT LIKE THE 'TITLE'. (THE "FERRETS" AS WE CALL THEM, ARE THE SECURITY POLICE WHO ARE CONTINUOUSLY INSIDE THE CAMP 'SNOOPING' AROUND AND PERIODICALLY CONDUCT THE SEARCHES). THIS STRENGTHENING OF THE GERMAN FORCES HERE IS DUE TO THE POSSIBILITY OF TROUBLE NOW THAT THE RUSSIANS ARE DRAWING SO MUCH CLOSER. THEY MUST BE NOW ONLY A LITTLE OVER 100 MILES AWAY – "NEARER EVER NEARER DRAWS THE COMING DAY". THE GERMANS ARE CERTAINLY 'JITTERY'. THIS AFTERNOON THERE WAS SOME AMUSEMENT WHEN ONE OF THE GUARDS IN THE SENTRY BOX DROPPED HIS RIFLE AND IT WENT OFF – CAUSING EVERY-ONE TO RUSH OUT AND ON FINDING OUT WHAT HAPPENED, PASSING SOME CAUSTIC REMARKS. JUST ONE OF THE AMUSING INCIDENTS THAT OCCUR NOW AND AGAIN. PRACTICED DROP KICKING AND PLACED KICKS WITH BOB WITH THE 'RUGGER' BALL, AT NIGHT WE GOT A THRILL OUT OF HEARING FOR THE FIRST TIME THE FAINT DULL ROAR OF BATTLE IN THE DISTANCE AND AS WE LAY LISTENING WE SPECULATED HOW MUCH LONGER WE WOULD BE 'HERE'. WE COULD NOT HELP BUT FEEL EXCITED AND GIVE VENT TO OUR FEELINGS. WHAT A TIME WE WILL HAVE GOING THROUGH RUSSIA – MOSCOW, ESPECIALLY, WE HOPE! (PARCELS TO-DAY).
26/7/44 PORRIDGE THIS MORNING FOR BREAKFAST FOR A CHANGE – THUS SAVING SOME OF MY BREAD RATION (1/6 OF LOAF!). ON PARADE WE CAN HEAR THE DULL EXPLOSIONS IN THE DISTANCE – DEFINITELY

31. AFFORD TO THROW STONES

MORE DISTINCTLY – IT MAY BE JOE'S ARTILLERY FIRE OR THE GERMANS ON DEMOLITIONING, BUT BELIEVE ME, WHICHEVER IT IS, IT SURE SOUNDS GOOD. NEWS THIS MORNING CAME THROUGH THAT THE CAMP WE WERE AT FIRST GOING TO AT IDABURG, IN THE POLISH CORRIDOR, HAS BEEN TAKEN BY THE RUSSIANS – UNLESS THE PRISONERS WERE TRANSFERRED, THEY WILL GET HOME FOR CHRISTMAS. COME ON, JOE, AND DO THE SAME FOR US! PLAYED BRIDGE MOST OF THE DAY WITH 'ROBBY' AS PARTNER IN THE TOURNAMENT, GETTING THE WORST OF THE DEALS NEARLY EVERYTIME - NEVERTHELESS WE JUST MANAGED TO BEAT TOM AND 'RODG' AND WE HAVE ANOTHER GAME TO FINISH AGAINST 'BALDY', ONE OF THE COOKS. WHILE PLAYING IN THE AFTERNOON WE PUT UP

THE USUAL CALL "FERRETS UP" AND HE CAME STRAIGHT OVER TO THE HUT OBVIOUSLY MAD AND PLAYED HELL IN GERMAN. I WISH WE COULD HAVE UNDERSTOOD HIM! WENT TO THE WHIST DRIVE AT NIGHT, BUT AS USUAL JUST DID AVERAGE AFTER MAKING A GOOD START. HAD A DING-DONG ARGUMENT ON NUMBER OF FIGHTING TROOPS GERMANY, RUSSIA, BRITAIN AND AMERICA, ALL OF US TAKING PART AND GOING LIKE THE HAMMERS IN HELL, EVEN OUTSIDE OPINION WAS CALLED IN! A BUNCH OF NEW LADS CAME IN DURING THE MORNING AND WE KNEW TWO OF THEM, SO WE SPENT QUITE A WHILE TALKING TO THEM, ASKING QUESTIONS ON THE NEWS, GERMANY'S "VI" WEAPON ETC. WE HAD ONE OF THEM TO TEA, AS THEY HAVE NO RED CROSS FOOD STUFFS YET.

<u>27/7/44</u> ROSE EARLY TO-DAY FOR SOME UNKNOWN REASON. GOT UP ABOUT 7.00, A RECORD FOR ME HERE! USUALLY IT'S A WONDER IF I'M UP FOR 8.00. THE HUT AND EVERYTHING WAS ALL CLEANED UP LONG BEFORE PARADE AND IT IS USUALLY A LAST MINUTE SCRAMBLE TO GET IT DONE. PORRIDGE AGAIN FOR BREAKFAST – SOMEBODY MUST BE LETTING HIS HEAD GO! HOWEVER, WHEN DINNER CAME ROUND THERE WAS ONLY BREAD, AS THERE WERE NO 'SPUDS'.

32   VIRTUE IS ITS OWN REWARD

WENT ROUND TO THE LIBRARY IN THE MORNING WITH MY BOOK, BUT GOT SUSPENDED FOR A FORTNIGHT (!) BECAUSE I HAD THE BOOK OUT SIX DAYS INSTEAD OF THE PRESCRIBED 5. FINISHED OFF A GAME OF BRIDGE WITH 'ROBBY' AS PARTNER AND COMMENCED ANOTHER GAME IN THE AFTERNOON, FINISHING IT OFF IN THE EVENING. LOST ROBBY'S PENCIL AFTER IT, OVER WHICH HE NATURALLY WENT 'CROOK'! SNEAKED IN A QUICK GAME OF CHESS WITH 'BALDY', BUT IT WAS A LITTLE TOO QUICK FOR ME! DURING THE DAY BILL MADE SOME PROPELLERS AND FIXED THEM ON THE ROOF AND THEY CERTAINLY WORKED WELL AND THE CANADIANS HAD A ROWDY MEETING IN THE EVENING!

<u>28/7/44</u> BILL GOT DOWN TO INCREASING HIS PROPELLERS TO FOUR INSTEAD OF TWO AND WHEN HE GOT IT UP IT MADE QUITE A DIN INSIDE THE HUT, THEN 58 HAD A GADGET THEY BROUGHT OUT – A PROPELLER WITH TWO 'MEN' ATTACHED, WHICH ALSO WORKED EXCEEDINGLY WELL – THE CRAZE IS GOING ON THROUGH THE CAMP! WELL, I DID P.T. THIS MORNING FOR THE FIRST TIME FOR SOMETIME, FOR PREVIOUS MORNINGS I HAVE GENERALLY HAD SOME EXERCISE WITH BOB WITH THE RUGBY BALL OR BADMINTON. IT WAS GENUINE EXERCISE TOO! PLAYED

BRIDGE AGAIN LATER IN MORNING AFTER 'ROBBY' HAD FINISHED HIS MEDICAL DUTIES. WHILE BEFOREHAND I GOT STUCK INTO BILL'S BOOK! HAD A 'WIZARD' DINNER WITH A SECOND IN ADDITION – THERE WAS CABBAGE AGAIN. "RED" (S.S.M. LLOYD) AND "PAUL" (SGT HILL), CAMP LEADER AND ADJUTANT, WERE SUDDENLY TAKEN AWAY WITH NO WARNING UNDER THE PRETENCE THAT THEY WERE BEING MOVED TO AN ARMY CAMP AS THEY WERE PARATROOPERS AND THEY COULD NOT TAKE THEIR PERSONAL BELONGINGS EVEN! AFTER THEY HAD LEFT THEIR HUT (HEADQUARTERS ALSO) WAS STRIPPED RIGHT DOWN BY THE FERRETS, BUT THEY NEVER FOUND A THING! POOR CLUELESS CREATURES! THE FERRETS HAVE BEEN WANDERING AROUND A LOT RECENTLY AND HAVE GOT THEIR HANDS ON A MAP OR TWO AND CONSEQUENTLY APPEAR TO BE IN WHAT IS COMMONLY KNOWN AS A 'FLAT SPIN'. HOWEVER, IT

33. HONOUR BEFORE HONOURS

SEEMS RATHER QUEER THAT THIS SHOULD JUST HAPPEN TO 'RED' AND PAUL ONLY TWO DAYS (OR RATHER LESS) AFTER A NEW BUNCH COMES IN, AMONG WHOM THERE IS A VERY SUSPICIOUS CHARACTER, APPARENTLY ALREADY KNOWN FOR HIS WILLINGNESS TO HELP 'JERRY'. ANYWAY, ENOUGH SAID FOR THE TIME BEING. TO CONTINUE – AFTER DINNER THERE FOLLOWED TWO HOURS OF STRAINED RELATIONSHIPS BETWEEN US AND 'JERRY' – ONE LITTLE FAT BOMBASTIC GERMAN SHOUTING AND GESTICULATING AT SOME OF THE BOYS, ANOTHER LAD BEING LEAD OFF TO ONE OF THE HUTS BY THE GERMAN W/O FOR A DRESSING DOWN AND ONE OF THE GUARDS THREATENING TO SHOOT! WHAT A LAUGH AND OF COURSE WE DIDN'T MISS THE CHANCE OF GIVING THEM A FEW REMARKS AND 'BOOS', WHICH NATURALLY DID NOT IMPROVE THEIR TEMPER! JOE MUST BE GETTING UNCOMFORTABLE CLOSE FOR THEM, SO I DON'T BLAME THEM FOR PANICING. PARADE CAME EARLY TO-DAY FOR SOME REASON(?) – AT 3.30. AFTERWARDS 'ROBBY' AND I SETTLED DOWN TO A GAME OF BRIDGE UNTIL TEA-TIME, THEN AT 5.30 WE HAD A CAMP MEETING, AT WHICH F/SGT THOMPSON WAS NOMINATED CAMP LEADER AND UNANIMOUSLY APPROVED AND F/SGT WALKTY TOOK ON THE DUTIES OF ADJUTANT. CONTINUES THE BRIDGE GAME UNTIL SUPPER-TIME WHEN WE COMPLETED IT ROUNDING IT OFF WITH A '2 NO TRUMPS' CALL ON A 224PTS HAND! PLAYED 'BALDY' AT CHESS IN THE FADING LIGHT AND GOT MY REVENGE FOR YESTERDAY'S DEFEAT. ENDED UP THE EVENING LYING IN BED DISCUSSING REDS HASTY DISAPPEARANCE BEFORE ROLLING OVER AND

GOING TO SLEEP BETWEEN TWO BLANKETS INSTEAD OF THREE WE HAD BEEN USED TO HAVING. WE HAD TO HAND ONE IN TO-DAY, OTHERWISE THERE WOULD BE INSUFFICIENT FOR THE NEW 'BODS' COMING IN TO-MORROW – WE ARE GOING TO GET ONE BACK FOR THE WINTER! IF WE'RE HERE!

29/7/44 THE MAJOR CAME ROUND ON ONE OF HIS HUT-TO-HUT INSPECTIONS, SO WE MADE AN EXTRA SPECIAL

34   TAKE CARE OF THE PENNIES AND THE SHILLINGS

CLEAN-UP AND AS USUAL TOOK A NOTE OF ALL ARTICLES BROKEN, SUCH AS BOWLS, MUGS, FORKS ETC. I DON'T SUPPOSE THEY WILL BE REPLACED, THOUGH, AS THEY TAKE A NOTE OF THEM EVERYTIME BUT NOTHING EVER COMES OF IT. BILL, NICK AND 'RODG' WENT ON RATION PARTY FOR SOME THING TO DO, BUT I HAD MY DIARY TO WRITE UP FOR THE LAST TWO DAYS. FATTY, THE GERMAN, IS AT IT AGAIN, BUT THIS TIME HE IS PLEASANT ABOUT IT AFTER HIS TELLING OFF YESTERDAY FROM THE COLONEL, AFTER THE MAN OF CONFIDENCE REPORTED HIM. PLAYED BRIDGE WITH 'BALDY' AS PARTNER AGAINST TOM AND RODG AND WE JUST MANAGED TO MAKE IT AFTER 'BALDY' HAD LET HIS HEAD GO ONCE OR TWICE AND OVERCALLED! WENT TO THE DEBATING SOCIETY'S EFFORT "THE BALLOON GOES UP" IN THE EVENING. WELL-KNOWN PERSONALITIES ARE IN A BALLOON AND ONE HAS TO GO OVERBOARD, SO EACH ONE STATES HIS CASE WHY HE SHOULD REMAIN IN IT. AT THE END THE AUDIENCE VOTE WHO SHOULD BE THROWN OUT! THIS FATE BEFELL COL. LINDBERGH, VOTING GOING THUS:-

COL. LINDBERGH 74   LADY ASTOR 61
DE VALERA 53   MARIE STOKES 20
M. MOLOTOV 5   DUKE OF WINDSOR 4
WALT DISNEY NIL

IT WAS A VERY LIVELY AND INTERESTING MEETING, REALLY ENJOYED BY ALL. PAUL WAS TO STAND FOR GEN. DE GAULLE, BUT OF COURSE PAUL IS NO LONGER HERE!

30/7/44 FRIED DRIED EGG FOR BREAKFAST WHICH SURE WENT DOWN WELL. PARADE AT 10.00 AS USUAL ON A SUNDAY AND THEN A DEBATING SOCIETY COMMITTEE MEETING WHERE THE COMMITTEE HAD CARICATURES MADE OF THEM BY THE OFFICIAL ARTIST!

35. WILL TAKE CARE OF THEMSELVES

JUST BEFORE DINNER A THUNDERSTORM PASSED OVER AND AT THE SAME TIME AN AIR-RAID WARNING CAME THROUGH SO WE WERE CONFINED TO OUR HUTS, AS WE HAVE BEEN ON PREVIOUS OCCASIONS. OCCUPIED MY TIME CALCULATING HOW MUCH I WOULD BE WORTH AT THE END OF AUGUST – I WILL HAVE ENOUGH TO GO ON LEAVE WITH, ANYWAY!! PLAYED THE SECOND LATE GAME OF THE BRIDGE CONTEST IN THE AFTERNOON AND AFTER A CLOSE GAME, ENDED UP WITH A FLOURISH. TOM, RODG AND BOB WENT INTO TOWN FOR SOME THINGS REQUIRED TO BE BROUGHT UP TO THE CAMP AND FOUND THAT THE 20 OF THEM HAD TO HAUL 3 CARTS LADEN WITH GOODS UP TO HERE - A DISTANCE OF ABOUT 2½ MILES!! WERE THEY CHEESED WHEN THEY GOT BACK? OR WERE THEY? AT NIGHT WENT TO THE CONCERT, WHICH WAS VERY GOOD, PARTICULARLY A TURN "I WAS AN ACTOR" – WE HAD GREEN, MAC AND OGILVIE TOGETHER AGAIN AND CONSEQUENTLY 10 MINUTES OF RIOT!

31/7/44 RODG'S WEDDING ANNIVERSARY TO-DAY – MARRIED ONE YEAR. AFTER PARADE PREPARED TO WRITE OUT RADIO-LETTER FORMS FOR THE BOYS. BUT THE IDEA WAS 'SCRUBBED' OWING TO LACK OF CERTAIN KNOWLEDGE REGARDING THEM, AS THEY ARE HANDLED BY "JERRY". LISTENED TO THE EXPERIENCES, SOME TRULY AMAZING, OF ONE OF THE LADS WHO HAS BEEN ON ANOTHER CAMP FOR TWO YEARS AND JUST ARRIVED HERE YESTERDAY. SAW ONE OR TWO PHOTOGRAPHS HE POSSESSED OF THEIR ACCORDION (IN EVENING DRESS!!) BAND AND GROUPS OF LADS. "PATIENCE IS A VIRTUE", SO I GOT DOWN TO CULTIVATING IT AND SAT DOWN TO A SESSION OF PATIENCE WITH THE CARDS UNTIL DINNER. WORKED OUT A CONVENTION WITH RODG FOR BRIDGE AND ENDEAVOURED TO PUT IT INTO PRACTICE IN THE EVENING, BUT WE

36. SILENCE IS GOLDEN

DID NOT GET THE CARDS! WE PLAYED UNTIL SUPPER TIME, THEN I CAME BACK TO OUR HUT TO FIND THAT NICK HAD A VISITOR, WHO HAILS FOR SOUTH SHIELDS. HE WAS ONE OF THE OLD-TIMERS ARRIVED YESTERDAY SO WE HAD A CHAT

AND A WALK ROUND THE COMPOUND BEFORE THE WHISTLE BLEW FOR EVERYONE TO BE IN THEIR HUTS. BILL HAD BEEN OUT TO SUPPER WITH A LAD WHO COMES FROM HIS HOME TOWN, SO WE LAY TALKING OF THIS OTHER CAMP AND ARGUING HOW LONG WE WOULD BE HERE IN THE LIGHT OF MORE INTERESTING REVELATIONS CONCERNING THE RUSSIAN FRONT. BETS ARE FLOWING FREELY BETWEEN THE OPTIMISTIC AND THE PESSIMISTIC!

1/8/44 WENT FOR A CHAT WITH THE "GEORDIES" AMONG THE NEW LADS AND THEN MET SOME OF THE OLD ONES TOO, TALKING OF THE TIMES, TOWN AND PALS, DANCES, FILMS AND THEATRE SHOWS. AFTER A GOOD DINNER - NICK AND I HAVING SOME OF 58's AS THEY COULD NOT EAT IT ALL (!) – "ROBBY" AND I FINISHED OUR LAST BRIDGE GAME OFF, WINNING EVENTUALLY AFTER BOTH SIDES HAD GONE DOWN DOUBLED AND OCCASIONALLY REDOUBLED! GOT ON PARADE LATE THROUGH PLAYING THE LAST GAME, WHICH WAS THE DECIDER. THE MAJOR (THE COMPARATIVELY NEW ONE) THREATENED TO KEEP US STANDING ON PARADE AN HOUR IF WE DID NOT KEEP QUIET. QUIETNESS REIGNED! SORTED OUT OUR RED CROSS PARCELS ON RETURN AND THE ADDITIONAL TINS OF FOOD WE RECEIVED FROM 'JOKERS' TRANSFERRED HERE FROM THE OTHER CAMP – QUITE A CONSIDERABLE AMOUNT. IT WAS CERTAINLY VERY WELCOME. IT WAS HARD ON THEM, THOUGH, TO THINK THAT THEY HAD SAVED UP ALL THAT FOOD ONLY TO COME AND GET EVERY TIN PUNCTURED BY JERRY HERE. HENCE THE REASON FOR SHARING IT OUT. BILL AND I PLAYED "TOMBOLA" (HOUSEY-HOUSEY) IN THE EVENING AND LOST 9 CIGARETTES NOT WINNING A THING BETWEEN US. TALKED OF THE OLD TIMES AGAIN BACK ON THE STATION AND BROUGHT UP THE OLD LAUGHS.

37. HE CONQUERS WHO ENDURES

2/8/44 COMMUNIQUÉ LOOKS EXCEEDINGLY GOOD AGAIN – JERRY TAKING A PASHING ON ALL FRONTS. PLAYED MONOPOLY WITH 58 ON THEIR HOME-MADE BOARD, WHICH IS A VERY GOOD EFFORT AND THEN WENT DOWN TO THE CENTRE OF EDUCATION TO ENTER MY NAME FOR THE VARIOUS SUBJECTS I WANTED TO TAKE – MERCANTILE LAW, BOOK-KEEPING, ECONOMICS AND FRENCH. HAD ANOTHER GOOD DINNER – NEW POTATOES, WHICH WERE DELICIOUS BUT THERE WASN'T ENOUGH, BUT AFTER WAITING IN THE

QUEUE FOR ABOUT ½ HOUR I JUST MANAGED TO GET A SMALL SECOND. IT IS LOUSY OUTSIDE, RAINING MOST OF THE TIME, SO SPENT MOST OF THE AFTERNOON IN THE HUT WRITING UP MY DIARY AND PLAYING PATIENCE AND THINKING NOT A LITTLE OF HOME, JEAN AND THE MANY WIZARD LEAVES I'VE HAD. GRAND THOUGHTS AND NEVER-TO-BE-FORGOTTEN MEMORIES. ON PARADE AT 4.30 IT POURED WITH RAIN AND AS WE HAD JUST COMMENCED THE SYSTEM WHEREBY THERE WERE ONLY TWO DIVISIONS INSTEAD OF THE USUAL SIX, JERRY COULD NOT COMPETE WITH THE COUNTING AND GOT INTO A FLAT SPIN, CONSEQUENTLY KEEPING US THERE FOR ABOUT AN HOUR, COUNTING AND RE-COUNTING. IN THE END HE GAVE UP (!) AND CONFINED US TO OUR HUTS FOR A CHECK-UP ON ALL THE HUTS. WHEN THAT WAS COMPLETED THE RAIN HAD CEASED SO HE HAD US ON PARADE AGAIN, THIS TIME IN THE SIX DIVISIONS, SO HE GOT THE NUMBER CORRECT FIRST TIME!! EVENTUALLY WE HAD OUR TEA ABOUT 7.00, BUT WITH NO HOT DRINK, AS THE PUMP HAD BROKEN AND THERE WAS NO WATER! NO DRINK FOR SUPPER EITHER. ALL WE HAD WAS THE DOUBTFUL WATER TO DRINK FROM THE OTHER PUMP. AT NIGHT WE PULLED BOB'S LEG ABOUT ALL HIS GIRLS IN VARIOUS PARTS OF THE WORLD AND OF COURSE HE RETALIATED!
3/8/44 WOKE UP TO THE TUNE OF SOME HEAVY EXPLOSIONS NOT SO FAR FROM HERE, WHICH RESOUNDED THROUGH THE CAMP. THERE WAS ONE IN PARTICULAR JUST AFTER PARADE, AND EVERYONE CHEERED.

38   A STITCH IN TIME SAVES NINE

SHOUTING REMARKS SUCH AS "JOE'S-A-COMING", "HOIST THE RED FLAG", "YOU'VE HAD YOUR TIME JERRY" AND THE GUARDS WERE SOMEWHAT PERTURBED! TINY CAME OVER TO PLAY CRIB FOR A WHILE, AND THEN I WENT ROUND TO SEE THE GEORDIES THAT RECENTLY CAME HERE. CHATTED AND GOT THEIR SIGNATURES IN THE BOOK AND IN ADDITION I GOT A COLLAR AND TIE FROM THE SUNDERLAND LAD! SPENT THE AFTERNOON REPAIRING MY SOCKS, TROUSERS, SEWING ON BUTTONS AND MY COLLAR ON TO MY SHIRT. LOUSY DAY AGAIN, BUT IT CLEARED UP TOWARDS EVENING. WALKED ROUND THE COMPOUND WITH BOB SEVERAL TIMES DISCUSSING THE WAR FRONTS AND TO-DAYS COMMUNIQUÉ – QUITE A GOOD PICTURE ALL TOLD.

4/8/44 WEATHER NONE TOO GOOD AGAIN, SO PLAYED BRIDGE, CRIB AND PATIENCE DURING THE DAY. WROTE HOME AND TO JEAN. WANDERED AROUND ENDEAVOURING TO FIND OUT THE NAME OF THE ROAD JEAN, MY COUSIN, LIVES IN WHICH HAD GIVEN ME QUITE A LOT OF THOUGHT. EVENTUALLY THOUGHT OF IT MY SELF AND GOT SAME CONFIRMED. TEA WAS NOT UNTIL 7.00 OR THEREABOUTS OWING TO OUR MEAGRE BREAD RATION NOT ARRIVING UNTIL THEN! TURKEY HAS BROKEN OFF DIPLOMATIC RELATIONS WHICH DOUBTLESS WILL HAVE SERIOUS CONSEQUENCES FOR JERRY, AND ALONG WITH OTHER ITEMS THE COMMUNIQUÉ IS ANOTHER GOOD ONE TO-DAY. TOMMY EXPOUNDED TO US WHAT COURSE THE WAR WAS NOW GOING TO FOLLOW AND WHEN IT WOULD END! HOME FOR CHRISTMAS IS HIS CRY TOO! QUITE A LOT OF NOISE GOING ON TO-NIGHT IN VARIOUS PARTS OF THE CAMP.

5/8/44 PREPARED FOR THE COLONELS INSPECTION AFTER ROLL CALL. HOWEVER, WHEN WE RETURNED TO OUR HUTS AFTER PARADE, GUARDS AND FERRETS HAD SHUT OUR HUTS PRIOR TO SEARCHING THEM. OF THIS THE COLONEL WAS UNAWARE (!!!) SO HE HAD TO CANCEL HIS INSPECTION AND SOME OF THE HUTS WERE THOROUGHLY SEARCHED – THEY

39. THE APPAREL OFT PROCLAIMS THE MAN

SAY THAT THE NOISE GOING ON LAST NIGHT WAS OF A SUSPICIOUS NATURE! HUT 52, NEXT DOOR, WAS IN AN UPROAR – BUT AS USUAL THEY HAD NO CLUE AND FOUND NOTHING – NOT THE FIRST TIME! GOT ROPED IN THIS MORNING FOR FATIGUES, DOING A HEAVY MORNINGS WORK CARTING BRICKS. HAD TO STAND A TELLING OFF FROM OFFICIOUS FAT, BOMBASTIC GERMAN, WHO IS GETTING VERY POPULAR HERE – AND THEN HE CAME OUT WITH WHAT HE CALLED JOKES! BY, HE'S ON THE LIST. DID ALL MY NECESSARY WASHING WITH BOB AND RODG. IN THE AFTERNOON, EACH OF US FIGHTING OVER THE SCRUBBING BRUSH! PLAYED BRIDGE LATER AND THEN WENT OVER TO THE COMPOUND ENTRANCE TO SEE THE NEW CHAPS ARRIVE AND GET SOME NEWS – WE GOT IT ALL RIGHT! PREPARATION FOR VICTORY PARADES IN ENGLAND IN NOVEMBER! JOE'S TAKEN WARSAW AND CRACKOW AND IS HEADING THIS WAY! FLORENCE HAS FALLEN! BOY OH BOY! THE RUSSIANS MUST BE ONLY ABOUT 60 MILES AWAY, FOR CRACKOW IS ONLY 70. IT IS POSSIBLE TO HEAR THE GUNFIRE REGULARLY, WHEN THERE IS NOT TOO MUCH NOISE. HEARD

ALSO THAT THE LADS AT IDABURG CAMP (WHERE WE ORIGINALLY WERE POSTED FROM TRANSIT CAMP AND IT WAS CANCELLED AT THE LAST MINUTE) WERE RELEASED BY JOE AND ARE NOW ON THEIR WAY BACK TO 'BLIGHTY'. LUCKY BLOKES, BUT IT WILL BE OUR TURN SOON – IN FACT EVERYONE THINKS VERY SOON. THEN JOE SAYS HE IS GOING TO BE IN BERLIN IN SEPTEMBER – I HOPE HE SUCCEEDS.
6/8/44 ROSE EARLY FOR A SUNDAY MORNING AND GOT CLEANED UP, SHAVED, BATHED AND PUT ON MY BEST BLUE (INCLUDING MY RECENTLY ACQUIRED COLLAR AND TIE!) AND AFTER PARADE AND A SHORT DEBATING SOCIETY COMMITTEE MEETING, WENT TO CHURCH. IT WAS A GRAND SERVICE AND HELD IN THE NEW COOKHOUSE, WHICH IS SOON TO BE COMPLETELY FOR OUR USE. IT WAS PROMISED TO US A MONTH AFTER OUR ARRIVAL.

40   HE HOW WISHES TO GOVERN OTHERS MUST
AND ITS STILL PROMISED! WROTE A LETTER HOME AGAIN AND ALSO SENT A P.C. TO JEAN, MY COUSIN, FOR HER BIRTHDAY IN NOVEMBER. BILL AND I WENT TO THE WHIST DRIVE IN THE EVENING AND WE BOTH WON SOME CIGARETTES – BILL WINNING THE FIRST HALF "LADIES" PRIZE AND I WON THE FIRST HALF GENTS PRIZE (12 CIGARETTES EACH) – VERY WELCOME! WE ONLY JUST DECIDED TO PLAY AT THE LAST MINUTE TOO! ARGUED AT NIGHT OVER INCOME TAX – THE WAY ITS PAYABLE AND TYPES OF INCOME – THEN NICK AND BILL, HAVING NO INTEREST IN IT, COMMENCED TO BARRACK BY USING "MONOPOLY" PHRASES, SAYING "MORTGAGE IT", "OH, GO TO JAIL" ETC. RATHER A BEDLAM FOR A WHILE! LISTENED FOR JOE'S GUNS AFTER!
7/8/44 UP EARLY AGAIN TO-DAY, HAVING BREAKFAST AT 7.15, AS PARADE WAS EARLY – AT 8.30, BECAUSE WE ARE HAVING A SPORTS DAY OF SORTS BEING IT'S AUGUST BANK HOLIDAY. FIRST ON THE PROGRAMME WAS A BASE BALL MATCH BETWEEN II & III DIVISIONS AND I & IV DIVISIONS, WHICH II & III WON BY 27-25 AFTER A VERY EXCITING GAME. THE CRICKET MATCH, ENGLAND V AUSTRALIA WAS ABOUT TO COMMENCE AT 11.00 WHEN AN AIR RAID WARNING CAME THROUGH AND EVERYONE WAS CONSEQUENTLY CONFINED TO THEIR HITS, WHERE RODG, BILL, TOM AND I PLAYED

BRIDGE. THE ALL-CLEAR CAME ABOUT ¾ HR LATER, BUT HANG ME IF ANOTHER AIR RAID WARNING DIDN'T COME THROUGH A FEW MINUTES LATER, WHICH KEPT US IN OUR HUTS UNTIL 1.30pm PREVENTING US FROM HAVING OUR DINNER UNTIL THEN, ALTHOUGH IT HAD BEEN READY AN HOUR. WELL, AFTER DINNER THE CRICKET MATCH EVENTUALLY COMMENCED WITH ENGLAND GOING IN TO BAT FIRST. IT APPEARED AS THOUGH IT WAS GOING TO BE A COMPLETE ROUT FOR THEM, FOR WITH THE SCORE 14 FOR 5, EAST WENT IN

41. FIRST LEARN TO GOVERN HIMSELF

AND SCORED 36 AND ONLY A FEW OF THEM WERE SINGLES. ENGLAND SCORED A TOTAL OF 65 RUNS AND AT THE CLOSE OF PLAY FOR THE DAY AT 4.30 (ROLL CALL TIME) AUSTRALIA WERE 46 FOR 4 – PLAY TO BE CONTINUED TO-MORROW. DURING THE AFTERNOON SIDE-SHOWS WERE ERECTED – "KNOCK THE CANS OFF", SKITTLES, HOOP-LA, "COUNT THE RAISINS!, BURIES TREASURE, CROWN AND ANCHOR, "THROW YOUR CIGARETTES ON THE SQUARES TO WIN, DICE THROWING ETC. IT WAS GOOD FUN, YOU PAID FOR YOUR TRIES IN CIGARETTES AND RECEIVED CIGARETTES BACK AS PRIZES,. THEY WERE ALL RUN BY THE ENTERTAINMENTS COMMITTEE AND THEY COMMENCED WITH THEIR PREPARED POOL OF CIGARETTES. AT 6.15 THERE WAS A BOXING SHOW, TO WHICH THE COLONEL AND THE THREE MAJORS CAME, PLUS LUDWIG, THE COOK, AND SEVERAL "FERRETS".

RESULTS:- (ALL CONTESTS 3 TWO MIN. ROUNDS)
1 **FLYWEIGHT**
SGT. SMART, BROMLEY BEAT SGT LATCHFORD, SALFORD, ON POINTS.
2 **LIGHT-HEAVY WEIGHT**
F/SGT WILLMOT, MANCHESTER BEAT SGT CLIFF, MANCHESTER, ON POINTS.
3 **NEEDLEMATCH**
THE TWO CLOWNS F/S STURGESS, LEICESTER, AND SGT LYNCH, ISLEWORTH BOTH ENDED UP KNOCKED OUT. A GOOD LAUGH. IN THIS "BOUT" SOME WATER WAS THROWN IN THE AUDIENCE AND ONE LOT THROWN

CAUGHT THE OBERVELTWEBEL (DON'T ASK ME IF THAT'S THE

42   A ROLLING STONE GATHERS NO MOSS

CORRECT SPELLING!) – THE "FERRET-IN-CHIEF" AND HE DIDN'T SEE THE JOKE, BUT AT LEAST HE DID NOT SAY ANYTHING, BUT IF LOOKS COULD KILL – WELL!!!

4 EXHIBITION MATCH
SGT YARDLEY, CAMBUSLANG (SCOTTISH WELTER-WEIGHT CHAMPION) V SGT WRAY, MANCHESTER (RAF NORTHERN AREA CHAMPION). (A VERY GOOD EXHIBITION TOO).

5 LIGHT-HEAVY WEIGHT
SGT. GRUBB, ISLEWORTH BEAT W/O LANE, WESTON-SUPER-MARE, ON POINTS.

6 CATCHWEIGHT
SGT. PARRY-JONES (ALLIED SERVICES CHAMPION) BEAT SGT LLOYD, CHESTER (POLICE WELTER-WEIGHT RUNNER UP) ON POINTS.

7 WELTER-WEIGHT
SGT McBURNEY, SASKATCHEWAN, BEAT SGT MINIFIE, B. COLUMBIA, ON POINTS.

IN THE HUT WE WOUND UP THE DAY HAVING A CHAT ON BATTLESHIPS – CLASSES, DEEDS ETC. AND THEN ROLLED OVER FOR SLEEP SOMEWHAT EARLY THAN USUAL. TOMMY WANTED TO START AN ARGUMENT ON POLO, BUT NO ONE TOOK HIM UP – THANK GOODNESS!

8/8/44 THE CRICKET MATCH WAS CONTINUED THIS MORNING, THE REMAINDER OF THE AUSTRALIAN TEAM SOON GOING ALL OUT FOR A TOTAL OF 68 RUNS. ENGLAND WENT IN AGAIN AND WERE ALL OUT BY DINNER TIME FOR A SECOND INNINGS TOTAL OF 111, EAST SHINING WITH A GRAND SCORE OF 40. IT WAS QUITE EXCITING, THE LAST MAN OF ENGLAND'S HOLDING HIS END UP TO ENABLE "BLONDIE" (EAST) TO BRING THE TOTAL OVER

43.   A MAN'S FATE LIES IN HIS OWN HEART

THE CENTURY MARK AND THEN A 'WIZARD' CATCH BY THE "AUSSIE" BOWLER CLOSED "BLONDIES' INNINGS AND ENGLAND'S TOO. AUSTRALIA NEEDS 109 TO WIN THIS

AFTERNOON – IT SHOULD BE PRETTY CLOSE AND EXCITING, IT'S A LOVELY DAY AGAIN AND THERE IS NO LACK OF SPECTATORS, WHO GO SUNBATHING TOO. DINNER OVER, EVERYONE TRAMPED OVER TO SEE THE "AUSSIES" BAT, AND THEY SAW A VERY GOOD EXHIBITION BY THE TWO OPENING BATSMEN - TOMMY AND OHLSEN, THE PARTNERSHIP SCORING 32 BEFORE OHLSEN WAS BOWLED. FROM THEN ON IT WAS ONE BATSMAN DISMISSED AFTER ANOTHER AND AUSTRALIA WERE ALL OUT FOR 63 – NICHOLIN AND BILL DOING ALL THE DAMAGE, "NICK" CLEAN BOWLING SIX BATSMAN. HOWEVER, DESPITE THE RATHER DISAPPOINTING ENDING IT WAS A VERY KEEN AND INTERESTING GAME. THERE WAS ONE INCIDENT THAT DESERVES A MENTION – WHEN ENGLAND WAS BATTING THE SECOND TIME, W/O LANE WAS ADJUDGED TO HAVE HIT THE BALL WHEN THE WICKET-KEEPER (TOMMY) CAUGHT IT AND WAS GIVEN OUT BY ENGLAND'S UMPIRE. OUR NEXT BATSMAN CAME IN, BUT IN THE MEANTIME THE "AUSSIES" HELD A CONFERENCE AND DECIDED TO RECALL W/O LANE, WHO CAME OUT TO CONTINUE BATTING. A VERY SPORTING GESTURE ON THE AUSTRALIANS PART. APPARENTLY KEN LANE HIT THE GROUND WITH HIS BAT, BUT NOT THE BALL. AFTER THE MATCH THE EDUCATION CHAP CAME TO SEE ME AND HANDED ME THE TEXT BOOKS FOR TAKING THE BOOK-KEEPING CLASSES, DUE TO START NEXT WEEK. APPLIED MY MIND TO SAME FOR THE REST OF THE EVENING. HAD A DISCUSSION ON DIVORCE IN BED AND ALSO LISTENED TO THE GUNS IN THE DISTANCE, TRAINS PASSING THROUGH BANKAU, AND OTHER MEANS OF TRANSPORT.
9/8/44 PLAYED BRIDGE MOST OF THE DAY, DOING SOME STUDYING IN THE INTERVALS. THE OTHER PUMP BROKE, SO NO ONE HAS WASHED, BUT

44 IF "IFS" AND "ANDS" WERE POTS AND PANS, THERE'D BE MORE WORK FOR TINKERS

FORTUNATELY THE DRINKING ONE IS NOW O.K. (HOWEVER, WE ARE UNABLE TO USE IT FOR WASHING, AS IT IS OUTSIDE THE COMPOUND). THERE WAS A SHORT MEETING OF EDUCATIONAL INSTRUCTORS, WHEN THE PROPOSED TIME-TABLE WAS DISCUSSED. PLAYED WHIST IN THE EVENING AND WENT VERY NEAR TO WINNING THE "BOOBY" PRIZE – ONLY THE LAST FEW HANDS SPOILT IT. WENT FOR A WALK

ROUND WITH BOB – AT LEAST TO THE EXTREMES OF THE COMPOUND!

<u>10/8/44</u> SPENT THE MORNING STUDYING AND PLAYED CRICKET IN THE AFTERNOON – SCORED 7 WITH A TEAM TOTAL OF 75, THEN PLAYED WICKET-KEEPER. THEY REQUIRED SIX TO WIN WHEN THEIR LAST MAN CAME IN AND THEY GOT THEM, TO WIN A VERY EXCITING GAME. A NO-BALL COMPLETELY BOWLED ONE OF THEIR BATSMEN WHEN THEY STILL NEEDED TWO TOO!! WENT TO THE QUIZZ IN THE EVENING OVER IN THE NEW COOKHOUSE. I HAD CHARGE OF THE GONG ALONG WITH MR PHILLIPS, THE TIME-KEEPER. THIS TIME IT WAS A DIVISIONAL CONTEST WITH EACH MEMBER OF A TEAM SPECIALISING IN ONE SUBJECT, THE SUBJECTS BEING:- ART, HISTORY, MUSIC, LITERATURE, GEOGRAPHY, GENERAL KNOWLEDGE. IF THE TEAMS COULD NOT ANSWER THE QUESTION THEN THE AUDIENCE WERE ASKED AND WHOEVER ANSWERED CORRECTLY RECEIVED A CIGARETTE. THE WINNING TEAM RECEIVED 30 CIGS AND THE WINNING INDIVIDUAL 10 CIGS. RESULTS WERE:-

    1.   DIVISION VI 19½   2. DIVISION I 18½
    3.   DIVISION III 16   4. DIVISION II 15
    5.   DIVISION VII 14   6. DIVISION IV 13
    7.   DIVISION V 12½

    INDIVIDUAL PRIZE: SGT SINDALL (DIV II)

THERE WERE 14 ROUNDS CONSISTING OF ONE QUESTION TO EACH TEAM PER ROUND. THE QUESTIONS WERE CERTAINLY NOT EASY!

<u>11/8/44</u> WENT DOWN TO THE EXCHANGE MARKET AND EXCHANGED 10 RAZOR BLADES FOR 50 CIGS. AND THEN WENT FOR A HAIRCUT – CHARGE 3 CIGS. JOHNNY PRICE CAME ROUND TO SEE ME AND AFTER SOME MORE BARTERING WE HAD A SHORT SESSION OF BRIDGE BEFORE DINNER. LATER I WENT DOWN TO SEE GEORGE (THE EDUCATION BLOKE) AND WENT OVER THE BOOK-KEEPING WORK WITH HIM, UNTIL HE HAD TO LEAVE TO PLAY CRICKET. I CAME BACK TO THE HUT AND GOT DOWN TO THE FIRST BRIDGE GAME IN THE THIRD OR FOURTH BRIDGE CONTEST WITH ROBBY STILL AS MY PARTNER, WHEN IT WAS REFLECTED THAT OUR COMBINATION WAS GETTING BETTER RESULTS AS TIME GOES ON. FINISHED THE

GAME OFF IN THE EVENING (WITH A HANDSOME LEAD) AND THEM WENT DOWN TO SEE GEORGE AGAIN. I WAS INVITED TO SUPPER AND REMAINED THERE UNTIL THE WHISTLE BLEW AT 9.00. BACK IN THE HUT A HEATED ARGUMENT COMMENCED ABOUT WHETHER "THE GERMAN SOLDIER WAS THE BEST FIGHTING MAN IN THE WORLD". TOMMY UPHOLDS THAT THE GERMAN IS! IN THE END THE ARGUMENT WAS ENDED BY NICK AND RODG PLAYING "MACNAMARA'S" BAND OVER AND OVER!! WHAT A ROW!"

12/8/44 SWOPPED MY SLIPPERS WITH "CHEGGA" FOR A BAR OF CHOCOLATE(!) (REPRESENTS 35 CIGS). AFTER WRITING UP MY DIARY AND TIDYING UP, ROBBY AND I PLAYED ANOTHER BRIDGE CONTEST GAME AND LOST BY 410 PTS AFTER A GRAND START. THE GAME WAS VERY INTERESTING AND WAS OVER BEFORE DINNER. DID SOME "GENERAL" WORK IN THE AFTERNOON ALONG WITH SOME STUDY. THEY'VE GOT MACHINE-GUNS UP IN THE SENTRY BOXES NOW – PROBABLY AFTER YESTERDAY'S INCIDENT WHEN SOMEONE JUMPED OVER THE SAFETY FENCE AND DUCKED UNDER THE INNER BARBED-WIRE FENCE TO TURN ROUND TO SEE THE SENTRY AIMING AT HIM. HE IMMEDIATELY THREW HIMSELF ON THE GROUND AND THE SENTRY MISSED HIM, FORTUNATELY. HE WAS NOT TRYING TO ESCAPE, BUT MUST OF FORGOTTEN THE CIRCUMSTANCE UNDER WHICH WE LIVE, FOR HE WAS ONLY AFTER THE CRICKET BALL! ABOUT

46   HE WHO HESITATES IS LOST

TEA-TIME A HS126 CREATED SOME INTEREST WHEN IT LANDED IN A FIELD NEXT TO THE CAMP HERE. THERE WAS ACTIVITY THERE, WHERE BEFORE IT APPEARED THERE WAS NONE. ABOUT AN HOUR LATER IT TOOK OFF AGAIN. ALSO TO-DAY WE SAW AN ITALIAN AIRCRAFT FLY OVER – AN S.M.81. IT WAS REALLY HOT TO-DAY – I THINK HOTTER THAN IT HAS BEEN BEFORE – SO NICK AND I WENT TO THE PUMP FOR A SHOWER. TOMMY, RODG (A PARTNERSHIP WITH A NEW CONVENTION) AND I PLAYED BRIDGE (CUT THROAT) UNTIL DEN MADE UP THE FOUR AND WE SHOWED HIM HOW TO PLAY. AFTER SUPPER BOB, NICK & I HAD A WALK ROUND TO FIND THE COMPOUND HAS BEEN EXTENDED – QUITE A LONG WALK ROUND NOW! TALKED OF OUR OLD PALS IN BED UNTIL WELL AFTER 11.00, TOM AND BOB HAVING A DISCUSSION OF THEIR OWN! NO ARGUMENTS!!!

13/8/44 ROSE EARLY FOR SUNDAY – MUST HAVE BEEN ABOUT 7.45, SHAVED, WASHED AND TIDIED UP. WENT TO THE

SHORT DEBATING SOCIETY COMMITTEE MEETING AFTER PARADE AND THEN PLAYED BRIDGE UNTIL ABOUT 7.15 AT NIGHT, COMMENCING A BRIDGE CONTEST AFTER THE 3.00 PARADE AND CONTINUING AFTER TEA. NEEDLESS TO SAY RODG AND I LOST AGAIN! BY THE WAY, A LOT OF TIME WAS WASTED ON PARADE TO-DAY DUE TO 8 LADS SLEEPING IN – THE MAJOR DID NOT LIKE THEM TURNING UP SOME 30 MINS LATE! WENT TO THE RAFFLE DRAW AFTER THE BRIDGE GAME, BUT NONE OF '53' WERE LUCKY.

CAME BACK TO SUPPER AND A REAL TREAT, FOR BILL HAD GOT A LOAN OF A GRAMOPHONE AND SOME RECORDS FROM ONE OF HIS OLD PRISONER PALS, SO WE SAT DOWN TO A SESSION OF MUSIC FOR ABOUT 2 HOURS UNTIL WELL AFTER 10.00 (WHEN WE HAVE TO BE SILENT). WE HAD ONE OF '58s' HOME-MADE CANDLES TO SEE BY. IT WAS REALLY ENJOYABLE TO HEAR THE MUSIC – FIRST TIME SINCE WE WERE TAKEN PRISONER. IT GAVE YOU A REAL HOME-SICK FEELING, RECALLING TO YOUR MEMORY ALL

47   YOU CAN'T HAVE YOUR CAKE AND EAT IT

THE VARIOUS DANCES YOU USED TO GO TO – ESPECIALLY THE ONES WITH THE GIRL FRIEND (OH BOY!). WE HEARD
    "BEGIN THE BEGUINE"
(TO BUY) – "YEA, MAN"
("   ) – "ALL OUR TOMORROWS WILL BE SUNNY DAYS"
"DEEP PURPLE"
"AT LAST"
"OUT OF THIS WORLD"
(TO BUY) – "ON THE SUNNYSIDE OF THE STREET"
"DARLING"

WE ALL WENT TO SLEEP WRAPPED IN OUR OWN REMINISCENCES.

<u>14/8/44</u> SCHOOL COMMENCED TO-DAY, SO I SPENT NEARLY ALL DAY WORKING! TOOK MY FIRST CLASS IN BOOK-KEEPING (STAGE II) AT NIGHT – I DID NOT REALISE IT WAS SUCH AN ORDEAL TO TEACH! THERE WAS A GRAMOPHONE CONCERT IN THE EVENING IN THE NEW COOKHOUSE, BUT I COULD NOT GO, OF COURSE; HOWEVER I WAS GLAD I COULDN'T WHEN TOM, BOB, NICK AND RODG TOLD ME WHAT IT WAS LIKE WHEN THEY CAME BACK – ALL CLASSICAL! BOB AND I HAD A WALK ROUND BEFORE RETIRING TO BED. BILL WENT OVER TO '58' TO PLAY

SOLO BY CANDLE-LIGHT UNTIL SOME "FERRETS" APPEARED FROM NOWHERE! ABOUT 11.00 TO BAWL AT ALL AND SUNDRY ABOUT LIGHTS. THE REST OF US TALKED OF THE SEVERAL TIMES WE HAD HAD LUCKY ESCAPES WHILE FLYING AND FROM THAT FOLLOWED A DISCUSSION ON "ARE WE GOING TO FLY AGAIN?"

15/8/44 WORKED MOST OF THE MORNING AND AFTERNOON EITHER IN SCHOOL STUDY OR SHOWING TWO LADS SOME OF THE INS AND OUTS OF BOOK-KEEPING WHO ARE IN MY CLASS. FIXED AN ASHTRAY UP NEAR MY BED. WENT FOR MY USUAL WALK WITH BOB AND BROUGHT MY DIARY UP-TO-DATE. RETIRED EARLY, TIRED!

16/8/44 AFTER PARADE EVERYONE HAD TO REMAIN ON THE RECREATION GROUND WHILE A BAND OF "FERRETS"

48   DISCRETION IS THE BETTER PART OF VALOUR

SEARCHED EVERY HUT IN THE CAMP FOR UNPUNCTURED RED CROSS TIN FOOD, EVERY ONE OF OUR UNPUNCTURED TINS WERE TAKEN – 4 TINS OF BULLY BEEF, 3 TINS OF SPAM, 3 TINS OF SALMON, TIN OF KLIM, MEAT PATTY, ORANGE FLAVOURING, MARGARINE AND JAM(!!) NEARLY A WEEKS SUPPLY FOR ALL OF US. WE HOPE TO GET IT BACK EVENTUALLY – PUNCTURED! WE HAD TO REMAIN ON THE PARADE GROUND UNTIL AFTER 12.00! WE HEARD AT THE SAME TIME THAT A LANDING HAD BEEN MADE IN THE S OF FRANCE, BUT WE HOPE IT ISN'T THE SAME TYPE OF RUMOUR WE'VE HAD A-ROUND HERE RECENTLY – FALSE. NO. ITS TRUE ENOUGH FOR THE GERMANS ADMIT IN THEIR COMMUNIQUÉ. WORKED IN THE AFTERNOON AND PLAYED WHIST IN THE EVENING AND AS PER USUAL WON 'NIX'. AFTER SUPPER BILL HAD THE GRAMOPHONE UP HERE FOR US AND ALL 'JAZZ' ENTHUSIASTS JOINED US FROM OTHER HUTS AND WE LAY ON OUR BEDS LISTENING UNTIL EASILY 11.00, BILL HAVING A SMALL CANDLE TO SEE BY. THERE WERE ABOUT 15 OF US, TALKING OF HOME, OUR FRIENDS, OUR SWEETHEARTS AS WE LISTENED. WE HEARD:-

    "LAMPLIGHTER'S SERENADE" (MUST BUY THIS ONE!)
    "BLACK MAGIC"   (SOMETIME!)
    "INDIAN LOVE CALL"   (- DO -)
    "SONG OF INDIA"
    "YOU BETTER NOT ROLL THOSE BLUE, BLUE EYES"

"STARDUST"
"STAGE DOOR CANTEEN"
"WHEN THE STORM IS OVER"   (TO BUY)
DID NOT FEEL TOO WELL TO-NIGHT, SO I GOT SOME POWDER FROM "ROBBY", WHICH I DULY TOOK. I WASN'T TROUBLED DURING THE NIGHT AS I THOUGHT I WOULD BE! THANKS TO THE POWDER, DREAMT I WAS INOCULATED – MUST

49. THE PROOF OF THE PUDDING IS IN THE EATING
BE BECAUSE THE WHOLE CAMP IS GRADUALLY BEING DONE. BOB AND I SHOULD GO ON FRIDAY.
17/8/44 WE WERE CONFINED TO OUR HUTS AGAIN AFTER PARADE SO THE "JERRY" COULD CHECK UP ON OUR IDENTITY CARDS AND PHOTOS. WHILE THUS CONFINED WE HAD THE OLD GRAMOPHONE GOING AT FULL SPEED, NOT WASTING A MINUTE. THE GERMAN CAPTAIN CAME ALONG AND LISTENED TO IT WITH US – HE IS QUITE A BOY! – AND SUGGESTED WE SHOULD HAVE A DANCE AND MADE ONE OR TWO CRACKS. HE IS DEFINITELY ONE OF THE BEST TYPE OF GERMAN AND MOST OF THE CHAPS APPRECIATE HIS EASY WAYS (HE HAS MORE MEDALS [INCLUDING THE IRON CROSS] THAN THE MAJORS OR COLONEL). YESTERDAY AFTERNOON ON PARADE HE WHIPPED ROUND THE BACK OF THE PARADE TO GET A LIGHT FOR HIS CIGARETTE FROM ONE OF THE BOYS IN THE RANKS!! AND THE MAJOR FORBIDS US TO TALK EVEN AND HE WAS TAKING THE PARADE AT THE TIME!! PLAYED BRIDGE TO FILL IN TIME AND LATER STUDIED. DID A LITTLE EXERCISE WITH BOB PLAYING FOOTBALL.
18/8/44 "ROBBY", RODG, BOB AND I PLAYED SOLO AFTER I HAD BEEN TO MY ONLY CLASS IN THE MORNING, AND CONTINUED AGAIN IN THE AFTERNOON. WORKED AT NIGHT AFTER WE HAD ARGUED WITH 58 AS TO WHERE THEY GOT THEIR SIX STOOLS FROM (THEY ONLY HAD FOUR THIS MORNING). THEN WE PLAYED WAR WITH 'TINY' FOR PINCHING OUR WATER (WARNING EVERYONE WHO WENT BY WITH WATER TO BEWARE OF HIM!) AND AFTER THAT WE HAD A GO AT THEM ABOUT TAKING THE TEA CAN BACK OCCASIONALLY! WHAT FUN! IT CAME TO MAKING A DEMARCATION LINE BETWEEN THE TWO HUTS!!
19/8/44 SUPPOSED TO BE A MAJOR'S INSPECTION THIS

MORNING, BUT ONLY THE SMALL, FAT, POMPOUS GERMAN CAME ROUND, SO LITTLE WAS DONE IN PREPARATION. BOB AND I WENT TO SEE PETE, THE CAMP LEADER, AFTER, TO TELL WE DID NOT INTEND TO MISS THE INOCULATION YESTERDAY

50   OUT OF SIGHT OUT OF MIND

AND THAT WE WOULD BE OVER ON MONDAY FOR IT. FILLED IN TIME PLAYING BRIDGE UNTIL DINNER, THEN WROTE HOME AND WROTE TO THE IRVIN PARACHUTE CO. (ON BEHALF OF US ALL EXCEPT BILL) APPLYING FOR MEMBERSHIP TO THE CATERPILLAR CLUB. TOOK MY SECOND PERIOD IN BOOK-KEEPING, WHICH WENT DOWN MUCH BETTER, PROBABLY BECAUSE I HAD MUCH MORE CONFIDENCE. HOPE EVERY LESSON GOES DOWN AS WELL! AFTER TEA I TOOK ONE OF THE LADS IN BOOK-KEEPING (PRIVATE LESSONS!) AFTER HE HAD MISSED THE CLASS THIS AFTERNOON. IT HAS BEEN A GRAND DAY AGAIN. AFTER PARADE THIS AFTERNOON THE MAJOR HAD THE "BAD BOYS" UP BEFORE HIM AND INFORMED THEM HE WAS GOING TO PLACE A GUARD OUTSIDE THEIR HUTS AT NIGHT AND RESTRICTIONS THEY WOULD HAVE TO COMPLY WITH ETC ETC! (N.B. WE STILL HAVEN'T GOT OUR TIN (RED+) FOOD BACK THAT WAS CONFISCATED).

20/8/44 ROSE EARLY AS I COULD NOT GET TO SLEEP AGAIN THROUGH THE FLIES (BLESS THEM!) – NICK AND RODG TOO, WERE UP EARLY, WHICH, INCIDENTALLY, PROVOKED SOME CAUSTIC REMARKS FROM BILL, BOB AND TOM. SPENT THE MORNING WITH GEORGE, TALKING BUSINESS FOR A WHILE, THEN HE SHOWED ME PHOTOS TAKEN AT HIS LAST PRISON CAMP AND OTHER SOUVENIRS HE HAS. THERE WAS AN AIR-RAID WHILE I WAS THERE, WHICH UNFORTUNATELY CAUSED THE CHURCH SERVICE TO BE POSTPONED UNTIL TO-NIGHT. SPENT THE AFTERNOON READING AND WRITING UP MY DIARY. HAD DINNER AT 4.30 TO-DAY INSTEAD OF 12.30 (WHY, I DON'T KNOW). PAID A COURTESY VISIT(!) TO THE TWO GEORDIES IN ONE OF THE HUTS LOWER DOWN; DISCUSSED THE WAR, HOME FRIENDS, IDEAS FOR THE DIARY AND PAY (LESS INCOME TAX!). BACK IN THE HUT PRIOR TO ROLLING OVER, THE SUITABILITY OF GIRLS NAMES WERE DISCUSSED AT LENGTH.

21/8/44 HANG ME, IF AFTER PARADE JERRY DIDN'T

CONDUCT ANOTHER SEARCH, SO WE HAD TO REMAIN ON THE

51. PATIENCE IS A VIRTUE

SPORTS FIELD. SAW GEORGE AGAIN AND WE SAT CHATTING AND LATER WE SAW GEORGE'S PACK BEING REMOVED FROM THE CAMP! HE'S HAD THAT UNTIL THE WARS OVER. ANOTHER CHAP ALMOST GOT A BULLET IN THE BACK WHEN HE DASHED OFF FOR THE FOOTBALL IN AMONGST THE HUTS. EVERYONE SHOUTED AND HE JUST GOT BEHIND THE HUTS IN TIME – WITHOUT THE BALL. THE REST OF THE PLAYERS GATHERED ROUND THE GUARD ARGUING AND SHOUTING, BUT THE GUARD STUCK TO HIS GUNS!! REMARKS FROM THE ONLOOKERS e.g. "LYNCH HIM" "THROW HIM TO THE DOGS" WERE THE SWEETEST ONES! CLASSES COMMENCED AT THE CONCLUSION OF THE SEARCH. AFTER DINNER I WENT DOWN TO THE PUMP FOR A SHOWER – THE HEAT BEING ALMOST UNBEARABLE. QUEUED UP FOR THE INOCULATION, BOB AND I BEING FIRST IN THE QUEUE – THE DOC TURING UP ½HOUR LATE AS BEFORE. I GOT SO INTERESTED IN A BRIDGE GAME AFTER TEA THAT I FORGOT ALL ABOUT MY BOOK-KEEPING CLASS UNTIL ONE OF THEM CAME FOR ME!

<u>22/8/44</u> SOME GOOD NEWS FLOATING AROUND TODAY, WHICH HAS COME FROM AN UNIMPEACHABLE SOURCE. AFTER A LITTLE RECREATION DID SOME SPECIAL WORK! AT NIGHT I WENT TO SEE IT THERE WAS ANYONE I KNEW AMONGST THE 109 NEW LADS JUST ARRIVED, BUT I DON'T RECOGNISE ANY OF THEM. WATCHED A SOCCER MATCH BETWEEN TWO DIVISIONS, THEN GOT BACK TO A LITTLE MORE WORK. LATER DISCUSSED TO-DAYS GOOD NEWS.

<u>23/8/44</u> PUT IN SOME GOOD WORK ON THE DIARY AND THEN BILL CAME ALONG WITH HIS TWO "COBBERS" AND GOT ME INTO A GAME OF BRIDGE UNTIL DINNER TIME. THE MEAT WAS SO HORRIBLE WHEN IT CAME UP THAT WE COULDN'T EAT IT (WE MUST BE GETTING "FINNICKY"!). CONTINUED MY WORK ON THE DIARY AND LATER GOT WORKING ON ONE OF THE "FERRETS" TO FIND OUT GERMANY'S PRESENT ATTITUDE TO THE WAR AND WHAT'S GOING TO HAPPEN TO THEM! QUITE REVEALING! THEY

HAVE NO RADIOS, SO THEY HAVE NO MORE NEWS THAN WE HAVE. POOR IGNORANT SINNERS.

52   YOU CAN LEAD A HORSE TO WATER, BUT YOU
HAD TO REMAIN ON PARADE FOR ½ HOUR AS "JERRY" COUNTED ONE TOO MANY FOR THE FIRST SIX COUNTS! CONTINUED ON SPECIAL WORK AND AFTER SUPPER WE ALL HAD A GOOD LAUGH ON RECALLING ONE ANOTHER'S MISTAKES AND FAILURES OF THE GOOD OLD DAYS! AN "AUSSIE", DEMENTED IN MIND BY THE GESTAPO, HAS ENDEAVOURED TWICE TO-DAY TO GET HIMSELF SHOT BY THE GUARDS BY JUMPING OVER THE SAFETY FENCE – THE GUARD ACTUALLY FIRING AT HIM ONCE. SOMEONE HAS TO REMAIN WITH HIM NIGHT AND DAY, THOSE AT NIGHT SITTING UP WITH HIM FOR HE REFUSES TO SLEEP OR EAT. <u>24/8/44</u> WOKE UP EARLY THIS MORNING AT THE SOUND OF TWO RIFLE SHOTS TO FIND THE "AUSSIE" BETWEEN THE SAFETY FENCE AND BARBED WIRE AGAIN. THOSE WHO GOT THERE FIRST SHOUTED AT THE GUARDS AND CALLED HIM BACK AND EVENTUALLY HE CAME BACK INTO THE COMPOUND (FORTUNATELY, AFTER YESTERDAYS INCIDENTS THE GUARDS HAD BEEN WARNED ABOUT HIM). CONTINUED MY WORK ON THE DIARY, STUDIES AND "SPECIAL", THE DIARY RECEIVING SPECIAL ATTENTION. AS THE NEWS CAME IN, WE STUDIED IT, AND………. BOB AND TOM BUILT A FIRE ROUND THE SIDE OF THE HUT FOR COOKING AND WE USED IT TO FULL ADVANTAGE FOR TEA AND SUPPER, FRYING SPUDS WE KEPT OVER FROM DINNER AND OTHER FOOD FROM OUR RED CROSS PARCELS. WALKED SEVERAL TIMES ROUND THE COMPOUND WITH BOB, BEFORE OUR COMPULSORY RETIREMENT TO OUR HUT AT THE "BOTTOM OF THE AVENUE" TO LISTEN TO SWEET HAWAIIAN MUSIC AS THE SUN WAS SINKING BELOW THE HORIZON – A MANDOLIN AND GUITAR DUET. WIZARD! THE SUNSETS ARE REALLY LOVELY IN THIS PART OF THE WORLD – THE SKY IN THE WEST VERY OFTEN ATTAINS A BRILLIANT RED AND THE PATTERN OF THE CLOUDS MAKES IT A LOVELY SIGHT. THE RISING OF THE MOON VIEWED FROM OUR CAMP TOO PROVIDES A LOVELY SCENE, AS IT COMES ABOVE THE TREES JUST EAST OF HERE.

25/8/44 ANOTHER "TEST" MATCH TO-DAY – SECOND IN THE SERIES ENGLAND v AUSTRALIA, BUT AS BEFORE JUST WHEN THEY WERE ABOUT TO COMMENCE PLAY, AN AIR RAID WARNING CAME THROUGH AND WE WERE CONFINED TO OUR HUTS. IN THE HUT I WAS QUIETLY GETTING ON WITH MY WORK, BUT BRIDGE IMMEDIATELY CAME ON THE

53. CANNOT MAKE HIM DRINK

SCENE ON THE WHISTLE BLOWING, SO RODG, BILL, TOM AND I GOT DOWN TO A SESSION UNTIL THE ALL CLEAR. MORE MAIL HAD ARRIVED TO-DAY, BUT IT IS ALL FOR THE OLD P.O.Ws AND STILL WE HAVE NONE. I HOPE IT COMES SOON FOR IT WORRIES ME TERRIBLY AT TIMES THINKING OF HOW THEY ARE AT HOME. APPLIED MY MIND TO WORK AGAIN AFTER DINNER AND AT NIGHT WATCHED THE FIRST PART OF A COMIC BASEBALL GAME (THE OLD "GEFANGERS" v THE STAFF) WHICH PROVIDED MANY A LAUGH, BEFORE GOING TO THE STATISTICS CLASS FROM 7.00 TO 8.00. TO-DAY THE COOKHOUSE WAS MOVED OVER TO THE NEW BUILDING (AT LAST!), BUT WE HAVE NOT BEEN OVER THERE YET – NOT UNTIL TO-MORROW MORNING. TOOK ON A BET TO-DAY WITH "CHEGGA" THAT THE WAR WILL BE OVER NEXT APRIL (HIS DATE – I WOULD HAVE MADE IT EARLIER!) – I PUT ON A RED CROSS PARCEL AND HE A KEG OF BEER. DISCUSSED AT NIGHT WHERE WE WOULD GO ON OUR RETURN TO QUIETLY BOOZE THIS PROMISED PRIZE!! WIZZO!!

26/8/44 SUPPOSED TO BE A COLONELS INSPECTION AGAIN TO-DAY, BUT IT BECAME THE USUAL FARCE. CRICKET MATCH CONTINUED WITH THE POSITION: ENGLAND 1st INNINGS: 64 2nd INNINGS 14 FOR 1, AGAINST AUSTRALIANS 1st INNINGS TOTAL OF 82. THE AUSSIES STARTED HOT FAVOURITES YESTERDAY AND DO NOT LOOK AS THOUGH THEY WILL DISAPPOINT. LET THE BATTLE CONTINUE AND MAY THE BEST TEAM WIN. POOR OLD BILL, ONE OF THE ENGLISH SELECTORS, HAS TO STAND A LOT OF CRITICISM ROUND HERE. IN ADDITION HE WAS OBLIGED TO DROP OUT OF THE ENGLAND TEAM AT THE LAST MINUTE AS HE HAS SPRAINED HIS "SPIN" FINGER. TOM, FOR "THE AUSSIES" IS NOW OUR ONLY TEST REPRESENTATIVE. THE TEST MATCH IS NOW OVER (2.45pm), ENGLAND HAVING DONE IT AGAIN - BY 12 RUNS! IN THEIR 2nd INNINGS ENGLAND SCORED 101, THUS

LEAVING AUSTRALIA TO MAKE 84 TO WIN AND THEIR LAST MAN WAS CAUGHT WELL OUT IN THE FIELD WHEN THEY HAD 71. IT

54   HE WHO LAUGHS LAST, LAUGHS BEST

WAS ANOTHER GRAND GAME. APART FROM WATCHING THE MATCH EVERY NOW AND AGAIN I SPENT MOST OF MY TIME WORKING, BUT I CERTAINLY WATCHED THE FINISH. THE DAY PASSED BY WITH NO NEWS COMING THROUGH WHATSOEVER-NO GERMAN COMMUNIQUÉ EVEN. QUITE OFTEN "JERRY" DOES NOT BOTHER TO BRING UP THE NEWSPAPER FROM WHICH WE GET IT. BOB AND I STROLLED DOWN TO A HUT AT THE BOTTOM TO LISTEN TO THE GRAMAPHONE AND WE WERE SO ENGROSSED IN THE MUSIC THAT WE DID NOT HEAR THE 9.00 WHISTLE AND IT WAS ABOUT 20 MINS LATER THAT WE CAME BACK TO BANKAU(!!). (I DON'T KNOW WHERE BOB WAS BUT I WAS "SOMEWHERE" IN ENGLAND!). WE THEN HAD A STROLL BACK TO OUR HUT AND THE GUARD, NOT TRUSTING US, KEPT US IN THE SEARCHLIGHT THE WHOLE WAY! WHAT A LIFE! AS USUAL WE CAME BACK TO AN ARGUMENT – ON THE ROTA FOR WHO WAS TO FETCH THE TEA AND RATIONS ETC. – 58 MUST DO THEIR SHARE!!

<u>27/8/44</u> PASSED THE MORNING AWAY WITH BRIDGE, DURING WHICH THERE WAS AN AIR RAID. FLAK COULD BE SEEN GOING UP IN THE DISTANCE SOUTH OF HERE AND IT COULD BE CLEARLY HEARD. KEEP AT EM "YANKEE"! FINISHED UP PLAYING BRIDGE SOLIDLY ALL DAY WITH BILL, TOM AND RODG. (WE NOW HAVE BILL COMPLETELY CONVERTED!). WROTE TO JEAN BEFORE PARADE IN THE MORNING; THAT SHOWS THAT I GOT UP EARLY TO-DAY.

<u>28/8/44</u> HAD TROUBLE WITH ANTS, SO PULLED MY SHELF DOWN AND EXTERMINATED ALL THOSE I COULD FIND – AND HAVING FOOLED THEM BY REMOVING THE SHELF FOR A COUPLE OF DAYS, I HOPE TO REPLACE IT AND HAVE NO FURTHER TROUBLE! HAD ANOTHER INTERESTING CHAT WITH ONE OF THE "FERRETS", WHO HAD BEEN IN ENGLAND AND AMERICA, AND CONSEQUENTLY HAS NOT A ONE-SIDED VIEW OF THINGS. HIS ENGLISH WAS INDEED A CREDIT, WE HAD A GOOD LAUGH WHEN HE TOLD US ABOUT HIS NIGHT OUT LAST NIGHT!! SWOPPED

54a

TWO TINS OF DRIED BEEF FOR BACON WITH BOB. HANGED IF BOB AND I DIDN'T GET INTERESTED IN ASTRO WHEN THE STARS GOT OUT JUST BEFORE 9.00!! ANOTHER ISSUE OF "ELEGANTES" TO-DAY.

29/8/44 STARTED THE DAY OFF WASHING ALONG WITH RODG; PERFECT HARMONY BETWEEN US OVER THE SCRUBBING BRUSH! POOR OLD RODG. WASHED HIS TOWEL AND PUT IT ON THE LINE AND THEN THE WIND BLEW IT OFF INTO THE DIRT! A RE-WASH WAS CALLED FOR WHICH WAS WORSE THAN THE FIRST. LATER I GOT DOWN TO SOME SEWING REPAIRS AND BEING "CHEESED" WITH WASHING I ALSO PUT MY INITIALS AND HUT NO. ON SOME CLOTHING WITH THE IDEA OF SENDING THEM TO THE LAUNDRY. "PARCELS UP" WAS THE NEXT CALL AND AFTER SORTING THEM OUT, "DINNER UP" CAME ALONG. BILL AND I PLAYED "HORSE RACING" – 3 HORSES EACH – OVER WHICH I LOST THREE CIGARETTES, BEING BEATEN "ON THE POST" EVERYTIME. SOME NEW LADS ARRIVED BUT I DID NOT KNOW ANY OF THEM, AS PER USUAL. AT NIGHT BOB AND I WENT DOWN TO KNOBBY CLARK'S HUT FOR A CHAT, TO FIND OUT THE NEWS FROM HIS PAL WHO JUST ARRIVED THIS AFTERNOON. WHEN WE GOT BACK TO THE HUT, BILL HAD THE GRAMAPHONE AND THE HUT WAS CROWDED, SO WE GOT IN SOMEWHERE AND SETTLED DOWN TO ANOTHER JAZZ SESSION, WHICH WAS MOST PLEASING TO THE HEAR. THE PERFORMANCE ENDED ABOUT 10.15PM AND BEING TIRED WE ALL WENT TO SLEEP ALMOST IMMEDIATELY.

30/8/44 PLAYED CHINESE CHECKERS AFTER BREAKFAST WITH RODG, TOM AND "RED" (AN OLD "COBBER" OF BOB'S), AND I JUST MANAGED TO NIP IN ON "RED" AT THE END. PAID A VISIT TO GEORGE, TO RETURN HIS HANDKERCHIEF, AND STAYED FOR A CHAT UNTIL THEY GOT DOWN TO BRIDGE, THEN I WENT TO SEE "KNOBBY" AND HE WAS PLAYING BRIDGE!! STAYED THERE FOR A LAUGH FROM KELLY AND POPPA PULLING EACH OTHERS LEGS. RETURNED TO A GAME OF BRIDGE MYSELF, NICK PLAYING! ONLY BOB TO CONVERT NOW! DURING THE AFTERNOON NICK AND I WENT FOR A SHOWER DOWN TO THE PUMP, THEN I WROTE A POSTCARD TO JEAN AND ONE HOME. EVERYONE WAS ISSUED WITH A SHAVING BRUSH AND A

PACKET OF RAZOR BLADES TO-DAY, WHICH HAVE JUST ARRIVED FROM THE RED CROSS. WENT TO THE WHIST DRIVE WITH

<u>54b</u>

KNOBBY AND THEN WHIPPED UP QUICK FOR SUPPER (IT NOT BEING NECESSARY FOR ME TO REMAIN BEHIND TO SEE WHETHER I HAD WON ANYTHING OR NOT!) AND THEN I WENT DOWN TO GEORGE'S WHERE WE CHATTED FOR A WHILE ABOUT THE WAR. GEORGE AND I WENT FOR A WALK ROUND AND HE TOLD ME ABOUT HIS JOURNEY THROUGH GERMANY WHEN HE WAS SHOT DOWN (2½YRS AGO) AND WHEN HE CAME HERE. "TINY" WAS IN WHEN I RETURNED TO THE HUT AND I LISTENED TO SOME OF HIS POLICE TALES. POOR OLD TEDDY HAS A RASH ON HIS FACE JUST NOW AND HAS A BANDAGE ON – LOOKS AS THOUGH HE'S WEARING A BONNET!

<u>31/8/44</u> CHASED AFTER NEWS BUT UNSUCCESSFUL SO NICK, BILL, 'RODG' AND I PUT IN A MORNING AT BRIDGE AND IN THE AFTERNOON PLAYED "DODGEMS". THIS GAME I SHALL GET FOR PETER WHEN I GET BACK, IF I CAN. HE SHOULD LIKE IT. I WONDER HOW HE IS- I EXPECT HE HAS JUST STARTED SCHOOL AGAIN. NEVER MIND, I'LL BE HOME AGAIN SOON – OH! FOR THAT DAY. NEARLY EVERYONE THINKS WE'LL BE HOME FOR XMAS – EVEN A LOT OF THE OLD "GEFANGERS" THINK THAT, AFTER BEING WHAT WE TOOK TO BE VERY PESSIMISTIC OUTLOOKS WHEN THEY FIRST ARRIVED. PUT MY SHELF BACK TO-DAY SO I HOPE THE ANTS HAVE BEEN FOOLED! SAT AND THOUGHT OF THE PRESENTS I WOULD BUY WITH THE MONEY THAT IS ACCUMULATING FROM THE R.A.F. – I'VE GOT SOME GOOD IDEAS, SO I HOPE THEY MATERIALISE. DID SOME "SPECIAL WORK" UNTIL WELL ON INTO THE EVENING, THEN AFTER SUPPER BOB AND I STROLLED DOWN TO THE HUTS BELOW, MET GEORGE AND CHATTED ABOUT POST-WAR ENGLAND, IMMIGRATION ETC. UNTIL LONG AFTER THE WHISTLE. "TINY" WAS IN OUR HUT AGAIN, "BALDY" TOO, AND WE HAD A FRIENDLY CHAT UNTIL 10.00. NEW GERMAN ORDER OUT RE-STORING UP FOOD.

<u>1/9/44</u> PANIC ON PARADE TO-DAY – FOR AFTER CHANGING THE COMPOSITION OF DIVISIONS THEY COULDN'T

BALANCE THE COUNT! THEY TURNED OUT THE OFF-DUTY GUARDS AND "FERRETS", WHO WENT THRO' ALL THE HUTS. THEN ALL OF A SUDDEN THEY DISMISSED US - WHERE THEY MADE THE NUMBERS UP I'M HANGED IF I KNOW. AFTERWARDS THEY HAD A "PUKKA"

54c

SEARCH OF SOME 24 HUTS, BUT IT DIDN'T INCLUDE OURS. PLAYED A GAME CALLED "OK". (SIMILAR TO "HOUSEY-HOUSEY") FOR ELEGANTES AND LATER BRIDGE. HARRY, "KNOBBY" AND I MET IN THE AFTERNOON AND DISCUSSED THE FORMATION OF A GEORDIE'S CLUB, THEN I WENT DOWN TO HUT 134 WITH GEORGE AND CHATTED OVER EXPERIENCES, PLACES IN ENGLAND ETC. AT NIGHT I WENT DOWN TO THE BOTTOM WITH BOB AGAIN TO COME BACK TO THE HUT LATER TO LISTEN TO BILL ON THE MOUTH-ORGAN. IT WAS LATE BY NOW BUT THERE WAS STILL NO SLEEP AND SO I HAD A CHAT WITH JIM OVER IN 57 AND EVENTUALLY SETTLED AT A LATE HOUR FOR HERE – ABOUT 11-00!

2/9/44 WORKED ON MY BOOK-KEEPING IN THE MORNING AND TOOK MY CLASS IN THE AFTERNOON. WENT ROUND TO SEE THE COMMUNIQUE AND FROM OUR POINT OF VIEW IT'S THE BEST WE'VE HAD. WE DISCUSSED IT FOR SOMETIME AFTERWARDS; THEN AFTER PARADE WE HAD TEA QUICKLY AND WENT DOWN TO THE MESS-HALL FOR THE CONCERT. IT WAS GREAT – ITEMS INCLUDED COMMUNITY SINGING, BAND, SOLOS, MONOLOGUES, SKETCH AND SOLO SINGING. ANYWAY, IF THERE WAS ANY ITEM WHICH "CHEESED" ME, I COULD LOOK OUT OF THE WINDOW AT THE SOCCER MATCH BETWEEN 2 AND 3 DIVISION. IT WAS CERTAINLY FIRST-CLASS ENTERTAINMENT TOO – SCORE 1-1. NO WATER TO-NIGHT AS THE SYSTEM HAS GONE FOR A "BURTON". SHOULD BE OK BY MORNING. BOB AND I WENT ON OUR USUAL WALK, THEN CAME BACK TO PULL TOM'S LEG ABOUT THE NUMBER OF CHILDREN HE'LL HAVE TO GO BACK TO! HE GOT HIS OWN BACK ON MOST OF US! – KNOWING US SO WELL AS HE DOES.

3/9/44 ANNIVERSARY OF THE COMMENCEMENT OF WAR – 5 YEARS AGO TO-DAY! THE ONLY CONSOLATION THAT BRINGS IS THAT IT WILL BE THE LAST ONE – THANK HEAVENS. I WANT TO GET OUT OF THIS 'JOINT' AND

GERMANY MIGHTY SOON. HOME FOR CHRISTMAS DEFINITELY. EVERYTHING IS JUST COLLAPSING ABOUT GERMANY NOW, AND SHE IS DOING HER BEST TO KEEP "JOE" OUT UNTIL THE ALLIES GET IN. I KNOW "JERRY" IS REALLY SCARED OF RUSSIA AND ADMITS THAT THEY WILL NOT BE ABLE TO HOLD

54d

THEM FOR ANY LENGTH OF TIME. WELL, HAVING COME TO THAT CONCLUSION AND PUT IT IN WORDS, I WENT DOWN TO 134 AND CHATTED WITH GEORGE, STAN AND VIC UNTIL DINNER (I WAS STILL THINKING IT WAS ABOUT 11.00 WHEN IT CAME – AT 1.00). BACK TO 134 FOR BRIDGE ONLY PARADE AT 3.00 INTERRUPTING US TO 5.00. ON PARADE, ONE MAN WAS MISSING, SO OF COURSE WE HAD TO STAY THERE UNTIL HE WAS ACCOUNTED FOR – IT WAS DAMN COLD TOO ALTHOUGH FINE. EVENTUALLY THE MISSING MAN WAS FOUND ASLEEP IN THE HUT! AT NIGHT WE PLAYED BRIDGE BETWEEN OURSELVES AND AFTER SUPPER BOB AND I WENT FOR A WALK ROUND AND THEN POPPED IN 134 UNTIL 10.00. CHATTED ABOUT THE PROGRESS OF THE WAR, NEW ZEALAND, ENGLAND ETC.

4/9/44 LABOUR DAY AND OUR SPORTS DAY - THE FINAL WIND-UP TO EIGHT DAYS OF ENTERTAINMENT. WATCHED THE SPORTS ALL DAY TO TEA TIME – RUNNING MYSELF IN THE SKIPPING RACE, THREE LEGGED RACE (WITH NICK) – NO CLUE IN EITHER. RAN IN THE ½ MILE (SECOND) AND 1 MILE (FIFTH). NICK WON THE SKIPPING RACE. WE HAD SOME GOOD FUN, THERE BEING SOME GOOD ATHLETES ABOUT. THERE WERE ALSO SIDESHOWS – CROWN AND ANCHOR, HORSE RACING, CRAP, "SLING-IT", "THE COLOURS YOURS" AND FORTUNE TELLING!! CIGARETTES FLOWED FREELY. WENT TO THE BOXING IN THE EVENING AFTER CHATTING WITH BOB AND GEORGE. SOME NEW LADS CAME IN AND WENT OVER TO SEE IF I KNEW ANY OF THEM DURING THE INTERVAL IN THE BOXING, BUT DID NOT RECOGNISE ANYONE. THEREFORE, IMAGINE MY SURPRISE WHEN BILL LATER TOLD ME THAT ANOTHER ONE OF OUR CREWS WERE IN – LEE'S CREW! POOR BLIGHTERS, WALKED ROUND AFTER SUPPER TO CHAT WITH THEM BUT FAILED TO LOCATE THEM.

TALKED OF THE NEWS THEY TOLD BILL AND OF THE GOOD WAR NEWS.

54e

5/9/44 WROTE UP DIARY, PUTTING IN THE CRICKET, BOXING AND YESTERDAYS SPORTS, THEN HAD A GAME OF LUDO, WHICH WE DID NOT FINISH BEFORE DINNER. IN THE AFTERNOON HAD A LONG CHAT TO GIBBONS AND THEIR ENGINEER, WHO CAME IN YESTERDAY, TALKING OF THE SQUADRON, THE LADS THERE AND THEIR OPINION OF THE WAR. WE KEPT THEM TALKING AT FULL SPEED FOR TWO OR THREE HOURS. GOSH HOW WE WISH WE WERE BACK. HAD OUR PREVIOUSLY ARRANGED NORTH-EASTERN CLUB MEETING AT 6.15, WHICH LASTED NEARLY AN HOUR. FIFTEEN OF US WERE THERE AND WE ARE RAKING THE REST OUT PRIOR TO THE MEETING IN THE MESS HALL AS SOON AS POSSIBLE. WENT DOWN TO HARRY'S HUT AFTER TO DISCUSS THE DRAFTING OF A LETTER TO THE LORD MAYOR OF NEWCASTLE, THEN SUPPER WAS CALLED FOR. BOB AND I PAID OUR USUAL VISIT TO 134 – SPENT MOST OF OUR TIME PULLING THEIR LEG, "REDS" ESPECIALLY! RETURNED TO THE HUT TO LISTEN TO THE REST OF THE GRAMAPHONE RECITAL ALONG WITH ALL THE OTHER BODDS WHO WERE CROWDED IN THE HUT. HEARD IVY BENSON, ONE OF BING, SEVERAL OF JOE LOSS AND OF COURSE, TOMMY DAWSEY, BENNY GOODMAN AND GLENN MILLER. A "WIZARD" CHANGE, BUT THE GRAMAPHONE CERTAINLY FEELS THE STRAIN OF CONTINUOUS USE!

6/9/44 HARRY AND I GOT TOGETHER OVER THE PROPOSED LETTER TO THE LORD MAYOR OF NEWCASTLE AND GOT A GRAND ONE DRAFTED AND THEN DECIDED TO SCRAP THE IDEA! CANVASSED HALF THE CAMP AFTERWARDS FOR NAMES AND ADDRESSES OF "GEORDIES" WHO WERE NOT PRESENT AT THE MEETING. IN THE AFTERNOON BILL AND I WENT DOWN TO 79 TO PLAY HARRY AND HIS PARTNER 'LES' AT BRIDGE – THREE RUBBERS GAME FOR 2 CIGS. (GOOD ONES!) APIECE. THEY WON ALL THREE RUBBERS (WITH THE CARDS!), BUT ONLY WON BY 270 PTS. PLAYED SOLO AT NIGHT FOR "ELEGANTES" AND AFTER SUPPER WENT DOWN TO GEORGES FOR A SINGING SESSION. BROKE MY BOWL TO-DAY (IT SLIPPED OUT OF MY HAND), SO I NOW HAVE TO USE

A "KLIM" TIN. HOWEVER, SOME HAVE BEEN USING THEM FOR MONTHS! CALLED IN AT 57 ON MY RETURN FOR A CHAT TO JIM – TALKED OF THE LATEST NEWS.

54f

7/9/44 PORRIDGE THIS MORNING, BUT IT WAS ALMOST UNEATABLE AND MOST OF IT WAS WASTED, OH BOY, WHAT A STINK WAS CREATED! THE POOR OLD COOKS ARE HAVING TO STAND UP TO SOME ABUSE, ALTHOUGH IT DOES NOT APPEAR TO HAVE BEEN THEIR FAULT. COMPLETED THE CANVASSING OF THE CAMP FOR "GEORDIES" ALONG WITH "KNOBBY". WROTE UP DIARY AND ODD N-E CLUB WORK BEFORE DINNER. (GOSH, I GET QUITE BUSY THESE DAYS). BILL AND I PLAYED A CHALLENGE GAME OF BRIDGE WITH GEORGE AND "RED" AND GOT TRULY BEATEN, BUT WE GOT OUR OWN BACK TO A CERTAIN EXTENT IN THE EVENING WHEN WE PLAYED ANOTHER TWO RUBBERS. WENT DOWN TO GEORGE'S, BOB AND I, FOR A CHAT AFTER SUPPER AND THEN RETURNED TO THE HUT TO ARGUE ON "THE AVERAGE WALKING PACE OF A MAN" AND ON "HOW LONG IT WOULD TAKE US TO COVER 100 MILES FROM HERE ONLY GOING AT NIGHT". STILL GOT SIX DAYS TO THE END OF MY100 DAYS! COME "MONTY", LET'S HAVE YOU!
8/9/44 WELL, WELL, AT LAST "JERRY" HAS FOUND A TUNNEL AFTER WE'VE BEEN LEADING HIM UP THE GARDEN PATH SO LONG. SOME CRAFTY WORK PUT IN BY "HANK" TO FIND THE PERSONS RESPONSIBLE, BUT WE HAD HIM TAPED ON THAT – HE WANTED TO TREAT IT AS A JOKE AND WASN'T GOING TO REPORT IT, ONLY HE JUST WANTED THOSE WHO DID IT TO FILL IT IN!! WHAT A HOPE. WE LEFT HIM TO DO IT AND WITHIN A FEW MINUTES NEARLY EVERY UNTER-OFFICER HAD BEEN OVER TO SEE IT AND IT WAS COMICAL TO WATCH THEM STANDING JESTICULATING AND SHOUTING AT ONE ANOTHER. LATER ONE OF THE "FERRETTS" TOLD US THAT THEY TOOK IT AS A JOKE, BUT ALSO AS AN OFFENCE AGAINST THEM. WOULD YOU CREDIT IT!! THIS TUNNEL WAS DONE PRACTICALLY RIGHT UNDER THE NOSE OF THE GUARD IN THE BOX! YOU'RE TELLING ME THEY'RE DIM. THEY DON'T TREAT IT SO MUCH AS A JOKE THOUGH FOR

54g

THEY HAVE POSTED A GUARD OVER IT. PLAYED SOLO FOR A WHILE AND WON SOME RENOWNED "ELEGANTES" (NEVERTHELESS THEY ARE GOING TO COME IN USEFUL NOW THAT WE ARE ONLY GOING TO GET 25 CIGS, ENGLISH OR AMERICAN, PER WEEK ALONG WITH ONE RED CROSS PARCEL A FORTNIGHT. WE'LL HAVE TO TIGHTEN OUR BELTS EVEN MORE. THIS IS AN ORDER FROM GENEVA OWING TO THE POSITION ON THE WESTERN FRONT – SUPPLIES UNABLE TO GET THROUGH) WORKED THE REMAINDER OF THE MORNING AND PART OF THE AFTERNOON, THEN WROTE A LETTER TO THE EVENING CHRONICLE WITH ALL THE N-E CLUBS MEMBERS ADDRESSES. WENT BACK TO OUR CHILDHOOD DAYS AND PLAYED LUDO AT NIGHT, THEN BOB AND I MADE OUR USUAL VISIT TO GEORGE FOR A SHORT CHAT ON "WHETHER TO TRY TO ESCAPE OR FOOL AROUND WITH NO INTENTION TO". GEORGE WAS DEAD AGAINST IT, BUT BOB AND I WERE ALL FOR IT. GOT BACK TO THE HUT SMARTLY AT 9.00 FOR DOGS ARE TO BE OUT TO-NIGHT (THEY WERE GOING TO BE LOOSE, BUT THEY HAD THEM ON A LEASH WE FOUND OUT). ALSO GUARDS HAD ORDERS TO FIRE AT ANYONE STROLLING AROUND. "TINY" WAS IN FOR A WHILE AND JUST AFTER HE LEFT, A JERRY CAME TO THE HUT WITH HIS REVOLVER OUT AND THE DOG(!) BESIDE HIM AND BAWLED SOMETHING IN GERMAN. WE DON'T KNOW WHAT HE WAS TALKING ABOUT, BUT IT WAS PROBABLY BECAUSE "TINY" IMITATED A DOG JUST BEFORE HE LEFT. POOR OLD BILL GOT A SHOCK THOUGH, BECAUSE HE WAS JUST GOING TO DO THE DOOR WHEN THE GUARD APPEARED! SILENCE THEREAFTER (EXCEPT FOR SOME MUFFLED LAUGHTER).

9/9/44 REALLY GOT DOWN TO "SPRING CLEANING", TAKING UP THE FLOORBOARDS AND SCRUBBING THEM, SWEEPING THE DIRT AWAY UNDERNEATH ETC. HAD A BATH AFTERWARDS AND THEN PLAYED SOLO UNTIL I WENT A "BUNDLE" AND WON 30 ELEGANTES, BECAUSE BOB DISCARDED THE WRONG CARDS! 'RODG' READ HIS BOOK THEREAFTER- NOT WISHING TO "WASTE" ANY MORE CIGS! DINNER.

54h

WORKED AND TOOK MY CLASS IN BOOK-KEEPING. LATER PLAYED SOLO AND HANGED IF I DIDN'T WIN THE "KITTY" AGAIN (60 CIGS ALTOGETHER) WITH MISERE OUVERT, AFTER A "BUNDLE" HAD BEEN CALLED AND "ROYAL ABUNDANCE"! TOM GOT ABUSED THIS TIME FOR A GRAVE MISTAKE. WHAT A CARD SCHOOL THIS IS – WONDER WE DON'T HAVE OUR RAZOR BLADES ALWAYS AT OUR ELBOW! CALLED IN TO SEE THE SOCCER MATCH BETWEEN 1,2,3,4 DIVISIONS (COMBINED) AND 5,6,7,8 DIVISIONS (COMBINED). OUR TEAM, THE FORMER, WON 2 –0.

10/9/44 GOT ALL SPRUCED UP THIS MORNING AND PUT MY COLLAR AND TIE ON FOR THE SECOND TIME SINCE I GOT IT. IT IS QUITE A NOVELTY FOR ANYONE TO WEAR COLLAR AND TIE AND TO LOOK ANYTHING LIKE SMART. BEFORE PARADE SEVERAL OF US STOOD WATCHING THE HORSE AND CARTS GOING ALONG THE ROAD JUST IN THE DISTANCE, WITH THE FAMILIES IN, ON A SUNDAY OUTING. OH, HOW WE WISHED WE COULD BE FREE TO WALK ROUND THE COUNTRYSIDE LIKE THAT. WENT TO THE CHURCH SERVICE AFTER PARADE – IT WAS CONDUCTED ON THE SAME LINES AS A PROPER SERVICE AND LASTED APPROXIMATELY 1 HOUR – BEING TAKEN BY A W/O FROM 5 DIV (ONE OF THE OLD LADS) AND HE SURE IS A VICAR. CHATTED WITH NICK AND JIM UNTIL DINNER, WHICH WAS VERY LATE – GONE 2.00. PARADE WAS AT 3.00, THEN WE HAD A MEETING OF THE N-E CLUB WHICH LASTED UNTIL TEA-TIME – THE REUNION AFTER THE WAR BEING THE MAIN TOPIC. VERY SUCCESSFUL. HARRY AND I HAD A CHAT ABOUT IT AFTERWARDS. AFTER TEA WE GOT THE SOCCER BALL OUT AND HAD A KICK AROUND UNTIL IT CAME ONTO RAIN TOO HEAVILY. IT WAS A VERY QUEER SKY, THE SUN SHINING LOW IN THE WEST JUST UNDER THE CLOUD, RAINING "CATS AND DOGS" HERE AND A BRILLIANT RAINBOW IN THE EAST, LATER JOINED BY A WEAKER ONE. SUPPER, THEN AS IT WAS COLD AND MISERABLE OUT I GOT INTO BED. THEN DEN CAME OVER FOR SOMEONE TO PLAY "SOLO" IN "58", SO I WENT OVER COMPLETE WITH OVERCOAT. PLAYED UNTIL SOME RATHER LATE HOUR, WINNING ANOTHER 30 ELEGANTES.

54I

11/9/44 MY GOSH, IT WAS COLD LAST NIGHT AND THIS MORNING (WHAT'S IT GOING TO BE LIKE IN THE WINTER – HELLS BELLS!). HOWEVER, IT GOT WARMER LATER ON. WORK TOOK UP ALL THE MORNING – NOTES FOR N-E CLUB, WRITTEN UP DIARY, WROTE TO BOB AND HOME AND COMPLETED LETTER TO EVENING CHRONICLE. WORK FOR BOOK-KEEPING CLASS THIS EVENING. AFTER DINNER (JUST AFTER!) THE AIR RAID SIREN SOUNDED AND WE HEARD "THE YANKS" GO OVER IN FORCE-UNFORTUNATELY WE COULDN'T SEE THEM AS THEY WERE WELL ABOVE THE CLOUDS. THIS IS THE FIRST TIME WE'VE HEARD THEM HERE, SO NATURALLY "JERRY" PANICKED AND HAD BLOKES PATROLLING IN THE CAMP ALONG WITH THREATS FROM THE SENTRIES THEMSELVES IF ANYBODY AS MUCH AS STUCK THEIR HEAD OUT OF THE DOOR – ALONG WITH THEIR RIFFLES "AT THE READY". CONTINUED WITH MY WORK, UNTIL AFTER THE EVENING CLASS. SUPPER AND THEN BOB AND I HAD OUR USUAL WALK AND CHAT AT THE BOTTOM. BED AND SLEEP EARLY, WITH PLENTY OF PREPARATION DEVOTED TO KEEPING OUT THE COLD. GOOD NEWS TO-DAY – 50 CIGARETTES TO BE ISSUED TO-MORROW, NOT TILL NEXT WEEK ARE WE TO BE CUT TO 25. ALSO 6,000 RED CROSS FOOD PARCELS ON THE WAY – THANK GOODNESS FOR WE ONLY HAD ENOUGH TO SEE US THROUGH THIS WEEK – I HOPE THEY DON'T TAKE LONG TO GET HERE. WE'RE STILL TO GET ONLY ONE A FORTNIGHT, THOUGH.

12/9/44 AN OFFICER OF THE GERMAN HIGH COMMAND COMING TO-DAY, SO WE HAD TO GET CRACKING ON CLEANING THE PLACE OUT BEFORE PARADE. WE WERE FINISHED LONG BEFORE 58! THEY'RE STILL BUSY AND I HAVE BROUGHT MY DIARY UP-TO-DATE SINCE WE FINISHED – AND THERE'S THE WHISTLE NOW. ALLEZ-TOUS! PLAYED CROWN AND ANCHOR FOR ELEGANTES AND LATER SOLO. IN THE AFTERNOON I PLAYED CHESS WITH "RED", BUT I HADN'T A CLUE! THE SWISS DELEGATES CAME ROUND AND A REPORT IS COMING OUT TO-MORROW. AT NIGHT GEORGE AND I HAD A FEW ROUNDS OF BRIDGE WITH STAN AND "BALDY" UNTIL IT WAS TIME FOR THEM TO FRY THE CHIPS FOR SUPPER. I WAS KINDLY INVITED TO SUPPER, SO I GAVE

THEM A HAND AND LATER ENJOYED A VERY NICE MEAL. SAT

<u>54j</u>

AND TALKED UNTIL 9.00, CHIEFLY ABOUT MAIL (AS SOME HAD JUST ARRIVED DOWN THERE TO-NIGHT). CAME BACK TO OUR HUT TO BED AND DISCUSSED THE POSSIBILITY OF GOING OUT TO THE FAR EAST ON OUR RETURN – IT LOOKS AS THOUGH THEY'RE GOING TO HAVE TO DRAG US OUT THERE – THIS DISCUSSION LATER DEVELOPED INTO AN ARGUMENT ABOUT THE QUALITY OF JAPANESE KITES. ARE THEY UP TO THE STANDARD OF GERMAN, BRITISH AND AMERICAN?.......MUCH LATER – SUDDEN SILENCE BROKEN A FEW MINUTES LATER BY SOMEONE SNORING AND THAT WAS THE LAST I KNEW.

<u>13/9/33</u> POOR NICK HAD A NIGHTMARE LAST NIGHT – OBVIOUSLY AFTER TALKING OF THE FAR EAST! I'M "JOE" TO-DAY FOR FETCHING THE TEA, WATER AND MEALS ETC. MY 100 DAYS ARE UP TO-DAY-LOOKS AS THOUGH I'VE HAD THE 50 CIGS! HOWEVER, IT'S NOT UP YET. (I STILL HAVE TWO OTHER BETS-EXCELLENT TERMS- 1. 50 CIGS. 2. 18 GALL. KEG OF BEER! WE'VE ALREADY DISCUSSED HOW WE ARE GOING TO CONSUME IT AND WHERE – THAT DIDN'T TAKE LONG!) WENT ROUND FOR A CHAT TO HARRY ON POST WAR HOUSING AND LOOKED OVER SOME OF HIS DESIGNS, CALLED IN TO SEE GEORGE, THEN SAW THE NE SPORTS REPRESENTATIVE. PLAYED SOLO TILL DINNER, THEN SIREN GOING ABOUT 12.00 WE SAW THE "YANKS" COME OVER (100'S OF 'EM) –LOOKING SILVER LIKE AS THE SUNS RAYS WERE REFLECTED- IN THE DISTANCE. THE FLAK WAS SURE THICK AND THEN, SURE ENOUGH, A KITE WAS HIT – SMOKE BILLOWING OUT AS IT WENT INTO A SWALLOW DIVE, THEN A SHEET OF FLAME, PROBABLY AN EXPLOSION, AND IMMEDIATELY IT WENT INTO A VERTICAL DIVE LEAVING BEHIND A LINGERING TRAIL OF SMOKE, WHICH A FEW SECONDS LATER, WAS THE ONLY EVIDENCE REMAINING TO SHOW THAT YET SOME MORE YOUNG CHAPS HAD 'BOUGHT IT'. HAD PARADE EARLY TO-DAY AS THERE ARE SOME NEW "BODDS" ARRIVING AND THEY WANT TO GET ROLL CALL OVER BEFORE THEY GET IN THE COMPOUND.

54k

MADE A FIRE AND COOKED SOME BACON FOR TEA, THEN AFTER WASHING UP ETC. WENT TO WATCH THE SOCCER MATCH, BETWEEN OUR DIVISION AND 1 DIV…(THE BIGGEST RIVALS). WE BARRACKED THEIR GOALIE WHILE THEY BARRACKED OURS. IT WAS A GRAND GAME, DIV 1 WINNING 2-0. (THE FIRST GOAL WAS A PENALTY FOR "HANDS", AND THE SECOND WAS DUE CHIEFLY TO 1 DIV'S EFFECTIVE BARRACKING!). KICKED THE BALL AROUND AFTER THEN INTO SUPPER AND THEN ENDED THE DAY HAVING A WALK ROUND THE COMPOUND WITH HARRY DISCUSSING CLUB PROGRESS.

14/9/44 DURING THE MORNING I WANDERED AROUND ORGANISING THE TRIAL SOCCER MATCH OF THE N.E.CLUB, HAVING A LONG CHAT TO NORMAN DELAYEN ABOUT NEWCASTLE AND THE OLD DAYS OF OXFORD AND OLD ASSEMBLY ROOMS. PLAYED "GOALIE" IN THE TRAIL IN THE AFTERNOON, THEN DISCUSSED THE PLAYERS AFTERWARDS. HAD A MEETING AT NIGHT OF THE SELECTION COMMITTEE WHEN WE COMPILED THE TEAM. WENT TO 134 LATER AND HAD A WALK ROUND WITH "RED" AND THEN GEORGE TOLD ME OF AN ARTICLE IN A GERMAN PAPER COMMENTING ON CHURCHILL'S STATEMENT TO ONE PRIME MINISTER THAT HE WOULD BE IN BERLIN BY THE MIDDLE OF OCTOBER SIGNING THE PEACE TERMS. I HOPE SO.

15/9/44 RUSHED AROUND WITH ROY AND ONE OR TWO OF THE TEAM REPRESENTING THE N.E., COMPLETING ARRANGEMENTS FOR A GAME WITH THE LONDON CLUB TO-MORROW AFTERNOON. THIS TOOK MOST OF THE MORNING. HAD A CHAT TO A CANADIAN I ONCE KNEW BACK IN ENGLAND, THEN WENT TO SEE GEORGE. PLAYED MATCH, IN THE AFTERNOON IN A 2 DIV. TRIAL MATCH, OUR TEAM WINNING 6 –1. CHATTED WITH '58' TILL PARADE, THEN AFTER TEA WENT DOWN TO SEE HARRY AND KNOBBY RE CLUB & FOOTBALL ETC., THEN WE ENDED UP PLAYING BRIDGE IN OUR HUT TILL DARK AND SUPPER. NEW ORDER TO-DAY – WE HAVE TO BE IN OUR HUTS WHEN THE "PERIMETER" LIGHTS GO ON, SO WE HAD NO CHANCE FOR A WALK ROUND AFTER SUPPER, AS THE LIGHTS WERE ON BY THEN-ABOUT 8.15! ARGUED OVER CHAPS OF OUR LAST

STATION – WHICH CREWS WERE WHICH & SO ON. GOT WELL WRAPPED UP FOR BED-ITS DAMN COLD!

541

16/9/44 DAD'S BIRTHDAY TO-DAY. I WONDER IF THE LETTER I SENT HIM ABOUT TWO MONTHS AGO ARRIVED IN TIME – I HOPE SO. I WONDER HOW MUCH LONGER I MUST WAIT FOR A LETTER – IF ONLY JUST ONE WOULD COME. HAD TO RUSH AROUND AGAIN, BECAUSE ONE OF OUR BEST PLAYERS CANNOT PLAY THIS AFTERNOON. GOT EVERYTHING NORMAL AGAIN FAIRLY SOON. WROTE UP DIARY AND DID SOME WORK. TALKED WITH BILL OF WHAT WE ARE GOING TO DO WHEN WE GET BACK-FLY AGAIN OR NOT? IT WAS A REAL HEART-TO-HEART CHAT AND IF THERE WAS ONLY OURSELVES TO CONSIDER THEN WE BOTH DEFINITELY WOULD FLY AGAIN…….BUT NOT OUT TO THE FAR EAST. NO DINNER, BECAUSE THE SPUDS DID NOT ARRIVE UNTIL LATE- HOT MEAL AT 5.00. HOWEVER, WE ALL GOT AN EXTRA ONE TWELFTH OF A LOAF. SO WE MADE GOOD USE OF THAT. PLAYED IN GOAL AGAINST THE LONDON CLUB IN THE AFTERNOON-A VERY GOOD GAME AND ALTHOUGH WE HAD ⅔ OF THE PLAY WE LOST 0-1. OUR WEAKNESS WAS AT INSIDE FORWARD AND WE UNDOUBTEDLY MISSED BELSHAW FOR SNAP SHOOTING. HAD A SHOWER UNDER THE PUMP AFTERWARDS, THEN THE HOT MEAL CAME UP- SPUDS AND CABBAGE. WENT TO THE CONCERT AT NIGHT, WHICH I THOROUGHLY ENJOYED – TURNS BY;- THE BAND, JOCK SINGING "THE HOLY CITY" AND "TREES", THE MOUTH ORGAN BAND WITH GUITAR, FIVE MINUTES OF SWING ON THE PIANO, PIANO-ACCORDIONIST, COMIC MONOLOGUE ON " THE SECOND FRONT" AND FRANK STURGESS WITH A FEW SONGS. WENT TO BED STRAIGHT AFTER SUPPER – 8.15, AS NOTHING ELSE TO DO – IT WAS DARK AND NO LIGHTS AND NO LEAVING THE HUT, SO WE ARGUED UNDER THE CLOTHES - WARMER TOO!

17/9/44 ROSE AND CLEANED UP - THE OTHERS LYING IN BED. ONE WOULD THINK IT WAS THE EARLY HOURS OF THE MORNING WHEN THEY GOT TO SLEEP, INSTEAD IT WAS ONLY JUST AFTER 9.00! "JERRY'S" PANICING AROUND HERE, AS JOE IS APPARENTLY GETTING CLOSER – UNDER 80 MILES AWAY NOW AND LESS THAN THAT ACCORDING TO "THE

FERRETS". THEY SEEM PRETTY "CHEESED", AS THE LAST TWO OR THREE NIGHTS THEY'VE HAD THEM OUT IN THE MIDDLE OF THE NIGHT FOR SOME REASON -SUPPOSED TO BE ANTI-PARACHUTE MEASURES AND ANTI–

54m

GUERILLA WARFARE MEASURES. WHO KNOWS WHAT AROUND ANYWAY? JERRYS OUT DIGGING TRENCHES- ALL AROUND THE CAMP THIS MORNING, THOUGH, AS WE CAN SEE – ONLY JUST THE OTHER SIDE OF THE WIRE. WROTE LETTERS AND WORKED ON DIARY. MRS.ASKEW AND "GRIFF" HAVE A LETTER TO COME TO THEM. THERE WAS SOME VERY NICE GRAVY TO-DAY WITH THE SPUDS FOR DINNER, BUT WHAT HAS HAPPENED TO THE MEAT? WE HAVE NOT HAD MEAT SINCE WEDNESDAY AND WE ONLY GET AN ATTEMPT AT MEAT TO-DAY. INVESTIGATION AT ONCE-ANOTHER ONE OF THOSE "RACKETS". YES, SURE ENOUGH, IT WAS LATER ADMITTED AT A MESSING COMMITTEE MEETING THAT 20 PORK CHOPS WERE COOKED FOR THE "STAFF" IN THE COOKHOUSE. SCANDALOUS-NEARLY 50% OF THE MEAT RATION FOR NEARLY 900 MEN OVER 3 DAYS GONE TO 20 IN THE COOKHOUSE. OTHER "RACKETS" NOW COMING TO LIGHT. BIG MUSIC BATTLE ON TOO WITH "MAESTRO" QUINN IN THE LIMELIGHT. ANOTHER ONE OF THOSE EARLY DAY "BUST-UPS". READ IN THE AFTERNOON AND PLAYED "MONOPOLY" AT NIGHT –A BATTLE ROYAL GOING ON BETWEEN TOM AND I WHEN WE HAD TO CLOSE DOWN OWING TO FADING LIGHT. BILL AND I WALKED ROUND THE COMPOUND THREE TIMES THEN RETIRED TO BED TO TALK OF OUR "YOUNGER" DAYS – EVENTS THIS TIME FIVE YEARS AGO. I WAS CHATTING WITH BILL LONG AFTER THE OTHERS WERE ASLEEP.

<u>18/9/44</u> SAW SOME DEER WANDERING AROUND JUST OUTSIDE THE CAMP. A NICE PIECE OF VENISON WOULD GO DOWN VERY NICELY RIGHT NOW. SOME NEW CHAPS CAME IN, BUT I DIDN'T RECOGNISE ANY OF THEM - ALL FROM HOSPITAL, I THINK. DOUG JENNINGS OUGHT TO BE ARRIVING SOON - HE BROKE HIS LEG WHEN CASSAN'S CREW BOUGHT IT. WENT TO WATCH THE CANADIAN'S PLAY A TRIAL GAME OF SOCCER AND SELECT A TEAM FOR THEM TO PLAY THE "AUSSIES". WORKED, THEN AFTER DINNER

QUEUED UP WITH "RODG" FOR SECONDS AS WE FELT PARTICULARLY HUNGRY. BY A STROKE OF GOOD FORTUNE WE MANAGED TO GET SOME DESPITE THE RACKETS! WORKED DOWN AT GEORGE'S ON ANOTHER BOOK FOR TO-NIGHT'S LECTURE. POSTPONED LECTURE LATER AS THE CHAPS WANTED TO SEE THE INTERNATIONAL. CONSEQUENTLY I SAW IT MYSELF –ENGLAND V SCOTLAND. EVEN, A 2-2 DRAW BEING THE BEST RESULT. HOWEVER, ENGLAND WERE DEFINITELY LUCKY TO

54n

DRAW AS THEY ONLY EQUALISED IN THE LAST THREE MINUTES THROUGH A SIMPLE GOAL. ENGLAND SCORED FIRST IN THE FIRST TWO MINUTES, SCOTLAND MAKING IT 2-1 IN THEIR FAVOUR BY HALF-TIME. USUAL EXERCISE LATER WITH BILL AND A DISCUSSION BEFORE PEACE AGAIN DESCENDED ON '53' FOR ANOTHER NIGHT. IT WAS A WIZARD SUNSET TO-NIGHT- A REAL PAINTER'S PARADISE. DOGS ARE STILL IN THE COMPOUND AT NIGHT.
19/9/44 SEARCH THIS MORNING FOR A SECTION OF THE CAMP – I WAS BEGINNING TO WONDER WHEN THE NEXT WOULD BE. WALKED ROUND WITH 'GIBBO' AND THEN SAW JIM AND TWO OF HIS MATES SITTING OUTSIDE A HUT AT THE BOTTOM, SO WE JOINED THEM. WE HAD A LONG CHAT AND AT THE SAME TIME LISTENED TO THE ACCORDIONIST PLAYING IN THE HUT. IT WAS WIZARD. 'GIBBO' TOLD US ABOUT WHAT HAPPENED IN ENGLAND WHEN THE INVASION STARTED AND LIFE ON THE SQUADRON TO WHEN HE CAME DOWN ON 25/8/44. HOW WE WISHED WE WERE BACK. IN THE AFTERNOON AND EVENING I BECAME ENGROSSED IN A BOOK AND VERY NEARLY FINISHED IT BEFORE DARK. SUPPER, THEN HARRY CAME UP AND WE HAD A WALK ROUND CHATTING ABOUT THE N.E.CLUB, THEN THE "RACKETS" – CAKES ETC. DOWN THERE NOW! ON RETURN TO THE HUT AT 8.30, WE DISCUSSED THE "RACKETS" AND HOW TO DISPOSE OF THEM WITH A CERTAIN AMOUNT OF RAGE!
20/9/44 FINISHED MY BOOK OFF BEFORE PARADE AND SHAVED ETC.- MUST HAVE RISEN QUITE EARLY, UNDER CRITICISM! SAW DIV 2 GET A HIDING AT SOCCER FROM 4 DIV – 3-0 WAS THE SCORE, LOUSY GAME. DISCUSSED OUR OWN

TEAM WITH ROY & EDDIE – BOTH UNABLE TO PLAY AND "ANDY" TOO IS CROCKED! ANYWAY, WILL GIVE US A CHANCE TO PLAY SOME OF THE "POSSIBLES". DINNER AND THEN A SESSION OF BRIDGE TILL PARADE TIME WITH TOM, BILL AND "RODG" – FIRST FOR A LONG TIME. GOOD GAME. FOR TEA WE HAD BIG RAW HORSE-RADISHES AND WERE THEY HOT! CHATTED WITH JACK ABOUT SCOUTING AND THEN WENT TO SEE THE SOCCER MATCH: CANADIANS V AUSTRALIANS AND OH BOY, DID WE GET A LAUGH – I HAVEN'T LAUGHED SO MUCH SINCE I LEFT THE MOTHER LAND. THE AUSSIES WON 2-0. THE CANADIANS A PENALTY WHEN ONE OF THE AUSSIES TEMPORARILY ACTED AS GOALKEEPER!! WALKED ROUND WITH HARRY AFTER SUPPER AND THEN A SHORT CHAT BEFORE SLEEP.

21/9/44 MESSED AROUND IN MORNING WITH DIARY, N.E. CLUB MEETING ON SUNDAY, WATCHING OATES AT SOCCER AND AT THE LIBRARY. SOWED UP MY SLEEPING BAG. HAD A TASTE OF CHEG'S TOMATO SANDWICH – IT WAS DELICIOUS! TALKED

TO JERRY GIBBONS. AFTER DINNER (A GOOD ONE, AS THERE WAS MEAT, CARROTS AND POTATOES AND IT WAS OUR TURN FOR SECONDS-AND WE GOT THEM), THEN I GOT STUCK INTO THE BOOK I GOT THIS MORNING. AT NIGHT I READ AND SAW PART OF THE SOCCER MATCH BETWEEN 1 AND 3 DIV., THE SCORE BEING 7-1 IN 1 DIV FAVOUR. WALKED ROUND WITH HARRY TALKING OF NEWCASTLE – MARGARET HUTTON CHIEFLY!! RETURNED TO THE HUT TO TALK (OR RATHER ARGUE!) ABOUT THE SCHOOL HERE. WROTE P.C. HOME TO-DAY.

22//9/44 ROSE VERY EARLY- MAKING SOME JAM WITH MY ORANGE JUICE BEFORE PARADE AS WELL AS TIDYING UP ETC. PLAYED "MONOPOLY", BUT IN THE MIDDLE OF IT, WE GOT SENT OUT OF OUR HUTS FOR A SEARCH. MADE FINAL ARRANGEMENTS FOR THIS AFTERNOON-QUITE A LOT TO DO, AS ONE OF OUR CHAPS CANCELLED IT, BECAUSE HE COULDN'T PLAY! PUT IT ON AGAIN AND FOUND OTHER PLAYERS-IN THE END THERE WAS ONLY THREE OF OUR REGULAR PLAYERS PLAYING-CHANCE TO FIND NEW TALENT! RETURNED TO HUT TO FIND IT HAD BEEN TURNED

UPSIDE DOWN. FINISHED OUR GAME, BOB WINNING. DINNER AND AGAIN OUR TURN FOR SECONDS-JUST GOT SOME-THEN PLAYED SOCCER FOR THE CLUB AGAINST LANCS & DIST. CLUB WE WON 2-1, BUT IT WAS A RATHER POOR GAME, BOTH CLUBS BEING MUCH WEAKER OWING TO INJURIES AND CALLS FOR LEAGUE MATCHES. WELL FOUGHT GAME, THOUGH. WASHED, WROTE UP DIARY ETC. BEFORE PARADE. SEVERAL COUNTS TO-DAY, SOMEONE OVERSLEPT! PLAYED "MONOPOLY" AT NIGHT, TOM AND I JUST ACQUIRED ALL THE PROPERTY BETWEEN US WHEN DARKNESS CAME AND IT HAD TO BE ABANDONED. SUPPER AND A STROLL WITH "NOBBY". TALKED ABOUT '58' AND 'DOWN BELOW' – THE NEW QUARTERS. DURING "JERRY'S" SEARCH TO-DAY THEY FOUND A TUNNEL IN ONE OF THE SCHOOL ROOMS, SO THEY BOARDED IT OFF. THE COLONEL DOES NOT REGARD IT AS A SERIOUS ATTEMPT TO ESCAPE, BUT IF IT OCCURS AGAIN HE IS GOING TO CLOSE THE SCHOOL, LIBRARY AND TAKE AWAY THE MUSICAL INSTRUMENTS! SO NOW WE KNOW!

23/9/44 CHATTED WITH HARRY AFTER PARADE ABOUT THE CAKE HE IS MAKING, THEN RETURNED TO THE HUT TO READ AND LATER PLAY "AVIATION" WITH TIM. DINNER. WORK. AFTER TEA PLAYED AVIATION WITH TOM AGAIN – IT TAKES SOMETIME ONE GAME – JUST FINISHED FOR SUPPER. I'M TWO GAMES UP ON HIM NOW. HAD AN ARGUMENT ABOUT "WHETHER AIRCREWS PAY SHOULD

84 DAY TO DAY DIARY (CONT)

23/9/44 BE STANDARDISED FOR ALL CATEGORIES". "58" CAME ACROSS TO JOIN IN AND WE WERE GOING AT "HAMMER AND TONGS" FOR NEARLY ¾ HOUR! WALKED ROUND WITH NICK AND "RODG" AND THEN RETIRED TO BED AFTER TALKING OF ANIMALS AND THEIR HABITS.

24/9/44 PLAYED "AVIATION" AFTER BREAKFAST WITH TIM, FINISHING IT AFTER PARADE. FINISHED READING MY BOOK AND DID A FEW ODDS AND ENDS UNTIL DINNER. DINNER WAS PRETTY LATE (AS WE ARE LAST TO BE SERVED) – ABOUT 2.00, SO WE HAD ONLY CLEARED UP AFTERWARDS WHEN IT WAS PARADE TIME. HAD A N.E. CLUB MEETING LASTING UNTIL TEA-TIME. THE ATTENDANCE WAS VERY DISAPPOINTING, BUT WAS TO SOME EXTENT DUE,

PROBABLY, TO THE FACT THAT PETE GAVE OUT ON PARADE THAT THERE WOULD BE A MEETING OF THE WEST COUNTIES CLUB IN MISTAKE! PLAYED BRIDGE DOWN AT '79' WITH "KNOBBY" AGAINST HARRY AND LES – WE GOT A TROUNCING. WE PLAYED OUTSIDE WHEN IT GOT TOO DARK TO PLAY IN THE HUT. AFTER SUPPER (ONLY HAD A CUP OF COCOA TO CONSERVE SUPPLIES!) WENT DOWN TO SEE GEORGE AND THE OTHERS IN "134". WAS OFFERED SOME PORRIDGE – VERY WELCOME. TALKED ABOUT SOCCER CHIEFLY. CAME BACK TO THE HUT TO COMMENCE A DISCUSSION ON THE SAME TOPIC-THEN WE HAD A GOOD CHAT ON SPEEDWAY TOO, BEFORE 'SWEET REPOSE!

<u>25/9/44</u> IT BLEW A GALE IN THE NIGHT AND WE EXPECTED OUR HUT TO TAKE OFF AT ANY TIME!! STILL MISERABLE AND RAINING WHEN WE GOT UP – ALL BUT "RODG" AND I STAYING IN BED UNTIL THE PARADE WHISTLE GOT THEM OUT! WORKED IN THE MORNING AND APPLYING MY MIND IN THE AFTERNOON TO ANOTHER BOOK I HAVE JUST GOT FROM THE LIBRARY-VERY APPROPRIATE- "BUSMAN'S HOLIDAY"! I DON'T THINK ONE COULD FIND A BETTER EXAMPLE THAN THIS LIFE, COULD ONE? WENT TO THE GATE TO SEE IF I KNEW ANY OF THE NEW "BODDS", SOME 80 IN NUMBER, BUT ONCE AGAIN NO. AND YET MANY HAVE MET PALS AND WERE CHATTING ACROSS THE WIRE AND SAFETY FENCE. "NOT BE LONG NOW" ONE SAYS. I SINCERELY HOPE NOT, FOR I GET VERY CHEESED HERE AT TIMES. HOWEVER, I HAVE ONLY TO THINK OF THOSE WHO'VE HAD 3 YEARS OF AN EXISTENCE LIKE THIS. MY GOD! AND YET THEY'RE VERY CHEERFUL, AND AS ALL ENGLISHMEN AND THOSE BORN OF ENGLISH STOCK, THEY JOKE OF THOSE YEARS. MANY'S THE TIME I DREAM OF WHAT I WILL DO BACK IN ENGLAND. LATE PARADE TO-DAY OWING TO THE NEW BOYS ARRIVING. MY CLASS AFTER TEA AND THEN SUPPER- WELL, ITS ????? AT 7.00 NOW. CALLED IN AT '79' FOR A CHAT AND THEN BACK

85	LOOK BEFORE YOU LEAP

TO HUT TO GET IN BED A BIT QUICK, BECAUSE ITS DAMN COLD- COLDER THAN ITS EVER BEEN TO-DAY. TALKED ABOUT WHAT EVERYONE IS TALKING ABOUT-ALL THE RED CROSS PARCELS, CLOTHING, CIGARETTES AND OTHER

NECESSITIES THAT HAVE ARRIVED. ALSO THE REPORT RE- THE INTERNATIONAL RED + REPRESENTATIVE'S VISIT. TALK OF EACH MAN GETTING 2 PARCELS EVERY 3 WEEKS INSTEAD OF ONE A FORTNIGHT. WE ALL PRAY IT COMES OFF.

26/9/44 PLAYED BRIDGE IN THE MORNING WITH NICK, "RODG" AND TOM, LATER GETTING THE NEEDLE AND THREAD OUT TO SEW SOME BUTTONS. NIPPED ALONG TO THE "39 STEPS" (BARBERS) FOR A HAIRCUT FOR 2 CIGS. JUST BEFORE DINNER. READ AFTERWARDS, FEELING COLD, UNTIL PARADE. COOKED MYSELF A DECENT MEAL FOR TEA – FRIED SPAM, BACON AND CHIPS! WIZARD, BUT IT ONLY WETS YOUR APPETITE! HAD A LITTLE BREAD AFTER IT FOR FILLING, BUT MUST LEAVE SOME OF MY $1/6^{th}$ OF A LOAF FOR SUPPER AND BREAKFAST TO-MORROW! WENT DOWN TO '79' AND PLAYED BRIDGE UNTIL 10.00, KNOCKING OFF FOR SUPPER AT 7.30 FOR 10MINS. PLAYED BY AN OIL-LIGHT (MARGARINE USED), BUT IT WAS NOT WITHOUT ITS DIFFICULTIES. SNEAKED IN AT 10.00 WITH ALL ASLEEP, JUST LIKE BEING BACK ON THE SQUADRON WHEN YOU CAME IN LATE! NO DISTURBANCE. BUT IN THOSE IT USED TO BE WELL GONE MIDNIGHT! DOGS ARE STILL USED BY JERRY ON THE LEASH INSIDE THE COMPOUND. IT WAS RAINING TO-NIGHT.

27/9/44 "KNOBBY" AND I PLAYED BRIDGE AGAINST HARRY AND LES BRINGING OUR NEW CONVENTION INTO WORK WITH QUITE GOOD RESULTS! FILLED IN A WHILE READING TILL DINNER, THEN CONTINUED AFTERWARDS. HAD ½ HOURS AMUSEMENT WATCHING THE POLISH GIRLS GATHERING POTATOES DURING THE AFTERNOON (ALONG WITH HALF THE CAMP!). WE EXCHANGED GREETINGS. OUTWARDLY THEY SEEMED QUITE HAPPY. TO-DAY – 1/3 OF A LOAF EACH! NEVER HAD THAT MUCH BEFORE IN ONE DAY. READ AND THEN HEARING GOOD REPORTS OF THE "JAZZ" SESSION, WENT TO THE MESS HALL TO LISTEN. IT WAS REALLY A SING-SONG AND I THOROUGHLY ENJOYED IT. OH! WHAT MEMORIES IT BROUGHT BACK TO ME - AND WISHES. SUPPER. CALLED IN AT '79' FOR A WHILE, THEN BACK TO BED.

28/9/44 GERMAN PORRIDGE FOR BREAKFAST. FINISHED READING MY BOOK, AND THEN WENT DOWN TO '79' AND GOT DRAWN INTO A GAME OF BRIDGE UNTIL DINNER. BY, I WAS COLD-WITH HUNGER I THINK. HAD SOME BREAD AND

BUTTER TO FILL THE HOLES DINNER LEFT AND FELT WARM THEREAFTER. BILL AND I PLAYED TOM AND "RODG" AT BRIDGE, THEN WROTE UP MY DIARY. RECEIVED OUR "DOG TAGS" THIS AFTERNOON (IDENTITY DISCS!). GREAT EXCITEMENT AS THERE IS

86   IMITATION IS THE SINCEREST FORM OF FLATTERY
SOME MAIL FOR "THE FIRST 70" – BUT ONLY FOR A FEW. NEVER MIND, THOUGH, IT HAS STARTED. IN 53 WE LOOK EAGERLY FORWARD TO THE NEXT LOT TO COME IN AS OUR HOPES ARE HIGH. PARADE AND THEN OUT WITH THE FOOD FOR TEA. CLEARED UP THEN WENT TO '79' TO FINISH OUR GAME OF BRIDGE, WHICH WENT ON UNTIL 10.30 WITH A SHORT BREAK FOR SUPPER DURING WHICH I HAD A CHAT WITH "CHEGGA" ON THE "COURSE OF THE WAR". SNEAKED IN AT 10.30 TO AVOID DISTURBANCES AND THE BEDLAM!
29/9/44 AFTER DOING SOME ODDS AND ENDS, "KNOBBY" CAME UP TO ASK ME WHETHER I FANCIED A GAME OF BRIDGE-TOO TRUE, SO OF I WENT UNTIL DINNER –TIME. WENT ROUND TO LIBRARY, WORKED, WROTE UP MORE OF MY DIARY AND AGAIN WATCHED THE POLISH GIRLS AT WORK-POOR LASSIES, THEY DO HAVE TO WORK. SETTLED DOWN TO A GAME OF "AVIATION" WITH TOM, FINISHING THE SAME AFTER TEA, LEAVING ME FOUR WINS UP ON HIM! AT NIGHT WENT DOWN TO '79' FOR OUR NOW USUAL SUPPER FOR 1/4HR. VERY EXCITING GAME FOR HARRY AND LES WON BY 30PTS AFTER 3 RUBBERS: 3090 TO 3060! CREPT IN ONCE AGAIN!
30/9/44 BY GAD, SIR, IT WAS COLD LAST NIGHT, COLDER THAN ITS EVER BEEN –AND AS FOR THE WATER, WELL! THIS NEXT WEEK WE ARE ALL GETTING A PARCEL EACH – THAT WILL RELIEVE THE OUTWARD PRESSURE ON THE STOMACH, SOMEWHAT. HAD A LOOK AT THE GOVERNMENT SCHEME OF RE-EDUCATION AFTER THE WAR – DISGUSTED. HELP FOR THE CHOSEN FEW AGAIN!! WENT FOR THE PARCELS AND CIGARETTES (50), WIZARD – THE ONE PARCEL TO LAST THIS WEEK ONLY. PREPARED MY DINNER- FISH CAKES- MADE FIRE AND COOKED THEM – PARTS OF THE HUT SUPPLYING THE WOOD! DINNER (VERY GOOD). WORKED AND THEN TOOK MY CLASS. TEA, MAKING SOME CHIPS FOR SAME WITH SPUDS SAVED FROM DINNER. CONCERT IN THE MESS HALL

AFTER WHICH NICK AND I WENT TO. IT WAS GRAND – "THE COMPOUND 'CARDS' BEING THE BEST ITEM (FLOTSAM AND JETSAM); THE BAND, MOUTH-ORGAN BAND, ACCORDIONIST AND SINGERS MAKING UP A GRAND SHOW. AFTER SUPPER HARRY, LES AND I WALKED SEVERAL TIMES ROUND THE COMPOUND TALKING OF OUR EXPERIENCES AND KEEPING A LOOK OUT FOR "FERRETS" WANDERING ROUND WITH THE "STREAM". ROLLED INTO BED FEELING PRETTY "TIRED" AFTER TWO LATE NIGHTS(!) AND THAT WALK. HAD SOME FUN WITH A MOUSE RUNNING AROUND UNDER OUR BEDS, BUT HE ESCAPED!

1/10/44 WELL, I WASH MY HANDS OF SEPTEMBER TO-DAY – ANOTHER MONTH NEARER TO GETTING HOME. WROTE HOME (A LETTER) AND ALSO SENT OFF TWO POSTCARDS. I NOTICED WHEN I WENT TO POST THEM THAT SINCE THE FIRST "KITE" CAME OUT 3 DAYS AGO THAT IT HAS NOW BECOME A "GEFANG" CRAZE – THE LATEST ONE!

SPENT THE REST OF THE MORNING WASHING AND AFTER A VERY APPETISING DINNER (MEAT, SPUDS AND CABBAGE), CONTINUES WITH MY WASHING AND HAD A BATH MYSELF AFTER 3.00 PARADE. OH, WENT TO AN INSTRUCTORS MEETING AT 2.30 IN THE SCHOOL. SAID I WOULD TAKE ON ANOTHER CLASS! PLAYED BRIDGE WITH "KNOBBY" AGAINST HARRY AND LES AND GOT EVERY BIT OF OUR OWN BACK! SUPPER AND THEN A LONG CHAT WITH JIM BEFORE RETIRING. RAINING "CATS AND DOGS" NOW AND DID MOST OF THE NIGHT.

2/10/44 ROSE FAIRLY EARLY, HAD BREAKFAST AND WASHED ETC. AND THEN DISCOVERED IT WAS ONLY 7.30! THE CLOCKS WERE PUT BACK AN HOUR LAST NIGHT AND NOBODY KNEW IT! ONLY THE "FERRET" TOLD US THIS MORNING-AWKWARD LOT THEY COULD HAVE TOLD US LAST NIGHT. DID PLENTY OF SEWING- PANTS (ALMOST GONE) AND DARNING ON SOCKS IN MUCH THE SAME CONDITION. AFTER "MUCH A DO ABOUT NOTHING" I FOUND THAT '79' WERE AT LAST READY TO PLAY BRIDGE, SO WAS DOWN THERE FOR THE REST OF THE MORNING AND MADE OUR LEAD OVER LES AND HARRY GREATER STILL. CONTINUED THE GAME IN THE AFTERNOON AFTER A GOOD ARGUMENT WITH "134"

(GEORGE ETC) ON THE R.A.F. BOMBING AND LENGTH OF WAR. TEA, NICK AND RODG MAKING A FIRE IN THE HUT AND ALL BUT SMOKING US OUT! MISERABLE WET OUTSIDE TO-DAY. STAYED IN '79' UNTIL THE COCOA CAME UP CHATTING AND "SHOOTING THE LINE", THEN AFTER I HAD COCOA I WENT DOWN TO 134 AND WE HAD A BIT OF A SING-SONG. BACK FOR 8.15 AND BED IMMEDIATELY AND AFTER MY NIGHTLY SMOKE OF A GOOD CIGARETTE, UNCONSCIOUSNESS! IT IS TERRIBLE AT NIGHT NOW WITH IT BEING DARK AT 6.00 AND NO LIGHTS – UNLESS YOU HAVE PLENTY OF MARGARINE.

3/10/44 ROSE FAR TOO EARLY AGAIN, THIS HOUR GOING BACK STILL "FOXED" ME. NO WATCH AND THEREFORE I HAD NO IDEA OF THE TIME. STILL RAINING HEAVILY AND GENERALLY MISERABLE. COFFEE SHOULD BE UP SOON NOW. ANOTHER 1/2HR IT WAS! PLAYED BRIDGE MORNING AND AFTERNOON IN '79' WITH A BREAK FOR DINNER! WIZARD DINNER – STEW; THAT I COOKED MYSELF WITH JERRY RATION AND RED CROSS FOOD. ALSO COOKED A GOOD TEA FOR MYSELF. A NEWCOMER HAS COME TO JOIN US IN '53' – A CANADIAN- TO ACCOMMODATE 48 NEW GEFANGS ARRIVED TO-DAY, THEY SPREAD THEM OUT- 7 TO A HUT. GOSH! BUT THEY ARE ALL VERY OPTIMISTIC- END OF THIS MONTH THE WAR WILL BE OVER ACCORDING TO MOST OF THEM. THAT'S CHEERING BECAUSE OUR OPTIMISM HAD BEEN SOMEWHAT SUBDUED WITH SUCH LITTLE PROGRESS BEING MADE. "CHEGGERS" IS SURE HE'S GOING TO WIN HIS RED CROSS PARCEL NEXT APRIL! WENT FOR A WALK ROUND WITH HARRY SEVERAL TIMES ROUND THE COMPOUND, AND MADE SOME ARRANGEMENTS TO MOVE IN WITH THEM WHEN WE GO DOWN TO THE NEW COMPOUND- SHOULD HAVE BEEN GOING DOWN TO-DAY, BUT "JERRY" FOUND SOME SHOVELS ETC. HIDDEN DOWN THERE FOR OUR USE, SO IT HAS BEEN POSTPONED UNTIL NEXT WEEK. SEPTEMBER 20TH WAS THE FIRST DATE AND THE RED CROSS COMMISSION SAID WE WERE TO BE OUT OF HERE BY OCTOBER 1ST – BUT HERE WE STILL ARE. IN TO BED FOR 8.30, NICELY PACKED IN CLOSE TO FOR WARMTH, NOW THAT THE NEW BLOKE HAS COME IN.

4/10/44 FIRST UP, AS USUAL. PARADE WAS OVER QUICKLY, AS WE HAD THE TWO MASTER-COUNTERS ON – "ROMMEL" (THE W/O) AND "THE BERLIN BOMBER" (PRIVATE 2ND CLASS). BRIDGE AGAIN TO FILL IN THE MORNING – I PLAYED WITH NORMAN AS "NOBBY" WAS PUNCTURING PARCEL CONTENTS. AFTER DINNER WENT DOWN TO '134' TO WORK WITH GEORGE, BRINGING AWAY SOME PROBLEMS TO WORK OUT. MADE A GOOD HOT TEA- A SORT OF STEW, AS HOT HEALS GO DOWN WELL AS IT SO COLD NOWADAYS. WALK ROUND WITH HARRY, THEN WENT TO HIS HUT FOR A CHAT. COCOA CAME UP, AFTER WHICH WE (NICK, RODG AND I) TALKED OF THE WIDE SUBJECT "MONEY" BEFORE RETIRING TO BED EARLY AS USUAL. JOHNNY, THEN NEW "PARTNER" IN HERE FEELING ILL AND WAS SURE SICK DURING THE NIGHT.
5/10/44 EVERYTHING CLEARED UP BEFORE PARADE, SO WORKED IMMEDIATELY AFTERWARDS, UNTIL THE SOCCER MATCH (KNOCK-OUT SEMI-FINAL) BETWEEN DIV 1 AND DIV 6 GOT STARTED, THEN WATCHED IT. BOTH TEAMS WERE UNBEATEN- LAST TIME THEY MET IT WAS A DRAW. DIV1 WON 5-2. AFTER THAT THE THIRD TEST MATCH ENGLAND V AUSTRALIA – OOH! CRICKET IN THIS WEATHER! HOWEVER, WATCHED IT, ALL WRAPPED UP, OF COURSE, AND IN THE AFTERNOON TOO. ENGLAND HAVEN'T A CLUE, BUT STILL THEY DID NOT WISH TO PLAY – NOT KEEN ENOUGH. COULD TELL IN THEIR PLAY. AT NIGHT I WENT TO '79' FOR A GAME OF BRIDGE BY OIL LIGHT UNTIL 9.00PM HAVING A BREAK FOR COCOA. BACK TO HUT TO BED.
6/10/44 WATCHED THE SOCCER MATCH WHICH COMMENCED IMMEDIATELY AFTER PARADE, BETWEEN DIV 2 AND 8 IN THE KNOCK-OUT COMPETITION SEMI-FINAL, DIV 8 WINNING 2-1 BOTH SIDES MISSING A PENALTY! ONE OF DIV 8'S MEN WAS CARRIED OFF HAVING BEEN KICKED IN THE FACE – NASTY GASH IT MADE. PLAYED BRIDGE WITH NOBBY TO FILL THE REST OF THE MORNING IN. AFTER DINNER, NICK, RODG AND I REARRANGED THE HUT AND CLEANED IT UP A LITTLE- IT CERTAINLY NEEDED IT. WENT OUT AFTERWARDS TO WATCH THE TEST MATCH; ENGLAND IN THEIR SECOND INNINGS, HAVING BEEN MADE TO FOLLOW ON. THE AUSTRALIANS WON BY AN INNINGS AND 13 RUNS! SHOCKING! THE "AUSSIES" SCORED 196 (TOMMY GETTING 80

AND LASTING UNTIL THE LAST WICKET), ENGLAND GETTING 87 AND 96. IN ENGLAND'S SECOND INNINGS THE

89   MANNERS MAKETH MAN

LAST WICKET STAND PUT ON 4 RUNS – IT LOOKED AS THOUGH THE "AUSSIES" MIGHT HAVE HAD TO GO IN AGAIN JUST TO MAKE A FEW TO WIN. BRIDGE AFTER TEA UNTIL 9.00, HARRY AND I, DURING A BREAK IN THE GAME, HAVING A SHORT WALK ROUND PRIOR TO CHANGE - IT WAS ACTUALLY VERY WARM IN THE SUN.

<u>7/10/44</u> IT PROMISED TO BE A NICE DAY AGAIN. WATCHED THE SOCCER, CLEANED UP, MADE A FIREPLACE AND DID SOME COOKING - CHIPS AND SALMON FOR DINNER. PARCELS WERE UP THIS MORNING - ONE AMERICAN TO LAST A FORTNIGHT. BILL MOVED DOWN BELOW SO WE HAD ANOTHER NEW CHAP IN THE HUT, WHO JUST CAME IN THIS MORNING WITH 80 OTHERS. TOOK THEM 6 DAYS TO GET HERE! SPENT SOME TIME QUESTIONING HIM. SAW THE SOCCER KNOCK-OUT FINAL BETWEEN DIV 1 AND 8, THE FORMER WINNING 4-0. DIV 8 UNFORTUNATELY ONLY HAD 10 PLAYERS MOST OF THE GAME, THE BEST PLAYER ON THE CAMP ("LITTLE GEORDIE" – LEFT HALF) BEING A "PASSENGER" ON THE RIGHT WING. VERY GOOD GAME. COOKED FOR TEA, PARADE TAKING A GOOD WHILE WITH THE SLOWEST OF COUNTERS, WHILE WE STOOD ON TENDER-HOOKS WITH OUR STUFF STILL ON THE FIRE – HOWEVER IT WAS OK. PLAYED BRIDGE IN '79' UNTIL THE COCOA CAME UP, THEN IMMEDIATELY WE HAD HAD SUPPER, THE SIREN WENT AND SURE ENOUGH IT WAS A FULL SCALE ALLIED NIGHT RAID. PLENTY OF EXCITEMENT AS THE SKY WAS FULL OF "KITES". IT WAS GRAND TO HEAR THEM AGAIN. LATER WE SAW THE TARGET WAY OVER WESTWARDS, PLENTY OF FLAK AND BOMB FLASHES, THEN THE BOMBERS CAME BACK OVER US AGAIN. ANOTHER "TERROR" RAID (FULLY EFFECTIVE!) AND HEAP OF LUCK TO THEM. HOWEVER, TOWARDS THE END OF THE RAID OUR HEARTS SADDENED AS WE SAW ONE OF THE PLANES SHOT DOWN IN FLAMES – FOR A FEW MOMENTS ALL WAS SILENT AS WE SILENTLY HOPED AND PRAYED THE BOYS WOULD GET OUT, THE SAME WAY AS SO MANY OF US HERE HAD BEEN LUCKY ENOUGH TO BE ABLE TO UNDER THE SAME

CIRCUMSTANCES. CLEANED UP BY OIL-LIGHT OWING TO THE MESS WE MADE. SCRAMBLING FROM ONE END OF THE HUT TO THE OTHER (THIS WAS AT 9.30 WHEN THE ALL-CLEAR SOUNDED!) THEN SLEEP.

8/10/44 ROSE EARLY (6.45!) TO TAKE THE DRINK CAN BACK (UNABLE TO LAST NIGHT OWING TO THE AIR-RAID) AND GOT THE COFFEE. PORRIDGE CAME UP LATER. BREAKFAST OVER BY 8.00 SO CLEANED UP AND WROTE UP DIARY AND THEN WENT DOWN TO '79' FOR BRIDGE UNTIL 10.00 PARADE. WORKED UNTIL DINNER, THEN WATCHED A SOCCER KNOCK-OUT FINAL ("B" TEAMS), DIV 1 AND DIV 3. SCORE 4-0 TO DIV 3, GOOD SHOW – DIV 1 HAVE BEEN DECISIVELY BEATEN. CHATTED TO BILL ABOUT CANADA AND THE BOOK-KEEPING. TEA AND OUR USUAL GAME OF BRIDGE IN '79' WITH A BREAK FOR COCOA. PLAYED UNTIL THE GUARD (WITH DOG) INDICATED TO US TO PUT THE LIGHT OUT (MUST

89   SARCASM IS THE LOWEST FORM OF WIT.

HAVE BEEN LATER THAN 10.00) WAITED UNTIL HE HAD GONE, THEN RETURNED TO BED. JUST LAID IN BED WHEN I HEARD A MACHINE-GUN GO (ABOUT 5 ROUNDS) AND THEN A TERRIBLE SCREAM. WHAT'S HAPPENED? I LAY AWAKE A LONG TIME WONDERING. HEARD PLENTY OF SHOUTING EVENTUALLY WENT TO SLEEP.

9/10/44 CANNOT FIND OUT WHAT HAPPENED LAST NIGHT, QUITE A NUMBER HEARD IT. I THOUGHT IT WAS ONE OF OUR LADS, BUT MUST HAVE BEEN ONE OF THE POOR RUSSIANS ("RUSCIS"). AFTER MORNING PARADE, BRIDGE THEN DINNER AND LATER WATCHED A SOCCER GAME. MISERABLE DAY; JUST FINISHED GAME WHEN THE RAIN CAME. WROTE UP DIARY ETC. UNTIL PARADE. TEA AND OUR USUAL BRIDGE GAME. THEY GAVE US A TROUNCING AND REDUCED OUR LEAD TO 850 FROM 12,450 SINCE YESTERDAY. HAD THE USUAL TROUBLE WITH THE LIGHT. ALL QUIET AT 10.30 IN THE HUT.

10/10/44 MISERABLE MORNING, BUT CLEARED UP NICELY AFTER DINNER FOR THE 4TH TEST MATCH BETWEEN ENGLAND AND AUSTRALIA (ENGLAND LEADING 201 UP TO NOW) JEAN COOPER'S BIRTHDAY TO-DAY, I HOPE SHE RECEIVED MY CARD IN TIME. BLESS HER. OWING TO

SHORTAGE OF SPACE I AM ONLY GOING TO RECORD ANY EVENTS OF INTEREST AND IMPORTANCE FROM NOW ON.
11/10/44 TEST MATCH CONTINUED THIS MORNING, BUT WEATHER TOO BAD IN AFTERNOON FOR CRICKET. VERY CLOSE GAME: AUSTRALIA- 1ST INNINGS, 97 AND 26 FOR 3 IN SECOND. ENGLAND 88. WHEN ARE WE GOING TO MOVE BELOW? HAD A "WIZARD" LONG CHAT IN 79 AND THEN IN OUR HUT (AFTER COCOA) AT NIGHT, ON LIFE BACK IN ENGLAND, CREWS, SONGS AND CHAPS WE KNEW.
12/10/44 PLAYED IN GOAL FOR N.E. CLUB V MIDLANDS CLUB IN MORNING, THE "GEORDIES" WINNING 2-0. "NOBBY" SCORED FOR US. DID A LOT OF COOKING AND THEN WATCHED THE SOCCER MATCH CANADA V AUSTRALIA. VERY GOOD ENTERTAINMENT AND EXCITING. THE "CANUCKS" WON 5-1. "MINNIE" PLAYED EXCEEDINGLY WELL. WE ARE MOVING INTO THE NEW CAMP TO-MORROW, SO PACKED AND SORTED OUT THE FOOD ETC., LABELLED PALLIAS' "THE AUSSIES" WON THE TEST MATCH BY 100 RUNS, NEAR ENOUGH. THEY SCORED 151 RUNS IN THE SECOND INNINGS AND ENGLAND ONLY 62 IN REPLY.
13/10/44 UP AT 5.00AM (WHAT AN EFFORT!) PARADE 5.30 AND THEN COMMENCED MOVE. WENT IN DIVISION 1 WITH "NOBBY", HARRY, LES, REG, AND JIM. ITS "WIZARD" IN THE NEW PLACE-LIGHTING, MORE ROOM, NO BENDING HEADS, GRAND LAVATORIES, 14 IN A ROOM AND A COMBINE OF SIX FOR FOOD. WHAT A LONG DAY IT SEEMED. NOTHING TO EAT OF DRINK FROM COOKHOUSE (NO BREAKFAST OR DINNER) UNTIL 5.00. HAD SPLITTING HEADACHE (THRO HUNGER PROBABLY!)

91 GET OVER WHAT YOU CAN'T GET THROUGH
14/10/44 ALL NICELY SETTLED NOW AND HAPPY. HAD A PROPER SHOWER EARLY (UNDER A REAL SHOWER) –FIRST SINCE WEZTLAR. AIR-RAID IN THE MORNING, DURING WHICH WE SAW THE AMERICANS, AWAY AND HIGH UP IN THE SKY- WHAT A LONGING I HAD TO BE WITH THEM INSTEAD OF HERE- TO RETURN TO FREEDOM AND LIFE AS I ONCE KNEW IT.
15/10/44 DIV 1 & 2 GOT NO PORRIDGE THIS MORNING, BECAUSE A BOILER FULL WAS BURNT. WHAT A ROW-LES AND NOBBY BEING PROMINENT-GOOD ON THEM; THEY GET OUR

RIGHTS! PORRIDGE FOR US TO-MORROW INSTEAD. PLENTY OF FUN AT THE CAMP MEETING-ALL AT 6S AND 7S.

16/10/44 WHAT A THRILL! I HAVE RECEIVED MY FIRST MAIL. A LOT OF US HAVE RECEIVED SOME. I GOT A LETTER FROM MARGARET- I READ IT OVER AND OVER AGAIN AND NEVER GOT TIRED. IT WAS GRAND. I WAS REALLYPLEASED TO KNOW THAT DAD HAD HEARD FROM ME. THEIR LETTERS MUST HAVE BEEN DELAYED, BUT I WILL GET THEM PRETTY SOON. MUST WRITE TO MARGARET NOW I KNOW WHERE TO WRITE. WRITTEN FOUR P.Cs. AND LETTER YESTERDAY AND TO-DAY. GOT TWO P.Cs GIVEN TO ME, WHICH CAME IN HANDY.

17/10/44 AIR-RAID LAST NIGHT, BUT NOT MUCH EXCITEMENT. FLAK IN THE DISTANCE ONLY. TAKING 2 CLASSES IN BOOK-KEEPING AS FROM TO-DAY, STAGE 1 AND 2. AIR-RAID THIS MORNING-TRAPPED IN THE SCHOOL, TEACHING, SO HAD A COLD DINNER! WROTE TO MARGARET.

18/10/44 HAD MY FIRST DANCING LESSON –FINAL WALTZ. "NOBBY" AND I MADE GOOD PARTNERS! I SURE LIKE IT IN THIS NEW CAMP WITH "NOBBY" HARRY, LES, ETC. I FEEL AS THOUGH I CAN WORK WHEREAS WITH THE OTHERS IN THE OTHER CAMP, I COULDN'T.

19/10/44 JERRY HAD A HAMMER TAKEN, SO PLENTY OF THREATS AROUND. CALLED ON PARADE EARLY IN THE AFTERNOON AND HAD TO REMAIN ON PARADE WHILE THEY MADE A SYSTEMATIC SEARCH OF ALL THE HUTS-WE WERE THERE 1½ HRS CARRYING ON. THEY DID NOT FIND IT, SO IT CONTINUES TO-MORROW. THEY HELD BACK OUR MAIL TOO, BUT WE GOT IT AT NIGHT. FIRST LETTER FROM HOME- OH BOY, AM I GLAD TO KNOW EVERYTHINGS OK. I GOT TWO LETTERS FROM MUM AND DAD AND ONE FROM DOROTHY. I KNOW MY FOUR LETTERS OFF BY HEART ALMOST, I'VE READ THEM SO OFTEN.

20/10/44 FINISHED OFF THE SECOND GAME OF THE DIVISIONAL BRIDGE KNOCK-OUT COMPETITION AN PASSED INTO THE 3RD ROUND WITH "NOBBY" AS PARTNER. SENT P.C. HOME RE LETTERS RECD. LORRY CAME INTO CAMP WITH SOME FOOD AND GOT STUCK IN MUD. HAD SOME FUN GETTING IT OUT! JUST A CHANGE FOR US, WITH SO FEW EVER OCCURRING.

21/10/44 YESTERDAY WE TOOK THE BLACK-OUTS DOWN AND LAST NIGHT WHEN THE LIGHTS WERE ON, IT JUST LOOKED LIKE PEACE-TIME. WIZARD! EXTENSIVE SEARCH AGAIN THIS MORNING, ALL OF US HAVING TO REMAIN OUTSIDE THE BARRACKS UNTIL IT WAS OVER- ABOUT 11.00! WENT TO A GRAND CONCERT AT NIGHT "TIN CANS FOR DRUMS" ITEM WENT DOWN EXCELLENTLY PLUS SOME SONGS MADE IN A P.O.W CAMP. WE ARE NOT ALOUD TO SING "GOD SAVE THE KING" SO WE SANG "LAND OF HOPE AND GLORY" TO THE FULLEST. WROTE THROUGH THE MAN OF CONFIDENCE, ASKING ABOUT MY COMMISSION, AS I HAD BEEN RECOMMENDED.

92   MARRIAGE IS A NOBLE DARING

22/10/44 N.E CLUB MEETING AFTER AFTERNOON PARADE. IT WAS VERY SUCCESSFUL, 25 PRESENT. "NOBBY" AND I INVITED GEORGE & HIS PARTNER OVER IN THE EVENING AND WE HAD A VERY PLEASENAT GAME OF BRIDGE-BEST FOR SOMETIME. JOE AND JEOF LOST 50 CIGS EACH PLAYING BRIDGE AT 1 CIG. A HUNDRED! POOR BLOKES!
23/10/44 MADE A GLORIOUS EXIT FROM THE BRIDGE CONTEST-HARDLY A DECENT HAND ALL NIGHT. "NOBBY" LOST 20 CIGS. OVER IT!
24/10/44 OH BOY, WHAT A LOVELY TEA WE HAD TO-DAY- STEW. A ONE NOT TO BE FORGOTTEN EASILY WHILE WE'RE HERE. WON 15 CIGS. AT BRIDGE.
25/10/44 MADE MY BIRTHDAY CAKE FOR TO-MORROW.
26/10/44 MY BIRTHDAY TO-DAY- AND THE CAKE. IT TAKES US ALL OUR TIME TO LEAVE IT UNTIL TEA-TIME. IT WAS DELICIOUS-I MELTED A CHOCOLATE BAR DOWN FOR ICING (ALONG WITH POWDERED MILK AND SUGAR). QUIET DAY OTHERWISE-ONE OTHER THING I HAD A FAINT HOPE FOR- MAIL. BUT NO, I'M SELFISH, FOR QUITE A NUMBER HAVE HAD NONE, INCLUDING POOR NOBBY, LES & REG. "NOBBY", -EX- BRICK-LAYER, MAKES A FIRE PLACE, SO WE HAVE A FIRE!
27/10/44 STRONG RUMOURS THAT WE MAY BE LEAVING HERE TO GO SOMEWHERE IN THE HEART OF GERMANY, POSSIBLY HAVING TO MARCH. I PRAY NOT. WE JOKE ABOUT IT JUST NOW, BUT…..LATER. JOE MAKES IT NECESSARY, FOR THEY ARE NOW N.W. AND S.W.OF HERE.

28/10/44 WENT TO THE CONCERT AT NIGHT-"BILLY HALL AND HIS ACCORDIAN BAND". IT WAS JOLLY WITH PLENTY OF SINGING. SAW SOMEONE I KNEW ONCE-YES "SPIKE" FROM BRIDGNORTH-CALLED HIM "BUTCH" WHEN I WENT UP TO HIM AFTERWARDS, BUT THAT WAS HIS CONFEDERATES NAME! TALKED AWAY LIKE THE "HAMMERS IN HELL"! LEARNT NEWS OF SOME OF OUR OLD PALS –I KNEW SOMETHING ABOUT HIS "MOB" HE JOINED. SEEING HIM TO-MORROW. 2 LETTERS WAITING FOR ME WHEN I GOT BACK TO MY ROOM-FROM HELEN SMITH AND AUNTIE DOT. QUITE A SURPRISE. HELEN'S GAVE ME A GOOD LAUGH, BUT I DON'T THINK IT WAS INTENDED TO!

29/10/44 LISTENED TO A GRAMAPHONE IN THE CORRIDOR, INCL. TWO RECORDS OF BING CROSBY'S. A VERY PLEASANT CHANGE. AFTER SUPPER WE HAD THE FIRST MEETING OF THE N.E. CLUB DISCUSSION GROUP WITH DAVID SCOTT RUNNING IT, "HUTCH" HAVING PLENTY TO SAY!

30/10/44 WROTE LETTER HOME. CONFINED TO BARRACKS IN THE MORNING FOR KIT CHECK OVER-THE 101ST APPROX!

31/10/44 PUT TWO PATCHES ON MY TROUSERS-IT WAS REALLY NECESSARY TOO!

1/11/44 SHAVED OFF MY MOUSTACHE THAT I'VE HAD FOR THE LAST 3 MONTHS- FOR TO-NIGHTS DANCE. GOT A STOVE IN OUT HUT, SO I'M HOPING WE WON'T BE SO COLD. OF COURSE, WE'VE BEEN PROMISED THEM SINCE WE GOT IN THIS NEW CAMP, SO THEIR PROMISE WAS NOT SO FAR OUT AS IS USUAL! AT NIGHT, I WENT TO OUR FIRST CAMP DANCE-DRESSED AS A WOMAN WITH "NOBBY" AS PARTNER. WE HAD A "WIZARD" TIME. I DASHED BACK FROM CLASSES AND WITH EVERYONE IN MY ROOM GIVING ME A HAND TO DRESS, WAS ALONG THERE FOR 7.30. EVERYONE SPLIT THEMSELVES LAUGHING AT THE WOMEN, AND

93.   WASTE NOT; WANT NOT.

SOME LOOKED REALLY "PRETTY". TO SEE SOME, ONE WONDERED HOW THEY MANAGED TO GET UP IN SUCH LADY-LIKE "RIG-OUTS", BLANKETS, TOWELS, SCARVES, HANDKERCHIEVES, RAGS, EXTRA LONG VESTS, LONG SOCKS, CARDBORAD (BRACELETS), CAPS, R.A.F.COATS INSIDE OUT (CLOAKS) WERE ALL USED TO BEST ADVANTAGE.

2/11/44 PULLED MY BED TO PIECES TO CLEAN OUT THE "DUD" STRAW AND NOW OUR BUNKS HAVE ARRIVED AT LAST, SO PREPARED THEM. 6 OF US HAVE BEEN WITHOUT THEM (THE UNLUCKY ONES IN THE CUT OF THE CARDS.) IT IS SURE GRAND IN THE TOP BUNK. RECEIVED LETTERS FROM JEAN, HOME AND BOB (ONE FROM EACH). I GET MAIL WHENEVER IT COMES IN - AND DO I LOOK FORWARD TO IT - OR DO I?
3/11/44 SOMEBODY MISSING ON AFTERNOON PARADE (NOW AT 4.00) AND THEN AFTER ½ HR A LAD CAME FROM THE WASH HOUSE, IN SHIRT SLEEVES. HE'D BEEN WASHING. WE ALL HAD A GOOD LAUGH. NOT TOO COLD THE LAST 2 DAYS.
4/11/44 THIS WEEK WE HAD OUR HOT MEAL FROM THE COOKHOUSE AT 5.00 – BUT DOES NOT AFFECT US NOW. WE HAVE A STOVE IN THE HUT AND THEN WE CAN USE THE RANGE IN THE COOKHOUSE IN THE MORNINGS AS WELL.
5/11/44 DRESSED UP IN SUNDAY BEST AND WENT TO CHURCH. AT NIGHT WENT TO HEAR A TALK ON "THE HISTORY OF PARLIAMENT" WITH N.E.CLUB DEB. SOC. IT WAS VERY GOOD. ON PARADE IN THE AFTERNOON FOR AN HOUR AS 10 MEN WERE MISSING AT FIRST AND WERE FOUND IN ONES AND TWOS. THE W/O COUNTED 5 TIMES ALL TOLD!! WAS HE CHEESED!
6/11/44 "JERRY" COMMENCED WORKING PARTIES TO-DAY FOR L.A.Cs AND UNDER. ANYBODY WENT AND WHAT A FARCE. THEY JUST CARRIED ON, WITH THE REST OF THE CAMP GETTING A HELL OF A GOOD LAUGH!
7/11/44 LOST 20 CIGS. AT BRIDGE! MEETING OF CLUB PRESIDENTS AT NIGHT.
8/11/44 SNOW!! RAIN, HOWEVER, SOON CLEARED IT UP. IT DID NOT MAKE IT VERY WARM, THOUGH. HARRY AND I HAD A LONG CHAT ABOUT N/C ETC. WROTE TO JEAN.
9/11/44 "JERRY" HAD A POLITICAL MEETING JUST OUTSIDE THE CAMP THIS MORNING, SO WE HAD TO STAY IN OUR ROOMS-JUST IN CASE! "JERRY" STOPPED OUR PARCEL ISSUE- BECAUSE HE HADN'T GOT IN ENOUGH EMPTY TINS!! HE HAS BEEN PRETTY STRICT ON THIS RECENTLY.
10/11/44 SNOW AGAIN! BLAST IT! LETTER FROM COLIN. WROTE HOME.

11/11/44 SHORT ARMISTICE AT 11.00 COMPLETE WITH BUGLE AND BUGLER. IT MADE A DEEP IMPRESSION ON US. ROOSEVELT STILL IN – GOOD.

12/11/44 TOMMY LAING CAME IN THIS MORNING WITH THE NEW CHAPS!! N.E.CLUB MEETING BEFORE AFTERNOON PARADE-W/O COLEMAN GAVE US A TALK ON "SHANGHAI". AFTER PARADE WENT TO AN INTERESTING TALK ON "AMERICA & THE ENGLISH" BY DICK GREEVE WITH WYNN JOHNSON MAKING A LIVELY INTRUSION.

13/11/44 HAD A LONG CHAT WITH TOMMY LAING. HOW I WISH I WAS HOME. WENT TO THE OPENING NIGHT OF "COMPOUND CAPERS"- A VARIETY SHOW WITH A FAIRLY SHORT PLAY "ROOKERY NOOK" TO FINISH WITH. "COMPOUND CADS", BILLY HALL, ORCHESTRA, FRANK STURGESS (VOCALIST), SOUTH SEA ISLAND MAGIC ETC. ALL WENT TO MAKE A TIP-TOP SHOW-WELL WORTH ALL THIS WAITING TO SEE. DIVISION 1 & 2 SAW IT. A "WIZARD" STAGE TOO.

14/11/44 SEARCH OF 49 (DIV 6 TO-DAY) TO CARRY INTO EFFECT THE GERMAN H.C ORDER RE-STORING FOOD, CIGS, CHOC. ETC - ONLY CAME OUT YESTERDAY! SNOW AGAIN, BUT IT DISAPPEARED LATER.

(CONTD. ON PAGE 54R)

54r

15/11/44 HELPED TO ORGANISE YORKSHIRE CLUB. "TIRPITZ" SUNK. DAMN GOOD SHOW. "JERRY" SAYS "IT WAS PUT OUT OF ACTION, BUT MANY PERSONNEL WERE SAVED"! WENT TO THE CAMP SHOW AGAIN TO-NIGHT WITH A COMPLIMENTARY TICKET TO RECEIVE THE Y.M.C.A. SPORTS BADGE AND CERTIFICATE. ENJOYED IT VERY MUCH AGAIN. THE GERMAN OFFICERS WENT.

16/11/44 WROTE HOME AND TO JEAN. ALSO WROTE A REQUEST P.C.TO THE B.B.C!! I WONDER WHAT COMES OF IT. "JERRY" STARTED ROLL CALLS IN THE BARRACK. VERY CONSIDERATE! SNOW-PLENTY.

17/11/44 GENERAL OFFENSIVE ON WESTERN FRONT HAS COMMENCED AS PER GERMAN NEWSPAPER - AN ENDEAVOUR TO "FINISH OFF" GERMANAY, THEY SAY. I

HOPE IT COMES OFF. RECD. A BOOK-KEEPING BOOK, FOR STUDYING!

18/11/44 SENT £100 HOME - NOTIFICATION TO PAY A/CS TO DO SO.

19/11/44 SNOW ALMOST COMPLETELY DISAPPEARED NOW. NEW LADS CAME IN-TWO IN OUR ROOM-WE PUMPED THEM FOR NEWS. CLUB MEETING IN AFTERNOON. VERY SUCCESSFUL.

20/11/44 HAD AN AIR-RAID WITH SOMEONE BEING FIRED AT AGAIN (QUITE A FREQUENT OCCURRENCE NOW!). INSTRUCTING LES MOST OF THE DAY IN BOOK-KEEPING (ALSO OCCURS REQUENTLY!)

21/11/44 HAD THE GRAMAPHONE AT NIGHT WITH SOME NEW RECORDS JUST ARRIVED TO-DAY. IT WAS WIZARD. WE WERE UP UNTIL 1.00AM LISTENING, LYING IN BED. HAD A CUP OF COCOA ABOUT MIDNIGHT. MAIL (600 LETTERS) CAME IN, BUT AGAIN I RECEIVED NONE.

22/11/44 TURNED DOWN THE OFFER OF ENTERING A PLAY COMING OFF-PARTS TOO SMALL! SEEMS TO ME THESE DAYS I'VE ALWAYS GOT SOMETHING TO DO - SEEING PEOPLE MOST OF THE DAY. CLUB WORK CONSIDERABLE-BOOK-KEEPING PLENTY- READING QUITE A LOT- LETTERS, DIARY AND PERSONAL CALCULATIONS TAKE UP A FAIR AMOUNT OF TIME- PERSONAL CONTACTS PLENTY!! PLENTY OF TALKING - MOST OF DAY, IF FACT.

23/11/44 JERRY CONDUCTED A SEARCH OF THE CHAPS IN V111 DIVISION AFTER PARADE THIS AFTENOON! WE'RE KEPT ON OUR TOES FOR COUNTER-MEASURES AT THE TIME!

24/11/44 NOT SO COLD RECENTLY, THANK GOODNESS.

25/11/44 WROTE HOME. JIM AND I ON DUTY IN ROOM T0-DAY.

26/11/44 N.E.CLUB MEETING-VERY INTERESTING TALK BY ONE OF OUR CHAPS ON "RADAR". WENT TO A CAMP TALK AFTERWARDS ON "A VOYAGE TO THE MOON". VERY INTERESTING INDEED. CRIB COMPETITION-KNOCKED OUT FIRST ROUND BOTH IN SINGLES AND DOUBLES, COMP. BRIDGE GAME AT NIGHT WITH HARRY AND LES! BAGS OF ERUPTION!

27/11/44 JERRY KEPT US WAITING ON PARADE THIS MORNING, BECAUSE WE HAVE CONSISTENTLY KEPT HIM WAITING. PLAYED COMPETITION BRIDGE MOST OF DAY.

28/11/44 WORKING PARTY THIS MORNING - DID A SOLID 2 HOURS OF MANUAL LABOUR. JIM WENT TO OPPELN ABOUT HIS EYES. HE HEARD SOME GOOD NEWS - HOPE ITS TRUE. NEWS PRETTY GOOD ALL ROUND.
29/11/44 NO MAIL AGAIN FOR ME, WHEN IT CAME THIS MORNING. I'VE GOT A HELL OF A COLD - I FEEL AS HEAVY AS LEAD.
30/11/44 ROSE EARLY FOR A CHANGE. HAD A SPECIAL PARADE AT 10.00AM AS 8 DIV HAVE BEEN FOOLING ON AGAIN -THIS

54s
TIME THEY GAVE IN VARIOUS FUNNY NAMES AFTER BEING CAUGHT SMOKING ON PARADE. WENT TO THE SHOW AT NIGHT- LEO MAKI'S "DANCING TIME". IT WAS MARVELOUS - I COULDN'T WISH TO SEE A BETTER SHOW IN "CIVVY" STREET. THERE WAS GEORGE FORMBY, "GERALDINE", LEO MAKI'S ACCORDIAN BAND ETC. OH BOY, WHAT A LAUGH AND WHAT A SWING.
1/12/44 MORE MAIL IN, BUT STILL I GOT NONE. GOT MY TROUSERS CHANGED!
2/12/44 OH BOY! WHAT AN AIR RAID TO-DAY. "THE YANKS" WENT OVER IN 100s UNMOLESTED - RIGHT OVERHEAD AND NOT SO HIGH, LEAVING VAPOUR TRAILS BEHIND. SAW ONE POOR CREW GRADUALLY GETTING FURTHER BEHIND THROUGH AN ENGINE BEING OUT OF ACTION. OUR HEARTS AND BEST WISHES WENT OUT TO THEM. GOD BLESS THEM. WE WERE ALL AS EXCITED AS KIDS. SAW THE ENGLAND V SCOTLAND SOCCER MATCH IN THE AFTERNOON. GRAND GAME. RESULT 0 – 0. IT WAS DEADLY COLD. ENGLAND MISSED HEAVENS KNOWS HOW MANY CHANCES.
3/12/44 GOOD LAUGH OUT OF "FRANK" (THE GERMAN W/O) ON PARADE THIS MORNING WHEN ONE CHAP TURNED UP LATE. N.E. CLUB MEETING, THEN WENT TO A LECTURE ON "LIFE IN IRELAND". THE DOMINIONS WON 3-0 AGAINST ENGLAND AT RUGBY. PLAYED GOALKEEPER FOR THE N.E.CLUB V MIDLANDS CLUB IN MORNING. WE LOST 0-6! PHEW, DEADLY! CAME NEAR TO BREAKING MY LEG AT NIGHT!

4/12/44 FELT LOUSY WITH COLD. WENT TO THE RADIO-STAGED PLAY OF "JOURNEYS END" AT NIGHT WITH HARRY, VERY GOOD.

5/12/44 PLAYED GOALKEEPER FOR 1 DIV v V1 DIV IN MORNING. WE WON 1-0. MAIL IN, BUT NONE FOR ME AGAIN – NEARLY A MONTH NOW SINCE I HAD A LETTER. AT NIGHT WENT OVER TO BOB, TOM, NICK ETC. FOR A GOOD CHAT.

6/12/44 SAW THE FILM "CORSICAN BROTHERS". DAMN GOOD. SILENT THOUGH, AS THERE WAS INSUFFICIENT POWER FOR THE SOUND ALSO! PITY, BUT I SURE ENJOYED IT, DESPITE THAT.

7/12/44 PARCEL SITUATION APPEARS GRIM - LAST ISSUE AT XMAS. "JERRY" RATIONS REDUCED AGAIN - SPUDS CUT 25% - BY HELL, WHAT A LIFE. ALWAYS A HUNGRY FEELING NOW. SHOWER TO-DAY. M.O'S INSPECTION.

8/12/44 WENT TO SEE THE FILM "CORSICAN BROTHERS" AGAIN AT 8.00 THIS MORNING WITH THE SOUND BETTER BUT STILL NOT ALTOGETHER AUDIBLE. SO WAS UP EARLY TO-DAY. NO MAIL FOR ME AGAIN TO-DAY. "POP" GOT MORE, AS USUAL. WHAT THE HELL GOES ON AROUND HERE? LOUSY WEATHER AGAIN.

9/12/44 DAMN COLD AGAIN. WORKED OUT MAIL STATISTICS!!

10/12/44 N.E. CLUB MEETING AT 1.30 AS USUAL- KEN LANE SPOKE ON "PROFESSIONAL FOOTBALL AND HIS DENMARK TOUR". AFTER PARADE THE PADRE SPOKE ON "PUTNEY TO MORTLAKE"- ROWING. HAD THE GRAMAPHONE BROUGHT IN AT 10.00, SO PLAYED IT IN THE DARK. I THOUGHT OF SO MANY THINGS - IT WAS HARD TO KEEP TEARS BACK AT TIMES. JEAN AND ALL AT HOME - I PRAYED FOR THEM.

11/12/44 RECEIVED 6 LETTERS. OH BOY, HAVE WAITED ONE MONTH FOR THEM. RATIONS NOW SO LOW, WE HAVE FRIED POTATO PEELINGS FOR SUPPER!!

The following pencil drawings have been scanned in from the diary.

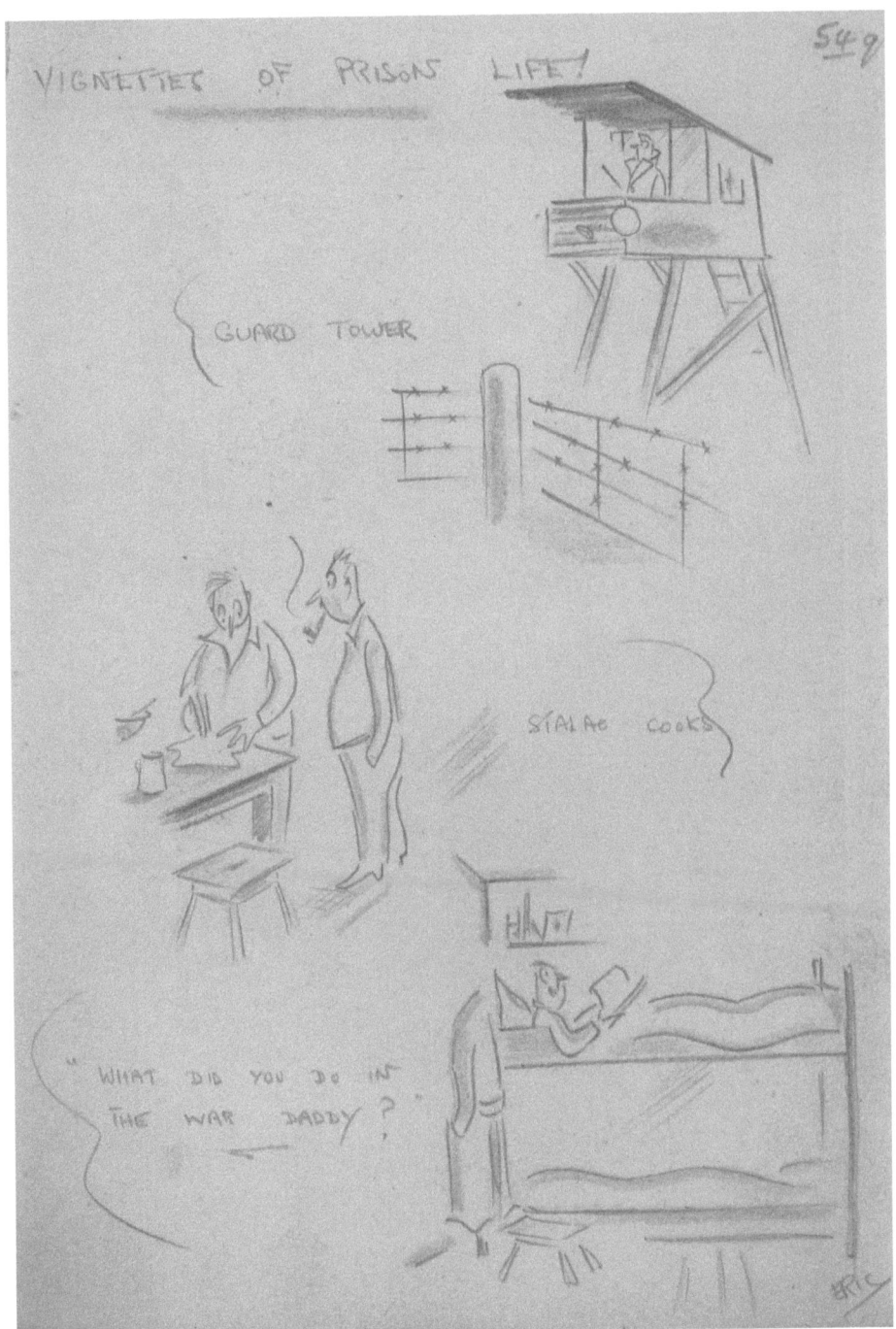

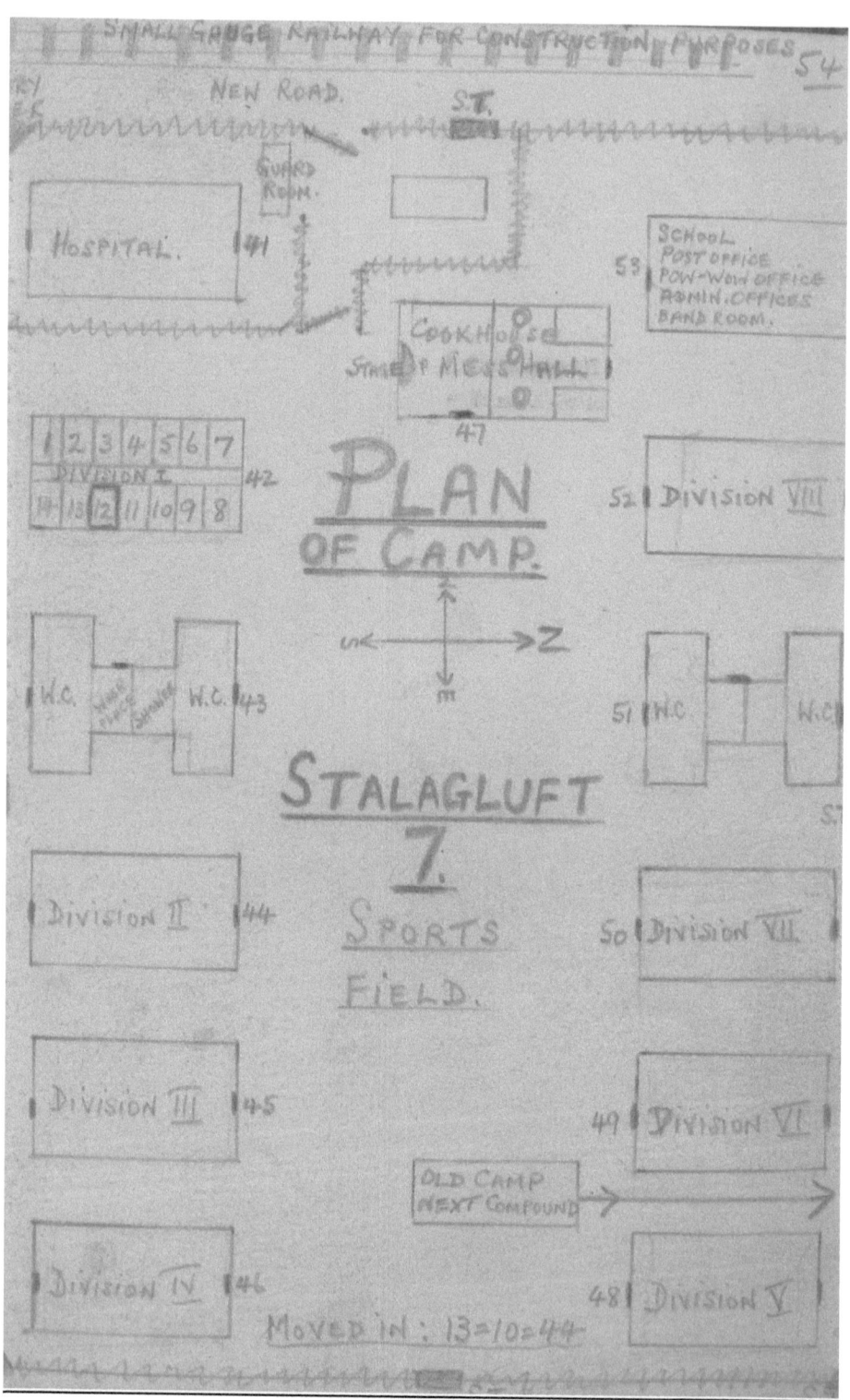

OCCUPANTS OF "42/12"
BARRACK 42 ROOM 12
LEYLAND O'LEARY F/S. (CAN)
GEORGE THOMSON SGT
NORMAN BRUCE W/O. (CAN)
TOM GLENN F/S.
JOE LUDWIG (CAN.) SGT.
HARRY MATE F/S.
"KNOBBY" CLARKE SGT.
GEOF FLAY (N.Z.) F/S.
JACK LINDSAY (AUS.) F/S.
VIC POPPA (CAN.) W/O.
LES KELLY F/S.
MICK FORD (CAN.) SGT.
REG. DALE SGT.
JIM BUTLER L.A.C
DIVISION I.
LEADER: PARRY-JONES
ROOM AREA 15' x 22'
LATE ARRIVALS IN 42/12
SGT. "LOFTY" LEE
SGT. GORDON NEEDON
SGT. ROY GREEN (AUS.)
SGT. (S.A.)
SGT. GEORGE KELLY.
(IN "KNOBBY'S" PLACE).
FRENCH WITHOUT TEARS
MARCUS SIMMONDS

HUT 53 AT ITS BEST !!

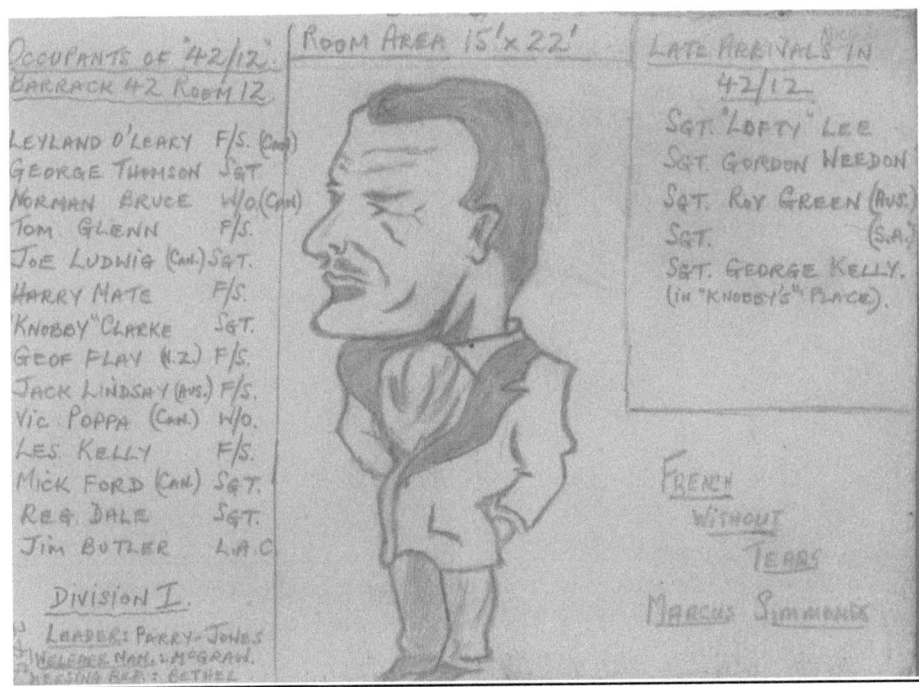

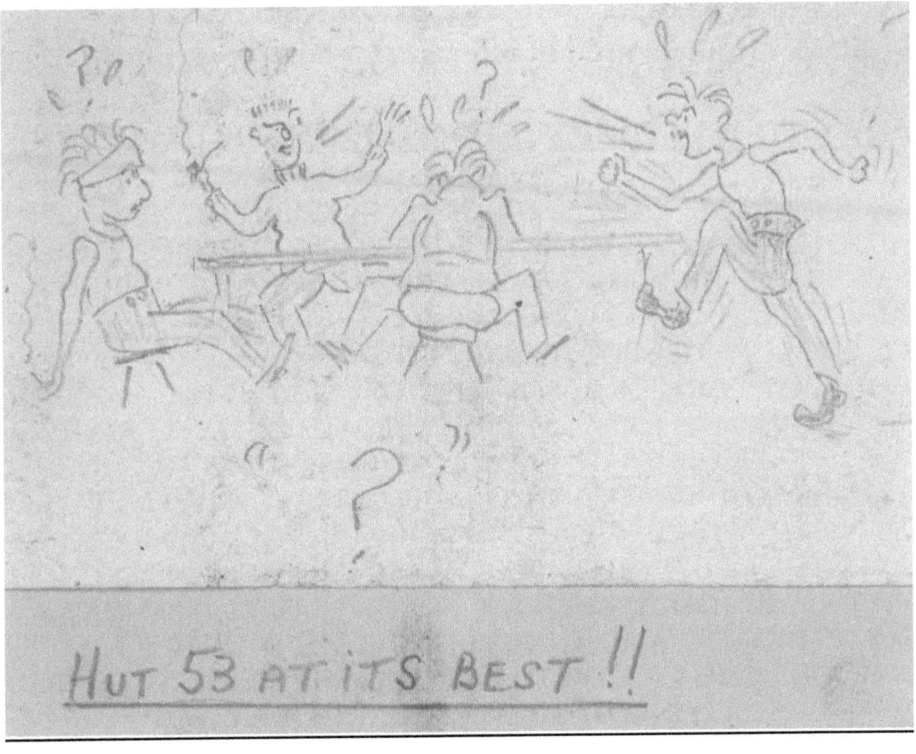

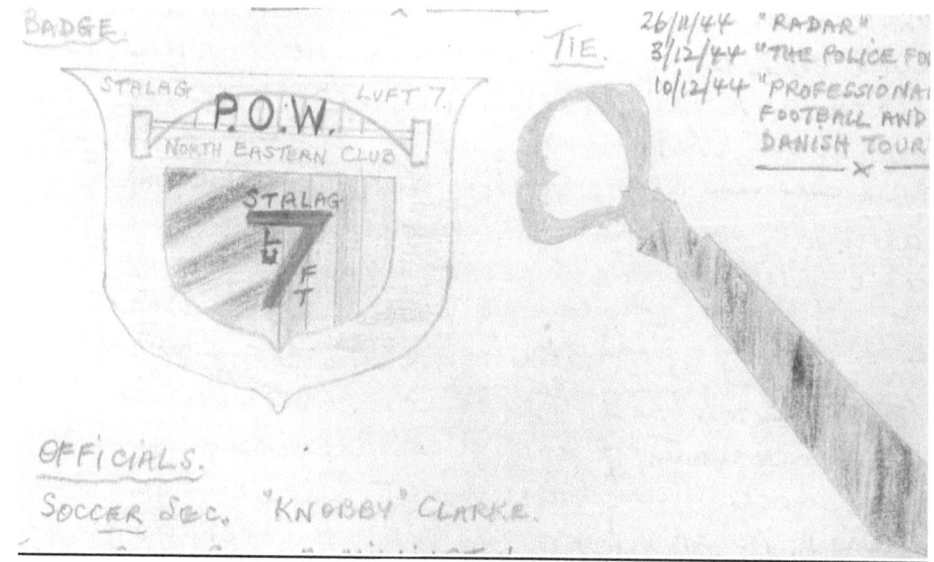

This is the tie and badge of the N.E. Club which held eleven meetings between 5/9/44 and 14/1/45. They wrote to the Evening Chronicle on 11/9/44 and had five talks, all mentioned in the diary, on various topics.

**The diary continued in a second book.
Page numbers are not relevant, so have been omitted.**

DAY TO DAY DIARY (CONTD FROM P.O.W.DIARY)

12/12/44 AN AIR-RAID THIS MORNING, WHICH MADE US AUTOMATICALLY CANCEL STAGE 1 BOOK-KEEPING CLASS. SAW NOTHING DURING RAID. WROTE TO JEAN AND BETTY. ALMOST RAN OUT OF CIGARETTES, SO GAVE LES HALF A BAR OF CHOCOLATE FOR 20 CIGARETTES. HAD A HAIRCUT FOR THE FIRST TIME FOR 3 MONTHS! DID I NEED IT?(!)
13/12/44 TROUBLE ON CAMP TO-DAY – THE CAMP-LEADER AND OTHER OFFICIALS RESIGNING OWING TO CERTAIN THINGS COMING TO LIGHT e.g. "HOOCH AFFAIR(!)". MEETING AT NIGHT, WHICH REPRODUCED RESULTS ALL OVER AGAIN, AS IN THE OLD CAMP! BALLOT TO BE TAKEN TO-MORROW. IT PRODUCED SOMETHING OUT OF THE ORDINARY, ANYWAY – SOMETHING TO AMUSE US! AT NIGHT WENT OVER TO HAVE A GOOD LONG CHAT WITH BILL AND THEN RETIRED TO BED WITH A "SPLITTING" HEADACHE. MADE OUR CHRISTMAS CAKE TO-DAY- ITS REALLY TURNED OUT GOOD TOO.

14/12/44 WROTE HOME. WENT TO SEE THE FILM "LIFE BEGINS FOR ANDY HARDY". IT WAS "WIZARD" – EVERYONE HAD A GOOD LAUGH. HAD TO CLEAN THE CLUBROOM OUT TO-DAY, AS IT WAS THE N.E. CLUBS TURN. HAD TWO LONG CHATS - BEFORE SUPPER TO EDMUND QUIGLEY AND AFTER SUPPER TO NORMAN DELAYEN RE A PROPOSED PERSONAL REUNION AFTER THE WAR - QUITE AN AMBITIOUS SCHEME. IT WAS TERRIBLY COLD TO-DAY, AN ICY EAST WIND BLOWING CONTINUOUSLY. TEMPERATURE AT TEA-TIME $-5°c$ COLD ENOUGH? HUH, IT GETS WORSE LATER.
15/12/44 SNOW! SNOW! SNOW! WHAT A LIFE – COLD AS HELL TOO. EAST WIND WHICH EVEN KEPT THE ROOM COLD. BED EARLY TO KEEP WARM - WAS "CHEESED" TOO.
16/12/44 QUITE A NICE DAY – SNOW STILL LYING DEEP, BUT ITS NOT TOO COLD. WENT TO THE SHOW "MODERNISTIC MOODS" WITH BOB BURNS AND GUEST ARTISTS (ALL-BAND SHOW). QUITE GOOD, BUT LES MAKI PUTS HIM "IN THE SHADE"!
17/12/44 AIR-RAID AT 12.00 LASTING UNTIL 1.45. SAW THE "YANKS" GO RIGHT OVERHEARD – 37 OF THEM. THREE BOMBS DROPPED ONLY 2 MILES AWAY, WHICH CAUSED QUITE A LOT OF EXCITEMENT. ABOUT AN HOUR AFTER THEY WENT OVER (JUST AFTER THE ALL CLEAR) LEAFLETS COMMENCED TO DROP AND EVERYONE TRIED TO GET ONE. HOWEVER, A "JERRY" WAS EMPLOYED TO PICK THEM UP AND THIS NOT BEING COMPLETLEY EFFECTIVE (OWING TO SOME GOOD "HOAXES") THEY CONFINED US TO OUR HUTS AGAIN. NO N.E.CLUB MEETING DUE TO THIS. AFTER 3.00 PARADE WENT TO A TALK ON "THE METROPOLITAN POLICE FORCE", WHICH WAS PRETTY GOOD. SAVING ALL MY CIGARETTE BUTTS, AS NEXT WEEKS ISSUE OF PARCELS ARE THE LAST, UNTIL SOME MORE ARRIVE – GOD KNOWS WHEN THAT WILL BE!
18/12/44 NEXT MONDAY CHRISTMAS DAY. WE ARE PRAYING FOR OUR NEXT-OF-KIN PARCELS TO ARRIVE IN TIME. IF ONLY WE COULD GET SOME CHOCOLATE AND CIGS TOO. SOON WE'LL BE CUTTING EACH OTHERS THROATS OVER THEM. AIR-RAID AGAIN - LOVELY DAY FOR IT WITH THE SUN SHINING (SNOW STILL AROUND, THOUGH, LIKE A CHRISTMAS CARD). SAW THE "YANKS" VAPOUR TRAILS WAY DOWN SOUTH AND THE DISTANT RUMBLE OF THE BOMBS.

BOB WAS CAUGHT OVER WITH US, WHICH CAME RIGHT IN THE MIDDLE OF SERVING UP DINNER. WENT BOB BURN'S SHOW AGAIN AT NIGHT, WHICH WAS MUCH IMPROVED AND I REALLY ENJOYED IT.

19/12/44 AIR-RAID WARNING AGAIN. JUST MANAGED TO GET BACK TO THE HUT IN TIME FROM STAGE 1 BOOK-KEEPING CLASS (PETE GIVING US A WARNING). SAW NOTHING BUT HEARD THE BOMB DETONATIONS IN THE DISTANCE. HAD AN ELECTION ON WHETHER CAMP LEADER AND MAN-OF-CONFIDENCE TO REMAIN IN OFFICE. CAMP LEADER REMAINING, BUT M.of C. GOES. NOMINATIONS FOR NEW ONE TAKEN. HAD A GRAND CHAT ROUND THE FIRE OF WHAT WE'RE GOING TO DO WHEN WE GET BACK - EAT, DRINK AND BE MERRY – OR, ALTERNATIVELY – EAT, WINE, WOMEN AND SONG.

20/12/44 SOME 80 ODD NEW CHAPS CAME IN TO-DAY -FIRST LOT FOR ABOUT A MONTH. THEY'RE 3-6 MONTHS FOR THE END OF THE WAR - NO CHANGE SINCE THEY CAME IN IN AUGUST!!!! IS IT NEVER GOING TO END? PUT IN OUR VOTE FOR THJE NEW MAN-OF-CONFIDENCE.

21/12/44 HEAVY FROST (CONSEQUENTLY DAMN COLD), BUT SUN SHINING AGAIN. IF ONLY IT REMAINS LIKE THIS THROUGH THE WINTER IT WILL NOT BE TO BAD - IF ONLY. SHOULD BE SOME MAIL IN TO-DAY - HAVEN'T HAD ANY THIS WEEK YET. YES, A 1000 LETTERS CAME IN, BUT I DIDN'T GET ONE. WENT TO THE SHOW "DIXIE DUGAN," WHICH I REALLY ENJOYED. THERE WERE TWO SHORT FILMS ON WITH IT. I HAD SEEN "DIXIE DUGAN" FILM BEFORE. GEORGE, NED AND I SPENT THE EVENING WITH A "FIRESIDE CHAT" ON OUR EXPERIENCES OF TRAINING DAYS. SOME BULK FOOD ARRIVED, WHICH HAS RELIEVED THE TENSION OVER WHAT WE WERE GOING TO DO FOR FOOD AFTER XMAS - IT'LL BE ENOUGH FOR 10 DAYS ANYWAY. WROTE TO MARGARET.

22/12/44 SENT AWAY FOR A STATEMENT OF A/C. "JERRY" SEARCHED OUR BARRACK TO-DAY AFTER AFTERNOON PARADE - TOOK NOTHING FROM OUR ROOM, THANK GOODNESS. BEEN FLOODING THE PROPOSED SKATING RINK ALL DAY. WENT TO BED FAIRLY SOON AFTER SUPPER FOR IT WAS SO DEADLY COLD - SOMEWHERE NEAR –10°c! SUPPER'S EARLY THESE DAYS - GENERALLY 7.00. TO-DAY IS JIM'S DAY FOR THE END OF THE WAR - WHAT A HOPE! LOOKS

AS THOUGH "KNOBBY'S" GOING TO BE THE NEAREST WITH MAY 8TH - AND TO THINK EVERYBODY LAUGHED AT HIM WHEN HE SAID THAT FOUR MONTHS AGO!

23/12/44 POOR OLD "KNOBBY" SHOULD HAVE BEEN MARRIED TO-DAY, IF HE HAD BEEN HOME! SEWED UP MY INNER BLANKET IN AN ENDEAVOUR TO KEEP WARM AT NIGHT. WENT TO A CAROL SERVICE IN THE AFTERNOON, WHICH I QUITE ENJOYED. PUT ICING ON THE CAKE AND WENT ROUND TO SEE SIMILAR EFFORTS IN OTHER ROOMS, SOME OF WHICH HAVE PROFESSIONAL TOUCHES. HAD A GAME OF BRIDGE AT NIGHT FOR A CHANGE.

24/12/44 OUR DIVISION WERE LATE ON PARADE THIS MORNING, SO "FRANK" KEPT US AND EXTRA HALF-HOUR OUT THERE – BY HELL IT WAS COLD. "KNOBBY" DODGED OFF (WITH ABOUT 5 OTHERS), WHICH KEPT US THERE LONGER, AS THEY CHECKED UP ON THE NUMBER. WHEN WE GOT BACK TO THE ROOM, AN ARGUMENT DEVELOPED WITH "KNOBBY" ABOUT THIS, WHICH EVENTUALLY LED TO A REAL "ROW" AND LATER BLOWS. "KNOBBY" WAS UNCONTROLABLE AND AFTER FURTHER TROUBLE, HE MOVED INTO ANOTHER ROOM. SPENT A LOT OF TIME DIVIDING UP THE PARCELS AND SAVINGS, AFTER WHICH WE SAW NO MORE OF "KNOBBY". WITH "POP" MADE A PLATE FOR MYSELF OUT OF COCOA TINS. PUT ICING ON THE CAKE AND TART AT NIGHT. AIR-RAID WARNING CAME THROUGH AT 9.00!! HEARD NOTHING MORE ABOUT IT. THOUGHT SPECIALLY OF YOU TO-NIGHT JEAN, AND I LONGED TO BE WITH YOU. I HOPE YOU ARE HAVING A GOOD TIME, DARLING. SAT UP AND CHATTED HAVING SOME COCOA AT 10.00 AND SOME GERMAN COFFEE AT 12.00. READ MY LETTERS OVER AFTERWARDS AND THEN TO BED AT 1.00. LIGHTS REMAINED ON UNTIL 1.30 FOR COMMUNIONS AND R.C SERVICE. QUITE A LOT OF MERRIMENT AROUND - ACCORDIANS, MOUTH ORGANS ETC. GOING WITH SINGING ("HOOCH" HELPING IN SOME CASES!).

25/12/44 ROSE AT 7.50 – PARADE AT 8.00 WAS THE REASON – HOWEVER IT'S THE ONLY ONE, THANK GOODNESS. COOKED BREAKFAST AND FINISHED ABOUT 10.00. CLEANED UP – SHAVE, COLLAR AND TIE ETC. FOR CHURCH AT 11.15. IT WAS A GRAND SERVICE – MY THOUGHTS WERE WITH THOSE AT HOME ALL THROUGH. DINNER, AFTER WHICH I REALLY FELT

FULL FOR THE FIRST TIME FOR MONTHS. READ FOR A WHILE, THEN WENT OVER TO SEE NICK, BOB ETC. TEA AT 5.30 - ANOTHER BIG MEAL FOR US (WE WERE SURE DOING OURSELVES WELL - ITS CERTAINLY BEEN WORTH STINTING OURSELVES IN THE PAST). OH, BEFORE TEA I WATCHED THE MATCH (SOCCER): THE CAMP V THE REST. SCORE 1-1. IT WAS AN EXCELLENT GAME. SAW BILL AFTER A RAID TO LET MY TEA SETTLE AND WISHED HIM "THE COMPLIMENTS OF THE SEASON" (MOST OF US CAREFULLY REFRAINED FROM WISHING EACH OTHER "A MERRY CHRISTMAS"!). SUPPER (HARRY BY THIS TIME BEING UNABLE TO EAT A THING!). HOWEVER, NED, JIM AND I WENT STRONG - REG TAKING IT EASY. SUPPER WAS LATE SO BED SOON FOLLOWED WITH LIGHTS GOING OUT NORMALLY AT 10.00. IT WAS A GRAND DAY, ALL CONSIDERED. MY STOMACH BEING SO SATISFIED, I HAD THE FEELING ALL DAY I HADN'T A CARE IN THE WORLD! WHAT A DIFFERENCE TO NORMAL!

<u>MENU FOR CHRISTMAS DAY 1944</u>

<u>BREAKFAST</u>	PORRIDGE. COFFEE
	EGG, SAUSAGE, MEAT ROLL
	BISCUITS, BREAD JAM.
<u>DINNER</u>	STEWED BEEF SOUP TEA
	SPAM, BULLY, ROAST POTATOES, CHIPS
	CHRISTMAS PUDDING, MILK
	GOOSEBERRY TART, CREAM
	BISCUITS, CHEESE
<u>TEA</u>	SOUP TEA
	FRIED MEAT, SPAM, ROAST POTATOES
	CAKE
<u>SUPPER</u>	BISCUITS, BREAD, JAM. COCOA
	GOOSEBERRY TART.

I COULDN'T UNDERSTAND HARRY BEING SO FULL, FOR I DIDN'T FEEL PARTICUALRLY FULL. LIKE HOME OF OLD AFTER A DECENT MEAL! ONCE WE GAVE A THOUGHT TO FEEDING IN A WEEKS TIME – AND SHUDDERED! JUST HAVE TO LET OUR STOMACHS SHRINK AGAIN THE HARD WAY!

<u>26.12.44</u> I GOT UP AND GOT A CUP OF TEA FOR ALL (FEELING ENERGETIC!), NEARLY EVERYONE LYING IN BED UNTIL PARADE TIME, WHICH WAS PUT BACK TO 10.00. "POP" GOT THREE PARCELS TO-DAY – CHOCOLATE, CLOTHING AND

FOOD – OH WIZARD. HE'S BEEN VERY LUCKY WITH LETTERS AND NOW HE GETS THE FIRST PARCEL. HAD AN AIR-RAID AGAIN WHEN SOUP WAS BEING GIVEN OUT (SAME TIME EVERYTIME) - SAW NOTHING, BUT HEARD THE DISTANT RUMBLE OF BOMBS. DID QUITE A LOT OF WASHING IN THE AFTERNOON, THEN PREPARED THE ROOM FOR TWO MORE NEW CHAPS COMING IN. AT NIGHT, BILL CAME OVER FOR A CHAT UNTIL SUPPER, AFTER WHICH I FINISHED MY WASHING. "POLISHED OFF" THE REST OF THE XMAS CAKE.

27/12/44 MET BOBBY ALLEN WHILE I WAS HAVING A WASH! HE CAME IN YESTERDAY – AM GOING ROUND TO SEE HIM LATER. AIR-RAID AT DINNER TIME AGAIN, SO OUR SOUP WAS LATE. DURING THE RAID ONE OF OUR CHAPS LEFT THE BARRACK AND WAS SHOT IN THE CHEST. NOBODY WAS ALLOWED TO PICK HIM UP UNTIL THE RAID WAS OVER. THE BASTARDS. THE POOR LAD WAS IN A BAD WAY. WE ALL HEARD WITH DEEP REGRET THAT HE DIED AN HOUR LATER. WE'LL HAVE TO WATCH OUR STEPS FROM NOW ON -THAT BEING THE FIRST TIME THEY HAVE APPARENTLY SHOT TO KILL. AT NIGHT HAD A LONG CHAT WITH BOBBY ALLEN AND THEN WENT OVER TO SEE TOMMY LAING. SUPPER AND TO BED TO READ.

28/12/44 JIM AND I ON DUTY IN THE ROOM TO-DAY, SO ROSE EARLY TO MAKE THE FIRE, BREAKFAST, WASH-UP, SWEEP UP ETC. READ AND HELPED CHAPS WITH BOOK-KEEPING PROBLEMS, WHO CAME IN TO SEE ME. SHORT AIR-RAID JUST BEFORE DINNER. READ, PREPARED MEALS AND CLEANED UP EACH MEAL. HARRY PREPARED A CAKE FOR NEW YEAR. HAD A NEW DISH FOR TEA - POTATOE AND BREAD PATES (FRIED). VERY GOOD - NEAREST APPROACH TO A SUASAGE WITHOUT USING MEAT. WENT TO SEE THE "ARTS AND CRAFTS" EXHIBITION DURING THE DAY.

29/12/44 GOT MY BED FILLED UP – IT'LL BE LIKE A FEATHER BED TO-NIGHT. WAS ON "ROCK BOTTOM" BEFORE. READ MY ECONOMICS BOOK MOST OF THE DAY. NO MAIL IN THIS WEEK YET?

30/12/44 CERTAILNY A DIFFERENCE IN THE BED LAST NIGHT. HAD A SHORT MEMORIAL SERVICE AFTER PARADE FOR OUR COMRADE KILLED ON WEDNESDAY. READ AND PREPARED DINNER. RECEIVED 9 LETTERS - GRAND - SOME WERE SENT VIA GENEVA AND POSTED LAST JULY AND AUGUST! LETTERS

FROM HOME (3), MICK (2), JEAN, KEN AND BETTY SMART (2). WENT TO SEE IF NICK ETC. HAD ANY- BOB GOT SOME ONLY. SCROUNGED SOME OF THAT RENOWED GERMAN CHEESE FROM THEM! HAD A SHORT GAME OF BRIDGE AFTER SUPPER.
<u>31/12/44</u> THOUGHT I WOULD SPEND A LITTLE MORE TIME IN BED, SO ROSE AT 9.15. BOTH PARADES WERE MESSED UP BY "JERRY", JUST WHEN IT WAS BITTERLY COLD TOO. FINISHED READING MY BOOK TO-DAY. HAD SOME OF OUR NEW YEAR CAKE AFTER TEA. IT WAS "WIZARD". COOKED MEALS - AND GOOD SUPPER AT 8.30. WAS INDICATED BEFORE GOING TO THE SCOTTISH CLUB'S SHOW AT 10.00. I RECEIVED TWO TICKETS, BEING PRESIDENT OF THE N.E.CLUB - HARRY WENT WITH ME AND LES SQUEEZED IN BETWEEN US! THE SHOW WAS GREAT AND LASTED UNTIL 12.30. ON RETURN WE HAD A CUP OF COFFEE AND THEN GOT TO BED BEFORE THE LIGHTS WENT OUT AT 01.00. ("FRANK" THE GERMAN W/O) CAME ROUND TO CHECK US OFF AT 1.00, WISHING US A "HAPPY NEW YEAR" – I BET! THE ST ANDREWS SOCIETY (SCOTTISH CLUB) PROGRAMME WAS:-

1. COMMUNITY SINGING LED "WEE MAC"
2. JOCK CAMPBELL SINGING
3. MONOLOGUES BY "STANLEY HOLLOWAY".
4. SKETCH "THE RECRUITING OFFICE"
5. FRANK SURGESS SINGING
6. SKETCH "PALM HOTEL"
7. SINGING BY THE WELSH CHOIR
8. BOB BURNS AND HIS ORCHESTRA WITH FRANK STURGESS, VOCALIST
9. ADDRESS BY ROY (ASSISTANT PREACHER-SCOTSMAN) AT 11.50 AND AT 11.58 TWO MINUTES OF MEDITATION BEFORE THE NEW YEAR ARRIVED. CHEERING AND BEST WISHES ALL ROUND THEN "AULD LANG SYNE".
10. "LEO MAKI'S HE CATS" WITH "JONNY" AS COMPERE AND "GERALDINE", SINGER WOUND UP THE PROGRAMME WITH AN ½ HOUR OF SWING, WHICH WAS REALLY SWELL. "LAND OF HOPE AND GLORY" TOOK THE PLACE OF THE NATIONAL ANTHEM. EVERYONE THOROUGHLY ENJOYED IT AND IT

WAS THE BEST POSSIBE UNDER THE CIRCUMSTANCES. <u>AND SO TO</u>

1945

(NOT MUCH NEED TO MAKE NEW YEAR RESOLUTIONS UNDER THESE CIRCUMSTANCES!! HOWEVER, SOME HAVE BEEN MADE-MOST OF WHICH COULDN'T BE BROKEN ANYWAY!)

<u>1/1/45</u> SCHOOL STARTED AGAIN TO-DAY, SO AFTER GOING TO THE LIBRARY WENT TO MY FIRST CLASS OF THE YEAR. WROTE HOME AND TO JOAN. ONLY ONE PARADE TO-DAY – AT 9.30. WE ARE GLAD TO HAVE THESE PARADES CUT OUT, BECAUSE WE GET SO DAMN FROZEN STANDING OUTSIDE FOR ½ HOUR OR EVEN MORE SOMETIMES. FINISHED OFF OUR NEW YEAR CAKE. REPORT OF MR SODERBERG'S VISIT (HE IS THE SWEDISH YMCA REP) YESTERDAY APPEARED TO-DAY. THERE ARE MANY HOPES WRAPPED UP IN HIM FOR THE FUTURE.

<u>2/1/45</u> WORKED THIS MORNING, AFTER WE HAD BEEN ON PARADE AN HOUR! APPARENTLY WE DID NOT GO ON PARADE EARLY ENOUGH, SO THE GERMAN OFFICER (OLD AND MONOCLED, BY THE WAY) AND "FRANK" WENT OFF AND LEFT US THERE. AFTER A WHILE WE WANDERED OFF AND SOON WERE CALLED BACK. "JERRY" ORDERED US TO HAVE ANOTHER PARADE AT MID-DAY, WHICH WE DULY HAD. "CHEESING", ESPECIALLY AS IT MESSED UP ONE OF MY CLASSES! RECEIVED A LETTER FROM JEAN - HER FIRST ONE WRITTEN (RECEIVED HER 2ND ONE A WHILE AGO). IT WAS MOST WELCOME. WENT ROUND TO 2DIV. AT NIGHT FOR A CHAT WITH BOB, NICK ETC.

<u>3/1/45</u> WROTE UP DIARY AND HAD A SHOWER (AT LAST –FOR OUR TURNS BEEN A LONG TIME COMING!). AFTER DINNER, WORKED AND THEN PREPARED TEA AND COOKED. CLASS SUPPER. A "WIZARD" ARGUMENT ENSUED IN WHICH THE WHOLE ROOM JOINED IN: TOPIC "WHICH COUNTRY HAS DONE MOST TOWARDS WINNING THE WAR", PLUS, 101 OTHER LITTLE ARGUMENTS THAT CROPPED UP. THIS LASTED FROM 7.00 TO 9.30.

<u>4/1/45</u> CHATTED, READ, SHAVED. ¼ LOAF OF BREAD TO-DAY; RECEIVED WITH OPEN ARMS. 500 PARCELS IN TOO, WHICH

WILL RELIEVE THE POSITION FOR A FEW MORE DAYS. EVERYONE CRYING OUT FOR CIGARETTES TOO - FORTUNATELY I HAVE ONLY BEEN SMOKING 5 A DAY, (PLUS A PIPE OR TWO OF TOBACCO SAVED FROM "BUTTS"!), WHICH LEAVES WITH A FEW YET. HAD "TOJO" IN THIS AFTERNOON QUESTIONING "ROY" ABOUT HIS 3 ESCAPES, SO "NED" AND I PULLED HIS LEG A BIT! COOKED THE TEA AND THEN WORKED. SUPPER. HAD A GAME OF BRIDGE WITH HARRY AGAINST GEOF AND LOFTY, TILL 9.45.

5/1/45 JIM AND I DOING FATIGUES IN ROOM TO-DAY, SO ROSE EARLY. HAD A JOB WITH THE DAMN FIRE. ALL LATE ON PARADE, SO PARADE AT 11.00, 2.00 AND 3.30 AS WELL! MY GOD, AND ITS DAMN COLD TOO. THE 2.00 ONE UPSETS MY BOOK-KEEPING (1) CLASS WHICH WAS THE SAME AS LAST TUESDAY. HOWEVER, THAT'S THE WAY IT IS – AND WAS! COOKING, CLEANING UP AND ODDS AND ENDS ALL DAY.

6/1/45 DID 6 "CIRCUITS" WITH REG FOR EXERCISE (JUST OVER 4 MILES!). MOST I HAVE DONE FOR A LONG WHILE. FELT LIKE A REST AFTERWARDS, SO READ ON MY BED. WORKED AND AT NIGHT HAD A GAME OF BRIDGE WITH HARRY, BEFORE RETIRING TO BED AT 9.30, TO LIE THERE THINKING OF HOME AND SATURDAY NIGHT, AND WHAT I NIGHT HAVE BEEN DOING AND WHAT I MIGHT HAVE DONE THESE LAST 7 MONTHS. OH WHAT'S THE USE OF THUS DREAMING. LET US HOPE AND PRAY.

7/1/44 ROSE EARLY FOR SUNDAY AND PREPARED THE BREAKFAST. WENT OVER FOR A CHAT WITH BOB, TOM, NICK AND THEN CAME BACK TO READ (WORK). AFTER DINNER WE HAD OUR 10TH N.E.CLUB MEETING AT WHICH I TENDED MY RESIGNATION AS CHAIRMAN. THE SECRETARY TOOK CHARGE OF THE MEETING. I WAS ASKED TO KEEP ON, SO AGREED TO DO FOR A MONTH AND IF I STILL WISHED TO GIVE IT UP, MY RESIGNATION WOULD BE ACCEPTED. GOT SOME PROGRAMME MAPPED OUT. NO PARADE THIS AFTERNOON – THANKS TO "JERRYS" KINDNESS! WAS GOING TO THE M.D's LECTURE AT 3.30, BUT COULDN'T GET IN! COOKED TEA, THEN WENT TO CLASS TILL SUPPER. WROTE UP DIARY AND ODDS AND ENDS TIL BED TIME. GOT A VERY WELCOME 15 CIGS TO-DAY (GOD KNOWS HOW LONG THEY HAVE TO LAST!). HOWEVER, AM HAVING 5 A DAY (GOT 20

LEFT) AND THEN…..WELL, IT'LL BE JUST TOO BAD. WEATHER A LITTLE WARMER AT THE MOMENT.

<u>8/1/45</u> NEWS OF MORE PARCELS COMING IN, WHICH WE SINCERELY HOPE TURNS OUT TO BE TRUE (OF COURSE, WHEN THEY ARRIVE IS ANOTHER MATTER!). WORK AND COOKING OCCUPIED THE DAY WITH A LONG CHAT WITH "NED" (OR "LES") AT NIGHT ABOUT HIS "CIVVY" JOB. BED EARLY TO FORGET MY HUNGER – AND FOR PEACEFUL THOUGHTS.

9/1//45 MADE A CAKE OUT OF CRUSTS OF BREAD AND A FEW BISCUITS AND THEN TOOK MY CLASS. AFTER DINNER PREPARED TEA AND MADE ARRANGEMENTS FOR THE NEW CHAPS COMING IN OUR ROOM (AND OUR COMBINE TO MAKE UP THE 6 – AS WE'VE ONLY HAD 5 SINCE "KNOBBY" LEFT). THE FIRST CHAP THAT CAME IN, WE DID NOT FANCY, SO WE ENGINEERED A CHAP IN FROM NED'S OLD SQUADRON, THE TWO SWOPPING ROOMS. CLASS AT NIGHT, SUPPER - AND THE CAKE. SOME MAIL CAME IN BUT NONE OF US RECEIVED ANY. OUR 5 MADE AN AGREEMENT TO SHARE OUR PARCELS (10% OF CHOC. TO EACH PARTNER AND BETWEEN HARRY, JIM AND I 20% OF CIGS. TO THE TWO UNFORTUNATES). WENT ROUND TO SEE IF NICK OR BOB GOT ANY MAIL. YES, NICK GOT ONE, OH, I NEARLY FORGOT, THE "FERRETS" FOUND A BIG TUNNEL IN PROGRESS IN VIII DIVISION LAST NIGHT AT 11.00 AND THEN PROCEEDED TO CONDUCT A LARGE SCALE SEARCH LASTING UNTIL 12.30. ALL THE CHAPS IN ONE ROOM WERE UP ON THE CARPET AND I UNDERSAND THEY ARE GOING TO GET A SEVERE SENTENCE, BUT WE DON'T KNOW YET FOR SURE.

<u>10/1/45</u> BAGS OF SNOW DURING THE NIGHT, SO IT WAS PRETTY THICK THIS MORNING - AND COLD TOO. SO "JERRY" CHOSE TO CHECK UP THE STOOLS IN EACH BARRACK - TAKING THEM ON MORNING PARADE WITH US. IT ONLY TOOK THEM ABOUT AN HOUR (BLAST THEM!) TO COUNT EACH LOT ABOUT TEN TIMES. WORKED AND COOKED DURING DAY. WROTE A P.C. HOME. WENT OVER FOR A CHAT WITH BILL AND THEN RETURNED TO BED.

<u>11/1/45</u> VERY COLD STILL. NICK AND TOM CAME ROUND IN MORNING, WHILE THEIR DIVISION WAS BEING SEARCHED, WE HAD TO GET OUT IN THE AFTERNOON FOR THEM TO GIVE OUR BARRACK THE ONCE OVER. SUPPER EARLY AS

SOME WENT TO "PANTO MANIA". READ AND TOOK STOCK OF GRUB. WORKED TOO! ARGUMENTS STILL FREQUENT!
12/1/45 WORKED AND WROTE P.C. TO JEAN. CLASS IN AFTERNOON AND THEN BACK TO COOK. WE CUT FOR THE AMERICAN PARCEL (AS ONLY TWO TO A ROOM OF 18). WE WON TOO – WHICH FROSTED OLD "POP". OUR NEWCOMER WENT INTO "DOCK" (GEORGE), AS HE IS NOT IN THE BEST OF HEALTH AND HAS A CARBUNCLE ON HIS NECK, WHICH HE IS TO HAVE REMOVED TO-NIGHT. THE DAY WAS DAME COLD - A HIGH EAST WIND BLOWING.
13/1/45 JIM AND I ON DUTY. ROSE AT 7.30 TO LIGHT FIRE AND GET BREAKFAST. CLEANING UP, COOKING, MAKING A PUDDING, CLASS IN THE AFTERNOON, SHAVE AT NIGHT OCCUPIED ALL MY TIME IN A FAIRLY FULL DAY. HAD A LOVELY STEW AT TEA-TIME (MADE WITH A TIN OF STEAK AND ONIONS (ARGENTINE FOODSTUFFS). DID ODDS AND ENDS AT NIGHT AFTER SUPPER - WRITING UP DIARY, N.E.CLUB WORK, AND MADE AN ENDEAVOUR TO SCROUNGE SOME GERMAN CHEESE FROM BOB & CO.
14/1/45 HAD BAKED BEANS ON TOAST FOR BREAKFAST- DELICIOUS. YOU WOULDN'T KNOW ME TO-DAY – ALL SPRUCED UP. DID 4 TOURS OF THE CAMP WITH "REGGIE", THEN RETURNED TO CHAT AND WARM UP AND THEN PREPARE DINNER. WENT TO N.E. CLUB MEETING AT 1.30 UNTIL PARADE. PREPARED TEA - WHICH WAS ALSO ABOVE AVERAGE (!) – THE CAKE BEING "POLISHED OFF". CLASS AT 6.00, THEN A DASH BACK FOR A LITTLE SUPPER BEFORE GOING TO SEE "PANTO MANIA" AT 7.15 WITH REG. IT WAS A GRAND SHOW - ACT 1, MUSICAL INTERLUDE AND ACT 2. A TWO-HOUR SHOW. LAST NIGHT, SO BOUQUETS WERE PRESENTED TO THE LEADING LADIES!! BACK TO ROOM FOR THE REST OF MY SUPPER AND BED.
15/1/45 SMOKED MY LAST GOOD CIGARETTE TO-DAY, SO I HAVE TO FALL BACK ON 40 ELEGANTES I HAVE SAVED FROM DAYS OF OLD! AFTER THAT – WELL, GOD KNOWS. SAVED THE DAY FOR A WHILE BY SELLING REG ½BAR AMERICAN CHOC. FOR 20 AMERICAN CIGS. BOUGHT TWO P.Cs FROM MICK FOR 10 ELEGANTES. COOKED AND MADE JIM'S BIRTHDAY CAKE FOR TO-MORROW. AFTER TEA DID SOME N.E.CLUB WORK AND READ. GOOD NEWS ON G. COMMUNIQUE REGARDING A NEW "PUSH" BY JOE DUE EAST

OF HERE. I HOPE HE WASTES NO TIME AND TAKES US BEFORE THEY HAVE TIME TO MAKE ARRANGEMENTS TO GET US OUT. OPTIMISTIC PETE!! GOT THE GRAMAPHONE AT NIGHT, WHICH JOE PLAYED UNTIL NEARLY MIDNIGHT, BUT I ONLY HEARD IT FOR A SHORT WHILE BEFORE I WAS ASLEEP.

16/1/45 ICED THE CAKE AND CLASSES, AND COOKED AFTER DINNER. ATE ½ JIM'S BIRTHDAY CAKE AT TEA AND THE ½ AT SUPPER. IT WAS REALLY DELICIOUS (EASILY THE BEST YET) AND THE ICING WAS CERTAINLY UP TO THE SAME STANDARD. CLASS AFTER TEA AND THEM MADE SUPPER. MADE THE PORRIDGE AT NIGHT. GOSH, THE NEWS IS GREAT TO-DAY, WITH EVERYONE PRETTY EXCITED OVER THE RUMOURS OF OUR INTENDED EVACUATION. QUITE A LOT OF "JERRY" AIR ACTIVITY TODAY? JOE IS ONLY ABOUT 60 MILES FROM HERE NOW ACCORDING TO TO-DAY'S COMMUNIQUE FROM "JERRY". GUN FLASHES IN THE DISTANCE, BUT WE DON'T KNOW WHERE THEY'RE FROM. IT MAY ONLY BE A RANGE (SAYS US WHO HAVE BEEN MISLEAD BEFORE NOW!) SOME WENT TO THE BOXING SHOW TO-NIGHT.

17/1/45 BREAKFAST AFTER PARADE AS THE PORRIDGE TOOK SO LONG. MOST OF US MAKING PREPARATIONS FOR GETTING OUT OF HERE. AT 11.00 A PANIC OCCURRED WHEN WE WERE TOLD TO BE READY TO LEAVE IN AN HOUR. PANDOMONIUM RAINED AS THE COOKHOUSE WAS RAIDED, LIBRARY, SPORTS STORE, CLOTHING STORE, HOSPITAL ETC. WE WERE PARADED OFTEN AND ON TENDER HOOKS ALL DAY. WE ATE LIKE LORDS, AS WE ALL HAD SURPLUS FOOD WE WOULD NOT BE ABLE TO TAKE WITH US AND THE "JERRIES" GAVE US EXTRA BARLEY ETC. FOR THEY COULD NOT FIND ANYTHING ELSE TO DO WITH IT. AIR-RAID AT NIGHT WITH THE BOMBS DROPPING RATHER CLOSE - LAID UNDER OUR BEDS ETC. ROOM IN A TERRIBLE STATE - ALL LITTERED UP.

18/1/45 JUST THE SAME AS YESTERDAY - TERRIFIC SUSPENSE - MIGHT MOVE ANY HOUR. EATING WELL WITH PLENTY OF BREWS. EATING ABOUT EVERY HOUR OR SO. RUMOURS ABUNDANT, ESPECIALLY CONCERNING JOE'S PROGRESS EAST OF US. PLENTY OF JOKING, BUT WE REALISE THE MARCHING IS GOING TO BE NO JOKE. ALL THOSE UNABLE TO MARCH GONE TO KREUZBURG.

19/1/45 STARTED ON THE MARCH THIS MORNING. OUT AT 5.00AM AND STOOD AROUND UNTIL 7.30 UNTIL WE GOT STARTED. THERE WAS A HOWLING WIND AND BY HELL IT WAS COLD. MARCHED ALL DAY WITH STOPS ABOUT 5 -7KMS. ARRIVED AT A SMALL VILLAGE ABOUT 5.00 AND SLEPT IN EITHER LOFTS OR BARNS. DEADLY, BUT WORSE TO COME.
20/1/45 ON THE ROAD AGAIN AT 6.00AM (WITH USUAL 1½-2 HRS WAITING). MARCHED 12KMS BEFORE WE WERE TAKEN OFF THE ROAD BY THE ARMY (AS WE, PLUS 100s OF REFUGEES, WERE BLOCKING THE ROAD) AND ORDERED TO REMAIN IN A BRICK FACTORY – NOW WRECKED – FROM MID-DAY ONWARDS. WE LIT FIRES IN THE YARD AND MADE BREWS AND STEWS ETC. I NOW HAVE STOMACH TROUBLE AND FEEL DEADLY. SAW THE M.O. NIGHT MARCH TO-NIGHT. WHAT AM I GOING TO DO? ALL OUT AT 8.30P.M AND WE STARTED OFF SOON AFTER 9.00. MY STOMACH WORSE AND HAD TO DROP OUT IN SNOW. LAY FOR ABOUT ¼ HR. 21.1.45 AS COLUMN PASSED, THEN GAVE IT ANOTHER GO AND IT SEEMED A MIRACLE HAPPENED FOR MY STOMACH GAVE ME NO FURTHER TROUBLE. MARCHED ALL TOLD 42 KMS WITH TEMP. -15ºC UNTIL WE ARRIVED AT 10.00AM AT A BIG BARN, SLEEPING SIDE-BY-SIDE WITH BULLS AND HORSES. IT WAS AT LEAST WARM THOUGH. WE CROSSED THE ODER DURING THE NIGHT - IT WAS TO DO THIS WE MARCHED SO MUCH. A LOT OF THE CHAPS "ALL IN". REST OF THE DAY WE SLEPT, EXCEPT TO GET UP FOR COFFEE FROM OUR 2 FIELD KITCHENS (WHICH HAS TO PROVIDE FOR THE 1500 ODD MEN!).
22/1/45 CALLED AT 1.00AM, BUT MANY CHAPS REFUSED TO MOVE. GRADUALLY THEY WERE TALKED "INTO IT", UNTIL ONLY A FEW REMAINED AND THEY SHIFTED THEM BY FIRING MACHINE-GUNS INTO THE RAFTERS. ANOTHER 23KMS TO-DAY. SOME FELLOWS LEFT BEHIND IN HOSPITAL WITH FROST-BITE, WATER ON THE KNEE ETC. BARN AT NIGHT - DAMN DRAUGHTY AND COLD ONE AT THAT. ½ CUP OF SOUP FROM THE FIELD KITCHENS PER MAN (1) –THOUGH ONLY A TASTE, IT WAS MOST WELCOME.
23/1/45 STAYED HERE RESTING TO-DAY – AND HAVE WE EARNED IT? RATIONS – ½ BISCUIT PER MAN (!). DAY BEFORE YESTERDAY WE GOT ABOUT 30 SMALL DOG BISCUITS! THAT IS ALL WE'VE HAD ISSUED AND IF IT WAS NOT RATIONS (PLUS

RED CROSS FOOD) RECEIVED BEFORE WE STARTED, WE'D BE STARVING NOW. MADE A FIRE, OUR COMBINE, AND HAD 2 OR 3 BREWS PLUS A TIN OF FISH WARMED UP ON TOAST. ANOTHER ½ CUP OF SOUP FROM THE "COOKERS".

24/1/45 OUT AT 4.00AM AND ON THE ROAD AT 5.30AM. FOR 30 KMS MARCH. WHAT A LIFE- IS THIS NEVER GOING TO FINISH NOW, FOR TRANSPORT SEEMS TO BE AS FAR OFF AS EVER. JUST ABOUT DEAD WITH FATIGUE WHEN WE REACHED OUR NEXT BARN TO STAY, SO AFTER RESTING WE JUST HAD SOME BREAD AND THEN WENT TO SLEEP.

25/1/45 LAY IN BED UNTIL WE HAD TO GET UP TO BE OFF ON THE ROAD AGAIN AT 11.00AM AND WE MARCHED UNTIL DARK. WHAT A SCRAMBLE TO FIND SOMEWHERE TO SLEEP IN THE BARNS IN THE DARK. ½ CUP OF POOR SOUP CAME UP FROM THE "COOKHOUSE" ABOUT 9.00. PRETTY COLD AND WE SEEM TO FEEL IT A LOT MORE NOW. ALTHOUGH VERY CROWDED FOR SLEEPING AND ANYTHING BUT COMFORTABLE, SLEEP CAME EASILY.

26/1/45 RATIONS TO-DAY AT LAST - BREAD, MARG. AND POTATOES (WE HAVE "FOUND" FOOD BEFORE NOW, WHICH HAS HELPED TO KEEP US GOING - SOME HAVE FAIRED MUCH BETTER THAN OTHERS - ESPECIALLY THE FRENCHMEN AND POLES WITH US). RESTED TO-DAY – WE CERTAINLY NEEDED IT - THOUGH IT MAKES IT WORSE ON STARTING AGIAIN. SPENT THE DAY MAKING BREWS AND ROASTING SPUDS ON VARIOUS FIRES (VERY GREAT SHORTAGE OF WOOD, SO LACK OF FIRES). HAD OUR FIRST WASH ON THE JOURNEY. MADE TWO SLEDGES OUT OF WINDOW FRAMES. RETIRED TO BED IMMEDIATELY THE SECOND ½ CUP OF SOUP (AND LAST) CAME UP FROM THE FIELD KITCHENS, ABOUT 6.00.

27/1/45 ROUSED ABOUT 4.30 AND ON THE ROAD AT 6.30 - FEELING NONE TOO GOOD - DON'T SEEM TO HAVE MUCH ENERGY. HAD BEEN SNOWING DURING THE NIGHT, SO OUR SLEDGES WERE HEAVY GOING. DISPOSED OF THEM AFTER 5KMS. "FOOTED" 21 KMS TO-DAY - ENOUGH FOR ME NOWADAYS. BY HELL, FORGOT TO MENTION THAT WE HAD TWO FULL LOAVES OF BREAD STOLEN YESTERDAY - ONE FROM JIM'S BAG AND ONE FROM HARRY'S. WHAT A LOSS – GOOD JOB WE HAD A LITTLE IN RESERVE TO MEET IT. FINISHED TO-DAY AT 1.00, BUT JUST LAY DWON ALL TIME

EXCEPT TO GET UP FOR ESSENTIALS, GOING TO BED EARLY AGAIN, AS THEY INTEND TO HAVE US UP EARLY AGAIN. 28/1/45 SURE ENOUGH WE WERE UP AND OUT BEFORE DAWN AND TRAMPING BEFORE 6.00 AFTER THE USUAL LONG WAIT ON THE ROAD BEFORE GETTING "CRACKING". DID 22KMS, WHICH SEEMED AS THOUGH IT WOULD NEVER END. HOWEVER, IT DID, AS THE WHOLE OF THIS NIGHTMARE MUST SOMETIME. WE PRACTICALLY LIVE NOW ON THE THOUGHTS OF THE GOOD MEALS WE WILL HAVE WHEN WE GET BACK TO ENGLAND. NOW WE LIVE ENTIRELY ON GERMAND RATIONS, FOR ALL THAT WE STARTED OUT WITH HAS GONE EXCEPT FOR ONE OR TWO SMALL ITEMS. ON MY LAST LEGS WHEN WE GOT TO THE OLD BARN, AS USUAL. MOST OF US ARE THESE DAY. ARRIVED ABOUT 1.00PM AND SOUP ABOUT 4.00 PLUS RATIONS (1/5 LOAF; 1/16 BLOCK OF MARG. AND 1/10 TINNED "BULLY"). TWO PIECES OF BREAD BEFORE SLEEP WAS JUST ENOUGH TO KEEP US GOING. 29/1/45 RESTED DURING THE DAY AFTER MAKING A "BREW" IN MORNING, AS THERE ARE RUMOURS OF A NIGHT MARCH. GOT 2½ CUPFULS OF SOUP FROM THE "KITCHENS" AND SOME "KNACKEBRUTTES" (BISCUITS) AS RATIONS. YES, SURE ENOUGH WE HAVE TO BE OFF TO-NIGHT AND WE HIT THE "TRAIL" AT 5.30PM AND WHAT A TRAIL. IT REALLY WAS A NIGHT OF HELL - OF HIGH WINDS AND SNOWDRIFTS WITH LORRIES AND CARS BLOCKING THE ROAD AND WITH OUR FIELD KITCHENS IN FRONT WE WERE AT TIMES STANDING FOR NEARLY AS MUCH AS AN HOUR. 30/1/45 OTHER TIMES WE WERE IN SINGLE FILE, "JERRY"
AND US ALL IN ONE, WITH JUST ONE IDEA; TO GET THROUGH AND NOT FALL OUT TO PERISH IN THE SNOW. PASSED A DEAD BODY (A CHEERING SIGHT!) AS WE GOT OVER ONE OF THE PASSES, BUT GLAD IT WAS NOT ONE OF OUR CHAPS. IT WAS ALMOST DAWN WHEN WE ARRIVED AT OUR DESTINATION AFTER DOING 29KMS! WE WERE ALL UTTERLY EXHAUSTED. TO "TOP" THE LOT THE SOUP PREPARED FOR US ON THE WAY IN THE FIELD KITHCHENS WAS SPILT OVER DURING THE LAST 2-3 KMS OF THE JOURNEY. SO WE WENT WITHOUT, AND STRAIGHT TO BED. HAD SOME "BREW" AND SOUP LATER IN THE DAY. PAID CIGARETTES TO GEOF'S CROWD FOR THEM TO MAKE A "BREW" FOR US, AS NONE OF US FELT UP TO IT. IT WAS

WORTH IT. HARDLY MOVED OUT OF BED AND LAY DOWN FINALLY AT 6.00 FOR A FULL NIGHT OF SLEEP FOR A CHANGE (NO EARLY CALL EITHER).

31/1/45 STAYED AT THIS BARN TO-DAY – VERY CRAMPED, BUT BETTER THAN MARCHING. MADE SOME "BREWS" AND ATE OUR RATIONS WITH CARE. FEELING DISTINCTLY "GROGGY" NOWADAYS. RUMOURS WE'RE WAITING FOR TRANSPORT FROM HERE (SOON SQUASHED FOR WE ARE NOW TOLD WE MUST GO TO GOLDBERG FOR TRANSPORT- ANOTHER 20KMS).

1/2/45 ROSE SOON AFTER DAWN TO START MARCHING AT 8.00 FOR GOLDBERG. WE'VE JUST ABOUT GIVEN UP HOPE OF TRANSPORT BUT THEY CANNOT MARCH US MUCH MORE AS CHAPS ARE PASSING OUT FREQUENTLY NOW, AS WELL AS MANY OTHERS BEING IN BAD SHAPE. THANK GOODNES WE ONLY DID 14KMS, BEFORE WE CAME TO OUR QUARTERS - IN SMALLER BARNS - MORE CROWDED THAN EVER. APPARENTLY HERE WE STAY UNTIL TRANSPORT DOES TURN UP AT GOLDBERG (ANOTHER 9KMS AWAY). JUST GOT OUT OF BED FOR THE SOUP TO-DAY, THAT'S ALL. DESPITE THE WAY WE WERE ALL DOUBLED UP TO GET IN, WE ALL SLEPT WELL.

2/2/45 SCROUNGED SOME WOOD AFTER PULLING DOWN A SHED AND MADE A FIRE. MADE A "BREW" AND SOME BARLEY SOUP FROM AN ISSUE OF BARLEY WE RECEIVED. USUAL 2½ CUPS OF SOUP FROM THE KITCHEN - DINNER AND LATE TEA-TIME! REST OF THE TIME RESTED.

3/2/45 PASSED THE DAY MUCH THE SAME AS YESTERDAY. ALWAYS ON THE SCROUNGE FOR ANYTHING EXTRA THAT MAY BE GOING. "NED" GOT A LITTLE EXTRA BREAD FOR CIGARETTES. EVEN RESTING DOES NOT SEEM TO GIVE US MORE STRENGTH AS THE RATIONS ARE SO LOW.

4/2/45 RUMOUR WE'RE GETTING TRANSPORT FROM GOLDBERG TO-MORROW - I HOPE IT'S TRUE AT LAST. STILL HAD ENOUGH WOOD LEFT TO MAKE A FIRE, SO MADE A COUPLE OF "BREWS", AND BOILED THE TWO SPUDS PER MAN RATION ISSUED TO-DAY! ALSO RECEIVED SOME BREAD AND MARG. (USUAL 1/5 AND 1/10!).

5/2/45 YES, OFF EARLY – "ROUSED" AT 5.00 – AND ON THE TRAMP AT 6.30AM FOR GOLDBERG STATION AND THE LONG AWAITED AND HOPED FOR TRANSPORT. WALKED 9KMS ARRIVING ABOUT 9.30 AND GETTING IN OUR CATTLE

TRUCKS AT 11.30 – 56 IN A TRAUCK. TERRIBLY CRAMPED, JUST ENOUGH ROOM TO SQUAT - WONDER HOW LONG THIS IS TO LAST. RECEIVED ANOTHER 1/12 LOAF PER MAN + SOME MEAT PASTE (1/5 TIN PER MAN). MOVED OFF ABOUT 3.00 AND STAYED THE NIGHT IN THE SIDINGS AT SAGAN.

6/2/45 SPENT A HELL OF A NIGHT, JUST GETTING A LITTLE SLEEP SITTING UP. IT SEEMED AS THOUGH DAWN WOULD NEVER COME. SPENT MOST OF THE DAY IN MORE OR LESS A DAZE. HAD NO WATER OR ANY DRINKS UNTIL TO-NIGHT, SINCE YESTERDAY MORNING ON THE WALK - WAS HELLISHLY THIRSTY. RATIONED OURSELVES CAREFULLY WITH BREAD ETC. SOME CHAPS EATEN ALL THEIRS ALL READY.

7/2/45 ANOTHER NIGHT OF HELL. SHOULD GET RATIONS TO-DAY, BUT NONE TURNED UP. PROGRESS ON THE TRAIN PRACTICALLY NIL. WE'RE SELDOM ALLOWED OUT OF THE TRUCKS EVEN THOUGH WE'RE STANDING FOR HOURS. SOME OF THE CHAPS IN BAD SHAPE WITH DYSENTERY, STOMACH TROUBLE, PILES ETC. AND YET NOTHING CAN BE DONE ABOUT IT. NEED HARDLY SAY THAT EVERYONE 8/2/45 ACHES IN EVERY LIMB AND THE MAJORITY FEEL VERY "TOTTERY" WHEN THEY STAND UP. NO RATIONS YET. ARRIVED AT OUR DESTINATION AT MID-DAY, AND AT LAST SAW BARBED WIRE - I NEVER THOUGHT I WOULD EVER BE GLAD TO SEE THAT! HUNG AROUND FOR HOURS AND EVENTUALLY GOT A SHOWER – HOW REFRESHING AFTER 3 WEEKS WITHOUT A STITCH OF CLOTHING COMING OFF. ONE SNAG - HAD TO GET DRIED ON MY ONE AND ONLY FILTHY TOWEL. OFF TO BILLETS AFTERWARDS - 300 IN ONE BIG ROOM - ON THE FLOOR - PRETTY CROWDED. BETTER THAN THE DRAUGHTY BARNS THOUGH. SOME IRISHMEN NEXT DOOR, WHO ARE EXCELLENT TO US. SOME SOUP AND POTATOES CAME UP AT DUSK AND DID WE GET STUCK INTO IT. I DIDN'T REALISE I WAS SO HUNGRY. GOT A FEW "SECONDS" OF SPUDS THAT HAPPENED TO BE GOING AFTER QUEUING. SAW "SPUDDER" HARRISON, AND OLD SCHOOL CLASSROOM MATE. HE MANAGED TO "SLIP" ME 20 CIGS (MOST WELCOME – "CAMEL"). SHARED THEM WITH HARRY AND JIM. HAD NO TIME TO TALK TO HIM. BED AFTER SOUP - COMPLETE OBLIVION.

9/2/45 SOME RATIONS AT LAST (2/5 LOAF PER MAN - 2 DAYS RATIONS, YESTERDAYS AND TO-DAYS - SOME DRIPPING TOO). SOUP ABOUT MID-DAY AND 4 OR 5 "SPUDS". LAY IN BED MOST OF THE DAY.
10/2/45 GOT STOMACH TROUBLE - WICKED PAINS AND (DIARHORIA!). ATE VERY LITTLE. WENT SICK AND GOT SOME MAGNESIUM TRISILICATE. RATIONS NOW 1/5 LOAF BREAD, 1/20 BLOCK MARG., MID-DAY SOUP, 4 OR 5 SPUDS AND ½ SPOONFUL OF SUGAR A DAY PER MAN! MY GOD, JUST ENOUGH TO BARLEY EXIST ON, AND CERTAILNY NOT ENOUGH TO RECOVER ANY LOST STRENGTH ON.
11/2/45 FELT A LITTLE BETTER. WENT SICK AGAIN. FEELING WEAKER. LAY IN BED MOST OF THE DAY.
12/2/45 STILL GOT THE PAINS ETC., BUT EATING MY RATIONS NOW. DID NOT FEEL WELL ENOUGH TO MOVE AROUND MUCH AND EVERY MOVEMENT IS A TERRIFIC EFFORT. AT LEAST THE NEWS IS GOOD.
13/2/45 FEELING MUCH BETTER IN THE STOMACH AREA AND SO GOT AROUND MORE. WENT OVER TO SEE NICK, BOB AND TOM, WHO ARE JUST MANAGING TO GET ALONG. AT NIGHT WENT WITH "NED" TO SEE A PLAY "DEEP DIGS THE DEVIL", PUT ON BY THE IRISHMEN IN THE FRENCHMANS' THEATRE, IT WAS PRETTY GOOD.
14/2/45 GOT 12 "BUCKSHEE" CIGARETTES PER MAN TO-DAY (WERE THEY WELCOME OR WERE THEY? – THEY'RE FROM OLD UNCLAIMED PERSONAL PARCELS OF YEARS BACK NOW). I GOT PLAYERS AND STATE EXPRESS. FELT BETTER AGAIN TO-DAY – DID TOASTING AND CHATTING TO THE IRISH CHAPS MOST OF DAY. COMMENCED GETTING MY DIARY UP-TO-DATE. TRIED TO LOCATE "SPUDDER" HARRISON WITHOUT SUCCESS. AIR-RAIDS HERE AT NIGHT COMMON, BUT WE DON'T HEAR ANYTHING OR SEE ANYTHING. HAD ONE DURING THE DAY TOO. HARRY GONE OVER TO THE SICK EVERYDAY AND THE M.O. HAS NO EQUIPMENT WHATSOEVER. WHAT A STATE OF AFFAIRS.
15/2/45 2 SLICES OF TOAST FOR BREAKFAST FOR THE FOUR OF US (NED, JIM, REG AND I). PAID HARRY A VISIT AND THEN SAW "SPUDDER" HARRISON, HAVING A SHORT CHAT TO HIM BEFORE THE GUARDS CLEARED US AWAY FROM OUR RESPECTIVE BARB-WIRE ENCLOSURES. WROTE UP DIARY TO-DATE. HAD SOME THICK SOUP TO-DAY FOR A CHANGE -

CAME UP AT 1.30 ALONG WITH THE USUAL 4 SPUDS. FEELING ABOUT AS WELL AS CAN BE EXPECTED, BUT HELLISHLY HUNGRY. WORKED OUT PAY AND BROUGHT IT UP-TO-DATE IN DIARY IN AFTERNOON. WROTE A P.C HOME. PREPARED THE TEA - SPUDS SAVED PEELING THEM AND CUTTING AND TOASTING THE BREAD. CHATTED WITH MAC ABOUT FOOD FOR A CONSIDERABLE TIME BEFORE RETIRING TO BED ABOUT 8.30.

16/2/45 REVELLE AT 6.30 AS USUAL, BUT AS I DON'T GO ON PARADE AT 7.30, I STAY IN BED UNTIL PARADE'S OVER AT ABOUT 8.00. MOST OF MORING PLAYED "CRIB" WITH REG. SOUP WAS GOOD TO-DAY, BUT WE'RE ALL SO HUNGRY IT MAKES LITTLE IMPRESSION ON THE ACHING GUTS. BREAD RATION CUT TO 1/7 (HALF) LOAF PER MAN - GOD! WHAT ARE WE GOING TO HAVE TO KEEP US ALIVE (WE GET 2 SPOONFULS OF FLOUR TO MAKE UP FOR IT!) BUT DIDN'T GET IT TO-DAY). SOME RED CROSS REPRESENTATIVES CAME ROUND WITH PETE THOMSON AND THE M.O INSPECTING WHAT HAS BEEN DESCRIBED AS OUR APPALLING CONDITIONS, BUT SAID WE CANNOT EXPECT THEM TO IMPROVE, BUT IF ANYTHING TO GET WORSE. WELL, NOW WE KNOW. NO SIGN OF ANY RED CROSS FOOD - JUST A ¼ PARCEL PER MAN WOULD GO A LONG WAY HERE. PLAYED "HEARTS" IN THE AFTERNOON (NED, REG, JIM AND I). TEA CONSISTED OF A SLICE OF BREAD WITH POTATO SOUP MADE WITH A FEW SPUDS WE SAVED FROM TO-DAYS ISSUE, HAD A BREW OF ENGLISH TEA WITH SOME SUGAR IN. AT NIGHT CHATTED TO SOME OF THE IRISHMEN, THEN HAD 1½ SLICES OF BREAD ABOUT 8.30 BEFORE GOING TO BED DEAD TIRED(!) AND YET WE'VE DONE NOTHING ENERGETIC. W/O FROM TO-DAY, I HOPE!

17/2/45 "JERRY" GAVE US BACK OUR 1/5 LOAF, THANK GOODNESS. GOT BREAKFAST READY (NOT MUCH TO DO (!), BUT IT TAKES A LONG TIME TO DO IT ON THE FEW FIRES AVAILABLE FOR US ALL). CHATTED TO THE IRISHMEN, MADE UP YESTERDAYS FLOUR RATION INTO SCONES (FLOUR, WATER, SUGAR AND COFFEE FOR FLAVOURING). HAD THEM ABOUT MID-DAY WHEN WE COULDN'T WAIT ANY LONGER FOR SOMETHING TO EAT. PLAYED HEARTS AGAIN. SOUP LIKE WATER TO-DAY- CRUEL- IT'S NOTHING FILLING, WHICH MEANS WE HAVE TO RELY MORE THAN EVER ON THE

BREAD AND SPUDS FOR SOME SATISFACTION. SMOKED MY LAST CIGARETTE, SO NOW HAVE TO RELY ENTIRELY ON "JERRY" ERSATZ TEA FOR A SMOKE. GOT A LITTLE EXTRA SOUP AND SPUDS FROM "PADDY" FOR A FAVOUR RENDERED YESTERDAY. IT WAS MOST WELCOME. HE IS ON THE WORKING PARTY, SO GETS A LOT MORE THAN WE DO. WROTE A LETTER HOME AND TO JEAN, AND WROTE UP DAIRY. RED CROSS PARCELS ARRIVED TO-DAY – FOR THE POLES, NOT US! AND WE ARE THE ONES REALLY IN NEED OF THEM.

18/2/45 A VERY NICE DAY ESPECIALLY CONSIDERING THE TIME OF YEAR. WANDERED ROUND TRYING TO GET A HOLD OF "SPUDDER", BUT FAILED. WENT ROUND TO SEE BOB, NICK AND TOM AND OF COURSE WE TALKED OF FOOD AND NOTHING BUT - OF DISHES WE HAD HAD AT VARIOUS STATIONS AND WHAT WE ARE GOING TO HAVE. EVERYONE IS TALKING OF FOOD ALL THE TIME. ENDEAVOURED TO SCROUNGE A CIGARETTE, BUT JUST MANAGED A COUPLE OF "DRAGS". THE OFFICERS OVER THE WAY HAVE BEEN GIVEN A RED CORSS PARCEL BETWEEN 5 BY THE NORWEGIANS. GOD FORBID – THEY'VE HAD NO END OF RED CORSS FOOD RECENTLY AND CIGARETTES AND WE'VE ONLY HAD THE BARE GERMAN RATION BUT THEY GET IT. THEY EACH BROUGHT (THE OFFICERS) AS MUCH FOOD AWAY WITH THEM THEY COULD AND THEY'VE COME NOTHING LIKE THE DISTANCE WE HAVE - AND THEY HAD ONLY A WEEK OF IT. GOT THE SCRAPINGS OF THE WORKING IRISHMENS URN TO-NIGHT. EVEN THAT WAS MOST WELCOME ALTHOUGH SO LITTLE. PLAYED CARDS PART OF THE TIME AND DOING TOAST AND "BREWS" OCCUPIES A LOT OF THE TIME. CHATTED TO SOME OF THE IRISHMEN AT DIFFERENT TIMES. HAD OUR 2 SLICES OF BREAD A PIECE EARLY - JUST BEFORE THE LIGHTS WENT OUT FOR AN AIR-RAID - AND GOT INTO BED, GLAD TO SLEEP TO TAKE MY MIND OF THINGS. LAY DREAMING OF FOOD FOR A WHILE.

19/2/45 DID NOT GET UP UNTIL AFTER 10.00, SO THAT I WOULD NOT EAT MY 2 SLICES FOR BREAKFAST TOO EARLY! CLEANED UP AND MADE UP BED, THEN TOASTED AND MADE SOME POTATO CAKES. WROTE UP DIARY. CHATTED TO MAC ABOUT LONDON AND GOOD PLACES TO GO TO FOR FOOD. PEA SOUP CAME UP AT 4.30 (PARADE TIME!) BECAME

GROUP-LEADER IN PLACE OF NICK FOR DISHING OUT RATIONS ETC. GOT THE PERMANENT FATIGUE PARTY SACKED AT NIGHT, WHICH CONSISTED OF SOME OF THE BIGGEST RACKETEERS. RATIONS STILL THE SAME - BREAD, SUGAR, MARG, PINT SOUP, 5 OR 6 SPUDS. WE ALSO GET ¼ BLOCK OF COAL PER MAN PER DAY! GOT A BIT OF GERMAN SOUP TO-DAY, BUT IT'S NO DAMN GOOD. AT NIGHT SPENT TALKING, AS USUAL – AN AIR-RAID CAUSING US TO CHAT IN THE DARK. ANOTHER AIR-RAID DURING THE NIGHT. HEARD THE GUNS TOO. COLD TO-DAY, BUT OTHERWISE O.K. DID A LITTLE TRADE WITH "PADDY".

20/2/45 PASSED THE DAY MUCH THE SAME AS YESTERDAY. MAC TOLD ME ABOUT LUMBERING AND THE VARIOUS TYPES OF "COOKIES" HIS MOTHER MADE. I NEARLY DROWNED WITH MY MOUTH WATERING SO MUCH. PLAYED A FEW HANDS OF "CRIB" WITH REG, COOKING AND TALKING, THUS OCCUPYING THE DAY. SOUP CAME UP EARLY- THE RATION OF SOUP HAS BEEN CUT! MY GOD, THEY CAN'T EVEN GIVE US A PINT OF SOUP A DAY - AND THIN STUFF AT THAT. JIM AND I SNEAKED OUT OF CAMP AT NIGHT AND WENT OFF TO THE FRENCH, SLAVS AND ITALIANS HUTS TO DO SOME TRADING (COCOA AND COFFEE). ENDED UP "FLOGGING" A PULLOVER EACH FOR 20 CIGARETTES EACH, BUT GOT NOTHING FOR THE DRINKS (TROUBLE BEING THEY HAD ALL JUST RECEIVED THEIR RED CROSS PARCELS). IT WAS QUITE AN EXPERIENCE, BUT BY HELL THEY'RE A TIGHT LOT. YOU GET NOTHING "BUCK SHEE". GOT BACK A FEW MINS. BEFORE THERE WAS AN AIR-RAID - JUST AS WELL. HAD A GOOD SMOKE FOR THE FIRST TIME FOR ABOUT A WEEK. BEEN A NICE DAY.

21/2/45 ROSE EARLY FOR A CHANGE AS EXPECTED HAVING TO GO ON PARADE (FOR THE FIRST TIME) AT 7.30, BUT IT WAS CANCELLED OWING TO RAIN. WROTE TO MARGARET AND WROTE UP DIARY, INCLUDING SOME OF MAC'S SUGGESTIONS OF EATS. HARRY CAME OUT OF HOSPITAL AND OVER FOR A CHAT, BUT HE COULD NOT COME BACK INTO OUR BILLET- NO ROOM. "SOUP" WAS REALLY GOOD (IF YOU COULD CALL IT SOUP FOR IT WAS JUST BOILED CABBAGE BUT THERE WAS QUITE A LOT OF CABBAGE). DISHED UP RATIONS (NO MARG, TO-DAY, BUT 1OZ OF SAUSAGE MEAT EACH INSTEAD), MADE TOAST, PEELED

SPUDS ETC. WENT OVER TO THE FRENCH CAMP AT NIGHT WITH JIM, BUT COULD NOT DO ANY TRADE. HAD A CHAT TO A FRENCHMAN WHO COULD SPEAK ENGLISH. HE TOLD US SOMETHING OF HIS LIFE AND WHAT HE HAS SUFFERED IN THIS WAR. GOT BACK ABOUT 8.00, HAD SUPPER AND GOT INTO BED QUICKLY AS THE SIRENS SOUNDED. QUITE A LOT OF ACTIVITY - LOOKS TO HAVE BEEN A GOOD RAID. THERE WAS ANOTHER ONE DURING THE NIGHT - THAT'S THE STUFF - GIVE 'EM HELL - BUT MY HEART ACHES TO BE UP THERE AND TO GO BACK WITH THEM - TO ENGALND, HOME, A GOOD MEAL, CLEANLINESS, FREEDOM AND A LIFE WORTH LIVING. HOWEVER, I PRAY, HOPE AND THINK IT WILL NOT BE LONG NOW.

22/2/45 UP AND DOWN ON PARADE FOR 7.30 TO-DAY. CAME BACK TO WRITE UP DIARY AND WRITE TO JEAN COOPER. CHATTED WITH "MAC" AND "ART" ABOUT THEIR PROPOSED VISIT TO MY HOME AND A COUPLE OF DAYS IN LONDON. TALKED OF MORE FOOD DELICACIES AND SWOPPING PARCELS AFTER WAR. "ART" TOLD ME ABOUT HIS DAYS IN ENGLAND. "SPUDS" AND SOUP RATION CUT TO-DAY, BUT NO EXTRAS TO MAKE UP FOR IT. I SUPPOSE BAD TIMES COME TO AN END AS WELL AS GOOD. SOUP CAME UP AT 2.30 AFTER IT WAS SUPPOSED TO BE UP AT 11.00. ALWAYS THE SAME - WE NEVER KNOW WHEN ITS COMING - ANYTIME BETWEEN 10.30 AND 4.30. SAUSAGE MEAT AGAIN INSTEAD OF MARGARINE, BUT MANAGED TO BUY ONE RATION FOR 2 CIGS. WENT DOWN TO THE FRENCH COMPOUND AGAIN WITH JIM AND MET OUR FRENCH FRIEND - SWOPPED ADDRESSES. GOT "DONE" BY A RUSSIAN FOR A TIN OF COCOA (THOUGHT HE WAS GIVING US 2 LOAVES FOR IT, BUT INSTEAD THERE WAS ONLY STUFFING IN THE PARCEL – THE - !). HAD TO GET BACK SMART, AS "JERRY" RAIDED THE FRENCH COMPOUNDS LOOKING FOR US CHAPS. GOOD JOB JIM AND I HAD ARMY GREAT COATS ON OR WE WOULD HAVE BEEN IN THE "BUNKER" NOW. AIR-RAIDS AGAIN + AVCTIVITY.

23/2/45 WE WERE OUT ON PARADE FOR LONG ENOUGH TO-DAY - BECAUSE WE WERE LATE GETTING OUT I SUPPOSE - AND THEY COULDN'T AGREE THE COUNT. DURING THE MORNING WE HAD OUR GRAND "LOTTERY" OF THE LITTLE RED CROSS FOOD GIVEN TO US - EACH MAN GETTING A PORTION OF ONE COMMODITY! I GOT 1/10 TIN OLEO

MARGARINE (JUST MY LUCK - THERE WAS ONLY ONE TIN TOO). HOWEVER, I SWOPPED IT FOR 1/10 TIN OF KLIM (POWDRED MILK). I BOUGHT A DAYS RATION OF GERMAN MARGARINE FOR 2 CIGS. FROM ONE CHAP IN HOSPITAL (THEY GET THE RATION, BUT ARE UNABLE TO EAT IT). THIS MIXED WITH THE KLIM AND SUGAR MADE A "WIZARD" SPREAD ON MY BREAD. OUR GROUP ALSO WON SOME EXTRA SAUSAGE (2 THIN SLICES EACH IT WORKED OUT TO) – THE EQUIVALENT OF A GERMAN RATION. GERMAN SOUP AND SPUD RATION VERY SMALL (BUT GOOD). EACH MAN GOT 22 CIGS AND SOME TOBACCO AT NIGHT FROM OLD UNCLAIMED PERSONAL PARCELS. CERTAINLY VERY WELCOME. AIR-RAID AGAIN AT NIGHT (SAME TIME AS USUAL), SO NED, JIM AND I HAD A GOOD ARGUMENT - IN FACT TO-DAY WE HAVE BEEN VERY "NIGGLY". GERMAN RED CROSS REPRESENTATIVE VISITED US TO-DAY AND SAID WE WERE IN PRETTY BAD SHAPE AND PROMISED TO DO HIS UTMOST TO INCREASE OUR RATIONS EITHER THROUGH THE GERMANS OR INT. RED CROSS - I HOPE SOMETHING GETS DONE ABOUT IT, FOR WE'VE BEEN WAITING LONG ENOUGH FOR PROMISED PARCELS ALREADY.

24/2/45 MADE BREW, TOAST ETC. IN MORNING, SOUP COMING UP EARLY FOR A CHANGE - 12.00. THERE WASN'T ENOUGH TO GO ROUND AND I WAS ONE OF THE UNLUCKY 15, BUT THEY MANAGED TO GET A LITTLE MORE, SO I WAS DULY SERVED (AND RELIEVED). IT WAS A VERY SMALL RATION, BUT IT WAS VERY NICE. "SPUD" RATION WORST YET. SALT TO-DAY FOR THE FIRST TIME. WROTE HOME TELLING THEM THE FULL MENU I'M LOOKING FORWARD TO ON ARRIVAL HOME. IT'S A "SUPER-DUPER" (TO USE ART'S TERM). DISCUSSED MENUS OVER TEA AFTER 4.30 PARADE. HAD A CONCERT IN OUR BARRACK AT NIGHT, BUT I ONLY HEARD A SMALL PART OF IT, AS I WAS IN TALKING TO ONE OF THE IRISHMEN MOST OF THE TIME. HE IS ONE OF THE WORKING PARTY. INTO BED AND A CHAT TO MAC BEFORE THE LIGHTS WENT OUT AT 10.00 - SOON AFTERWARDS THERE WAS AN AIR-RAID (LATE TO-NIGHT). HEARD SOME HEAVY STUFF GO DOWN NOT SO FAR OFF - CONTINUOUSLY FOR SOME 20 MINS.

25/2/45 ANOTHER DAY NEARER VICTORY AND HOME, FOOD AND COMFORT. OH! FOR THAT DAY. DID A FEW "CIRCUITS" WITH NED (ALSO KNOWN AS "LES"), THEN "CLEANED UP".

MENDED MY SOCKS AND PREPARED MY TOWEL FOR THE LAUNDRY. DISHED OUT RATIONS, WROTE UP DIARY AND PREPARED BREAKFAST AND DINNER. SOUP WAS GOOD AT 2.30. PLANNED A DAY IN LONDON WITH "ART" AND MAC AND CHATTED ABOUT FOOD AGAIN. AT NIGHT LAY TALKING AND WENT THROUGH TO THE IRISHMEN. WENT TO BED EARLY AND JUST GOT INTO BED WHEN THE LIGHTS WENT OUT FOR AN AIR-RAID.

26/2/45 WENT BACK TO BED TO SLEEP AFTER PARADE AT 10.30, THEN CLEANED UP AND MADE A BREW BEFORE EARLY SOUP, WHICH EVENTUALLY ARRIVED AT 1.30. PLAYED BRIDGE TILL PARADE, MAKING A SMALL SLAM TO TRUMPS. HAD TEA AND A CHAT, THEN WENT IN TO SEE TOM, THE IRISH CHAP, UNTIL HIS TEA CAME UP. PREPARED SUPPER, THEN TOM CAME IN FOR A CHAT, DURING WHICH THE LIGHTS WENT OUT FOR AN AIR-RAID – ACTIVITY IN THE DISTANCE. HE BROUGHT US A FEW VERY WELCOME BREWS OF GERMAN COFFEE AS WE ARE ALMOST OUT OF BREWS NOW. BED ABOUT 9.15 BEFORE THE LIGHTS WENT OUT AGAIN AT 10.00. BOUGHT A MARGARINE RATION TO-DAY FOR 2 CIGARETTES.

27/2/45 STOOD OUT ON PARADE FOR ABOUT AN HOUR THIS MORNING, AS 5 MEN WERE MISSING. I THINK "FRANK" GAVE IT UP AS BAD JOB IN THE END AFTER MANY DEMONSTRATIONS TO JOE WALKTY (WHO ALWAYS TAKES THE "CAN"). HAD A WALK ROUND WITH NED, THEN MADE TOAST, WROTE UP DIARY AND GOT CLEANED UP. SLIGHT CUT IN BREAD RATION TO-DAY - 16 MEN TO 3 LOAVES INSTEAD OF 15 (4 TO ¾ LOAF). THEY'VE JUST ABOUT CUT EVERYTHING NOW. AFTER ISSUING THE RATIONS (AFTER WE HAD A "BREW" AND 1½ SLICES BREAD! REPRESENTING BREAKFAST), DID SOME WASHING. SOUP LATE, 2.00. WORKED OUT VARIETIES OF BREAKFASTS! CHATTED TO MAC AND "ART" AND WITH NED AFTER TEA. BED ABOUT 9.00. AIR-RAID THEN AND ANOTHER DURING THE NIGHT.

28/2/45 2 OF OUR CHAPS SHOT LAST NIGHT, APPARENTLY, WHILE ATTEMPTING TO BREAK INTO THE "SERBS" RED CROSS STORE, AND A THIRD PUT IN THE "BUNKER". ONE IS SUPPOSED TO BE SERIOUS AND THE OTHER SLIGHTLY SHOT. YES, ALL THE SERBS, POLES, FRENCH AND EVEN ITALIANS(!!) GET RED CROSS PARCELS, BUT NONE HAVE COME

CONSIGNED TO US, SO WE DON'T GET ANY, (AND WE'VE NOW BEEN HERE 3 WEEKS). WHAT ANNOYS ME IS THAT IT'S AMREICA AND BRITAIN PAYS FOR THEM. THE SERBS GOT 3,000 YESTERDAY FOR ABOUT 300 OF THEM! WROTE UP DIARY AND CONTINUED MY LIST OF MEALS FANCIED. PASSED THE DAY MUCH THE SAME AS USUAL. WE WERE HANDED OVER TO THE ARMY AUTHORITIES ON 4.30 PARADE AND THEY CERTAINLY TOOK THEIR TIME. LIGHTS WENT OUT EARLY - ABOUT 8.00 AND I SAT CHATTING WITH NED WAITING FOR THEM TO COME ON, BUT THEY DIDN'T ALTHOUGH THE RAID WAS OVER. SO CRAWLED INTO BED NOT FEELING TOO WELL. HAD HEADACHE AND FELT HEAVY. WAS SOON ASLEEP AFTER THOUGHTS OF MY MENUS.

1/3/45 ROSE EARLY FOR PARADE - EVERYONE WAS OUT FOR 7.15, (BUT WE WERE OUT THERE FOR 1HOUR 20 MINS-GOD KNOWS WHAT THEY MESS ARROUND AT.) WENT TO BED AGAIN AND STAYED THERE UNTIL 11.00, WHEN WE HAD BREAKFAST (COFFEE AND THREE ½ SLICES BREAD - 1 WITH SUGAR). CLEANDED UP AND PREPARED DINNER FOR 2.00, WHEN THE SOUP CAME UP. CHATTED AND CONTINUED MY MENUS AND RECEIPES LIST. AT NIGHT WENT TO SEE TONY THE IRISHMAN AND LATER HAD SUPPER. BOUGHT A TO-MORROW'S SOUP RATION FOR ½ MARGARINE RATION (OVER WHICH I HAD A ROW WITH NED). OFFICIALLY TOLD TO-DAY WE ARE GETTING A ¼ PARCEL A MAN EITHER TO-MORROW OR SATURDAY AND ANOTHER SIMIALR ISSUE NEXT WEEK - THAT'S GREAT NEWS TO THE BOYS. HELL OF A DAY, ESPECIALLY AT NIGHT. AIR-RAID AGAIN PUT OUT LIGHTS EARLY, SO WENT TO BED EARLY. BOUGHT A SLICE OF BREAD FOR A CIGARETTE.

2/3/45 HELL OF A WIND STILL, SO WENT TO BED AFTER PARADE TO GET WARM. HAD AN EARLY "BREW" THANKS TO NED. GOT CLEANED UP ABOUT 11.00 AND THEN HAD BREAKFAST. MADE UP MORE MENUS AND CHATTED TO "MAC" AND "ART" UNTIL SOUP AND SPUDS CAME UP. THAT DOUBLE RATION OF PEA SOUP WAS "WIZARD". WROTE UP DIARY, AND CONTINUED WITH MENUS. PARADE AT 5.00 (A LITTLE QUICKER THAN USUAL). THEN TEA AND AFTER PREPARING MY BED ETC. WENT IN TO SEE TONY, THE IRISHMAN. CHATTED UNTIL THE LIGHTS WENT OUT ABOUT 8.00 FOR AN AIR-RAID, THEN GOT SUPPER IN A SCRAMBLE

AND WENT TO BED ABOUT 9.00. HAD A DAMN HARD JOB TO GET WARM AND GET TO SLEEP.

3/3/45 PARADED AT 7.30 AND AGAIN AT 8.30 FOR BLANKET CHECK. OH HELL! THE WAY THE "MASTER RACE" CARRY ON! WALKED ROUND WITH JIM TO GET WARM AS ITS DAMN COLD OUT. PREPARED BREAKFAST, THEN LAY IN BED WRITING UP DIARY AND MENUS. CHATTED TO MAC AND NED ABOUT POST WAR REUNIONS, MEALS ETC. LATER KEPT PRETTY BUSY DISHING OUT RATIONS, THEN SOUP AND SPUDS CAME UP. THICK BARLEY SOUP WITH A LITTLE MEAT AND PEAS. IT WAS PRETY GOOD. SCRAPED BOTTOM OF "KEEBLES" TOO, WHICH PRODUCED A LITTLE MORE FOR MY STOMACH. EXCITEMENT HIGH AS RED CROSS PARCELS ARE COMING UP AFTER WE HAD THOUGHT WE HAD "HAD IT" – THIS MORNINGS AIR-RAID HELD THE "FROGGIES" DISTURBANCE UP. THE PARCELS CAME UP AFTER PARADE AND THE CIGS AND CHOCOLATE WERE IMMEDIATELY DIVIDED OUT. SOME SAT DOWN STRAIGHT AWAY TO EAT THE WHOLE OF THEIR ¼! "BREWS" WERE MADE CONTINOUSLY ALL NIGHT UP TO 12.00 IN THE DARK(!) ALTHOUGH AN AIR-RAID AT 8.15 LASTING TILL ABOUT 9.30 HELD UP PROCEEDINGS. AFTER TEA (WHICH WE HAD BEFORE THE PARCELS CAME). I WENT FOR A CHAT WITH TONY AND "FLOGGED" OUR COFFEE THROUGH HIM (WE HAVE QUITE A LOT OF GERMAN COFFEE TO CARRY ON WITH). APART FROM THAT WE DID NOT TOUCH OUR PARCEL. GOT MY SUPPER IN THE DARK WHEN THE LIGHTS WENT OUT AND THEN WENT TO BED.

4/3/45 SUNDAY. PARADE (ALSO QUICKER ONE THAN USUAL), THEN PREPARED BREAKFAST. HAD GERMAN COFFEE WITH MILK (OH BOY, IT TASTED GOOD) THEN FRIED BREAD AND TUNA FISH (OH BOY). HAD MORE BREAD TOO, AS LAST NIGHTS TRANSACTION ALLOWED IT, AND WILL DO FOR A DAY OR TWO. HAD A CHAT TO "DIGGER" ABOUT FOOD ETC. SOUP UP AT 2.00, WITH SPUDS. NOT A REALLY BAD RATION, BUT SPUDS VERY SHORT. ¼ LOAF PER MAN TO-DAY, WITH USUAL MARGARINE RATION. WROTE UP DIARY ETC. TILL PARADE. TEA, THEN ORGANISED TO-MORROW'S FATIGUES. (HAD A SLAP UP TEA, BY THE WAY, BUT SPOILT BY ONE CLUMSY CHAP UPSETTING ONE OF OUR DIXIES OF TEA - HOWEVER, HE WAS GOOD ENOUGH TO REPLACE IT WITH A

"BREW" OF AMERICAN COFFEE, OF WHICH WE HAVE NONE). CHATTED TO TONY TILL NEARLY 9.00, THEN PANICED TO GET INTO BED BEFORE 9.00, BUT FAILED. WAS IN BED SOON AFTERWARDS THOUGH.

5/3/45 ROSE AT 1ST BUGLE TO GET MINT TEA (I WAS ONE OF THE 4 UNLUCKY TO HAVE TO GET UP EARLY). BUSY ORGANISING FATIGUES (OUR GROUP ON TO-DAY), UNTIL 12.30 AND DOING THEM, THEN SAT DOWN TO WRITE UP DIARY. WROTE TO HOME, BUT DID NOT GET IT FINISHED. FATIGUES AND PREPARING TEA. WHAT WITH THE EXTRA BREAD WE'VE GOT AND THE COMPLETE PARCEL BETWEEN THE 4 OF US WE'RE LIVING LIKE LORDS NOW. AT NIGHT THE PARCEL NEWS WAS GREAT - POSSIBILITY OF A PARCEL EACH PER WEEK FOR 3 WEEKS IN THE NEAR FUTURE - A PRISONERS DREAM. SPIRITS CERTAINLY ARE VERY HIGH COMPARED TO WHAT THEY WERE ONLY 3 OR 4 DAYS AGO. OUR GROUP DID WELL FOR SOUP AND GOT A FEW EXTRA SPUDS (MARBLES!). CLEARED UP AFTER TEA AND THEN WENT FOR A CHAT WITH TONY. CAME BACK AND MADE A BREW WITH JIM AND GOT SUPPER (ABOUT 8.00). LIGHTS WENT OUT FOR AN AIR-RAID AT 8.30, SO CAME BACK AND WENT TO BED. NED HAD A "BIND" BECAUSE HE WASN'T THERE FOR THE EVENING BREW AND IT WAS SUPPOSEDLY COLD.

6/3/45 AFTER PARADE HAD A WALK ROUND WITH MAC, CLEANED UP AND PREPARED BREAKFAST WHILE NED DID THE BREWS ON THE "BLOWER". BOUGHT A "BILLY CAN" FOR 5 CIGS. WROTE UP DIARY AND WROTE A LETTER HOME. PREPARED DINNER AND MESSED ABOUT AFTERWARDS. BOUGHT A SOUP RATION FOR A SLICE OF BREAD FROM "SMITHY" - THE SOUP COMING UP AT 3.00. ARGUED WITH NED OVER SOME SALT AND FUTURE COMBINE POLICY. PARADE. TEA (FRIED CORN BEEF SANDWHICH - WIZARD!). WENT IN FOR A CHAT WITH TONY, UNTIL THE LIGHTS FAILED. BY THE LIGHT OF A NEARBY CANDLE PREPARED SUPPER, BEFORE AN AIR-RAID PROHIBITS ANY SORT OF LIGHTS. HAD SUPPER JUST IN TIME, THERE FOLLOWING A VERY ACTIVE AIR-RAID. CRAWLED INTO BED EARLY IN THE DARK. SNOW THIS MORNING.

7/3/45 PREPARED BREALKAST (BAKED BEANS ON TOAST AND CHIPS. DELIGHTFUL). CLEANED UP BED, CUT UP BREAD AND BUTTERED, DISHED OUT BREAD AND MARG RATION,

PREPARED AND HAD DINNER AT 12.00 AND HAD A WALK ROUND WITH MAC. WROTE UP DIARY AND NOTES. NEWS CAME UP THAT WE ARE GETTING A COMPLETE PARCEL PER MAN TO-MORROW. OH BOY, THAT REALLY IS MARVELOUS NEWS AND IT SEEMS SO HARD TO BELIEVE. MOST OF US HAVE NEVER BEEN ON A COMPLETE PARCEL A WEEK AND I HAVEN'T SINCE ABOUT THE MIDDLE OF AUGUST! USUAL DAILY AIR-RAID TO-DAY AT 1.30. ARGUED OVER OUR PARCELS TO-MORROW TILL PARADE. TEA - 5.45-6.45, THEN PREPARED SUPPER. WENT THROUGH TO TONY FOR A FEW MINUTES, THEN CAME BACK TO ORGANISE A "BLOWER" AND GET THE SUPPER COOKED. TEA AND SUPPER WERE WIZARD (CORN BEEF HASH (TEA) AND MASHED POTATOES WITH MILK & MARG WITH FRIED BREAD (SUPPER)). AIR-RAID AT 8.30(VERY ACTIVE), SO TO BED I WENT.

8/3/45 JUST A USUAL DAY AGAIN – DISHING OUT FOOD, PREPARING MEALS AND CLAENING UP. KEPT UP MY CONTACTS AT NIGHT, USUAL AIR-RAIDS, RED + PARCELS.

9/3/45 NED NOT TOO WELL TO-DAY, SO THE THREE OF US WERE KEPT BUSY PREPARING MEALS FROM THE RED CROSS PARCELS RECEIVED YESTERDAY (ONE PER MAN) AND WE CERTAINLY GOT STUCK IN. SPAM, CHIPS AND FRIED BREAD AND AFTER BREAD, JAM AND CHEESE SANDWHICHES, BISCUITS, AMERICAN COFFEE WERE COMMON. IT WAS A GRAND FEELING TO FEEL SATISFIED FOR A CHANGE. USUAL AIR-RAIDS AND HAD NO TIME TO EVEN WRITE UP DIARY. AT NIGHT COULD NOT GET TO SLEEP UNTIL 2.30 (SIZE OF STOMACH TOO BIG PROBABLY!), SO LAY TALKING. THEN A CATASTROPHE – SOMEONE RIFLED MY CASE (ABOUT 4.00A.M.) AND STOLE 1 1/10 LOAF (RATIONS), ½ PACKET PRUNES AND 20 CIGS. DONE BY SOMEONE WHO MUST HAVE BEEN WATCHING ME PRETTY CLOSELY. FUNNY PART ABOUT IT, SO MANY PEOPLE SEEM TO HAVE BEEN AWAKE AT THE TIME AND HE WHO DID IT ACTUALLY SPOKE TO JIM IN ANSWER TO HIS QUESTION "HEY, WHO'S THAT"! WE HAVE OUR SUSPICIONS BUT THAT'S AS FAR AS WE CAN GET. BY HELL, I'D LIKE TO HAVE CAUGHT HIM RED-HANDED.

10/3/45 OH BOY, REALLY FEEL MORE LIKE MY OLD SELF WITH SOME GOOD MEALS IN ME. SOME OF THE MEALS:-

1. FRIED SPAM, CHIPS AND FRIED BREAD. TOAST AND CHEESE, BREAD AND JAM, COFFEE.

2. CREAMED TUNA, MASHED POTATOES ETC.
3. BAKED BEANS ON TOAST ETC.
4. PORK, MIXED VEGATABLES, ONIONS, BOILED SPUDS ETC. (STEW)
5. SARDINES ON TOAST
6. RAISINS AND THICK KLIM (PRUNES TOO)
7. MEAT PATE, POTATO, ONIONS, MASH ON FRIED BREAD AND TOAST.
8. BULLY BEEF RISSOLES, FRIED POTATO & ONION, SPAM & FRIED BREAD.

THE TRADING POSITION IS GOOD AT THE MOMENT. WE ARE NOW WELL OFF FOR FOOD – BOTH RED CROSS AND BREAD, THANKS TO THAT. USUAL AIR-RAIDS AND SCRAMBLE IN THE DARK. WENT TO BED TIRED TO-NIGHT.

11/3/45 SEEMED TO BE DOING SOMETHING ALL DAY – GROUP WORK, PREPARING & EATING MEALS AND CHATTING AFTERWARDS. HAD TIME JUST TO WRITE UP A LITTLE OF MY DIARY, BUT HAVE NOT GOT UP TO DATE. HAD A LONG CHAT TO TONY AT NIGHT AND LATER GOT CAUGHT WITH THE LIGHTS IN THE MIDDLE OF SUPPER.

12/3/45 USUAL DAY EXCEPT THAT WE VARY OUR MEALS – WE HAVE MEALS SOMETHING LIKE THIS:- 1. "BREW" STRAIGHT AFTER PARADE WITH A BISCUIT AND CHEESE. 2 BREAKFAST 9.30-10.00, WHICH IS JUST ABOUT AS SOON AS WE CAN PREPARE A BIG MEAL. 3. MIDDAY LUNCH 12.00-1.00 4. SOUP, WHICH MAY BE ANYTIME IN THE AFTERNOON. 5. TEA 6.00-6.30, AS SOON AFTER PARADE AS POSSIBLE. 6. SUPPER 7.30-8.00 BEFORE THE LIGHTS GO OUT. TEA AND BREAKFAST ARE THE BIG MEALS AND THE OTHERS SNACKS.

13/3/45 RISING EARLY NOW – AT 6.15 TO-DAY. WASHED, CLEANED UP ETC. FOR PARADE. WENT FOR PARCELS AFTER BREAKFAST – THAT WAS ABOUT 11.00. GOT THEM ISSUED AND THEN IMMEDIATELY GOT CRACKING, SWOPPING ITEMS AS WE HAD 4 TINS OF THE SAME JAM, 4 TINS PEA-NUT BUTTER (SWAPPED 3, THANK GOODNESS) AND 4 PKTS PRUNES. WE DID PRETTY WELL ON SWAPPING.

1. 1 TIN OF SPAM FOR 1 TIN BULLY
2. 2 GRAPE JAM FOR 2 PLUM.
3. 1 PEA-NUT BUTTER}   FOR {1 JAM (PINEAPPLE)
   1 PRUNES   }   {1 RAISINS)
4. 1 PEA-NUT BUTTER FOR 1 CHEESE

5. 1 PEA-NUT BUTTER FOR {1 PLUM JAM & 1 MEAT PATE
6. 1 PKT BISCUITS FOR 1 CEREAL
7. 1 PKT PRUNES & 10 CIGS FOR 1 SPAM

PRIVATE
80 CIGS FOR 2 CHOC.
1 CHOC & 20 CIGS FOR 1 COCOA
1 COCOA FOR COFFEE+ JAM

AFTER TEA WENT IN TO SEE TONY AND FOUND HE HAD BEEN SEARCHED COMING AND WE HAD OUR TRADE FOR TO-DAY. CHATTED FOR SOME TIME AND THEN SUPPER. AIR-RAID AS USUAL. NO SPUDS; MORE SOUP (WATER).

14/3/45 NOTHING IN PARTICULAR TO REPORT AGAIN TO-DAY EXCEPT THAT WE GOT SPUDS TO-DAY. HAD SOME "WIZARD" MEALS, AS ALWAYS NOW. HAD SUPPER WITH TONY AND HIS PALS, THEN AN AIR-RAID DOUSED THE LIGHTS. THEY CAME AGAIN AT ABOUT 10.30 FOR THE ARMY BOYS, AS A LOT OF THEM ARE LEAVING AT 5.00 A.M. IN THE MORNING FOR "KOMMANDOS". MANY GOT UP TO MAKE "BREWS" AND MOST TOOK ADVANTAGE TO EAT AGAIN – AS WE DID. RUMOURS GOING STRONG. WENT IN TO SEE TONY ABOUT HIM GETTING ME A BED IN THEIR PLACE. HE WILL IF HE CAN.

15/3/45 PARADE LATE, BECAUSE OF THE ARMY BOYS GOING. BREAKFAST WAS FINISHED AT 10.30. WROTE UP DIARY. NO SPUDS, SO HAD PLENTY OF SOUP, BUT IT WAS ONLY WATER. IT BLOATED ME OUT, AND DID NOT DO ME ANY GOOD. GOT TO STAY IN THIS PIG-STY FOR THE MOMENT, AS NO ONE CAN MOVE IN NEXT DOOR-APPARENTLY THEY'RE GOING TO DO SOME SHUFFLING AROUND.

16/3/45 FEELING BAD TO-DAY – BEEN SICK DURING NIGHT AND GOT A BAD STOMACH AGAIN. STAYED IN BED ALL MORNING, SLEEPING. CLEANED UP ABOUT DINNER TIME. "WIZARD" DAY, WARM WITH PLENTY OF SUN. CROWN & ANCHOR, HEADS & TAILS ETC. FIENDS GAMBLING AWAY CIGARETTES BY THE 100S. PREPARED TEA, AND HAD A WALK ROUND WITH NED AND REG. HAD TEA BEFORE PARADE AND AFTER IT WENT ROUND TO SEE TONY. SUPPER AT 7.30, THEN TO BED AT 8.00. FELT TIRED AND I CERTAINLY HAD A GOOD NIGHTS SLEEP.

17/3/45 FEEL GRAND TO-DAY, ROSE EARLY. 1/16TH LOAF AND NO SPUDS OR MARG. AGAIN TO-DAY. I SUPPOSE "JERRY" IS

SAVING ON THE RATIONS BECAUSE WE'VE GOT THE PARCELS. CRAFTY SOD. USUAL DAY OF RAIDS AND GETTING AROUND. SAW TONY AT NIGHT. MADE MYSELF A FEW CIGARETTES ON DEALS.

18/3/45 HAD A ROTTEN NIGHT AGAIN – SICK TWICE AND PAID COUPLE VISITS TO LATRINE. WENT TO BED FOR THE MORNING AND HAD NOTHING TO EAT AGAIN. SICK DURING AFTERNOON, WHICH MADE ME FEEL A LITTLE BETTER, SO I HAD A COUPLE ROUNDS OF BREAD. WENT TO BED ABOUT 8.00 AND HAD A GOOD NIGHTS REST. SPUDS AND GOOD THICK SOUP TO-DAY FOR A CHANGE.

19/3/45 FELT GRAND EARLY ON. GOT UP ON FIRST BUGLE, WASHED AND CLEANED UP BEFORE PARADE. BREAKFAST, THEN WENT SICK ABOUT MY STOMACH. JUST GOT TO GO ON EATING NORMALLY UNTIL IT SETTLES DOWN. FELT IT COMING ON AGAIN, BUT WAS GLAD IT WORE OFF LATER. RATIONS – $1/7^{TH}$ LOAF(!), DOUBLE SOUP (NO SPUDS), MARG. AGAIN AT LAST. SECONDS ON SOUP (THICK BARLEY) SO SAVED THEM TO USE AS PORRIDGE IN MORNING. WENT THROUGH WITH TONY IN EVENING (RECEIVED A GOD SEND!). BED ABOUT 9.30, LIGHTS BEING ON UNTIL 9.15! AIR-RAIDS WERE LATE TO-NIGHT (2). WROTE HOME.

20/3/45 ROSE EARLY AGAIN AND HAD A GOOD WASH BEFORE PARADE. WALKED ROUND. BREAKFAST. USUAL MORNING ODDS AND ENDS, SOUP AT MID-DAY – PURLEY BOILED CARROTS. RED CROSS PARCELS UP AT 3.00 AND SMARTLY GOT ROUND TRADING AND THUS BALANCED OUR 4 PARCELS UP NICELY (ONE OR TWO EXCHANGES NOT POSSIBLE). MOVED MY BED OFF THE GANGWAY, THANK HEAVENS, AS I MOVED IN TO TAKE ART & MAC'S PLACE. LATE TEA, THEN WENT IN TO SEE TONY UNTIL THE LIGHTS WENT OUT ON US. HAD OUR LAST BREW IN THE DARK AT 9.00, THEN CHATTED WITH NED UNTIL THE CANDLES LIGHTED AFTER RAID.

21/3/45 FIRST DAY OF SPRING AND ALTHOUGH COLD, IT WASN'T TOO BAD. EVERYDAY HERE IS MUCH THE SAME. SOUP (CARROTTS) AND SPUDS. DID SOME TRADING FOR TONY AT NIGHT – SOME RETURN FOR ALL HE'S DONE FOR ME. JUST MANAGED OUR LATE NIGHT BREW AT 8.00 BEFORE THE LIGHTS GO OUT. THE LIGHTS GRADUALLY GOING OUT LATER AND LATER – ABOUT 8.30 NOW WHEN THEY GO. OLD

NICK AND MAC HAD A GRAMAPHONE GOING ABOUT 10.00 – HEAVENS KNOWS WHEN THEY PACKED UP.

22/3/45 THURSDAY. LOVELY DAY. OUTSIDE TO-DAY IT WAS LIKE A FAIRGROUND. THERE WAS 5 EXCHANGE MARKETS, HORSE-RACING, 2 CROWN & ANCHORS, DARTS, HEADS-TAILS AND "TAKE-A-CHANCE" 1,000S OF CIGS ABOUT. GOT A LOT OF SOUP FROM THE IRISHMEN, AS THEY DID NOT WANT THEIRS (SORT OF A CABBAGE-SPRING SOUP). (WE KEPT THE CABBAGE ETC, DRAINING OFF THE WATER). NO MARG. TO-DAY AND A $1/7^{TH}$ LOAF! I DON'T KNOW HOW THESE CHAPS MANAGE ON A $1/7^{TH}$ A DAY. WITH TONY AT NIGHT. AIR-RAIDS COMING ROUND ABOUT 9.00 NOW, WITH THE MOON BEING UP EARLY – AND BRIGHT TOO.

23/3/45 USUAL DAY. HAD A TOUR OF THE MARKETS WITH NED AFTER BREAKFAST. $1/8^{TH}$ LOAF TO-DAY! THEY ARE A LITTLE BIGGER, THOUGH. REG'S 5th WEDDING ANNIVERSARY TO-DAY, SO SPENT AFTERNOON MAKING A CAKE AND AT THE SAME TIME MADE SOME PRUNE JAM. HAD THE CAKE AT NIGHT – WIZARD! JAM OK TOO. CHATTED TO TONY AND HIS PALS ARTHUR AND BILL, AFTER THEY HAD COME IN FROM WORK, ABOUT HORSE-RACING ETC.

24/3/45 ANOTHER WIZARD DAY. STARTED ON OUR SMALL GERMAN "WHITE" LOAF THIS MORNING TONY GAVE ME. IT DID NOT APPEAR TO HAVE MUCH TASTE. HAD A BATH, THEN "BREWED" UP FOR MID-DAY SNACK, WHICH WE HAD ALONG WITH SOUP (FIRST TIME WE'VE BEEN ABLE TO JUDGE IT PROPERLY!). PREPARED TEA, THEN WANDERED ROUND THE MARKETS WITH TONY. FOOLISHLY SQUANDERED 6 CIGS AT CROWN & ANCHOR. A GRAND DAY SO TOOK OFF SOME OF MY DIRTY CLOTHES - MUST GET WEAVING ON THEM TO-MORROW AND WASH THEM. USUAL AIR-RAID AGAIN. THERE WAS PLENTY OF "YANKS" OVER THIS MORNING TOO.

25/3/45 STILL A GRAND DAY. WASHED MY CLOTHING IN MORNING AND GAVE TONY, BILL AND ARTHUR A HAND TO MOVE INTO THE NEXT BARRACK IN AFTERNOON. HAD A LATE BREW AND MADE TONY ONE TOO, AS HE HAS NO FACILITIES AT THE MOMENT. CHATTED TO TONY AT NIGHT UNTIL THE AIR-RAID AT 8.00 (A LITTLE EARLIER THAN RECENTLY). WENT TO BED ABOUT 9.00 INSTEAD OF 10.00 AND 10.30 AS THE PREVIOUS 3 NIGHTS.

26/3/45 BREAKFAST AFTER EARLY BREW (WHICH WE HAVE IMMEDIATELY AFTER PARADE), THEN A TOUR OF THE MARKETS WITH "NED". WASHED OUT MY HANDKERCHIEVES (DID THEY NEED IT TOO!). MADE SOME MORE CIGS WHEN ANOTHER LOCK WAS SOLD THIS MORNING AND I PUT MY PEN ON FOR 50. NO SPUDS OR MARG. TO-DAY, SO SPENT A LOT OF TIME GOING ROUND BARTERING, WHEN NOT DISHING OUT RATIONS ETC. MADE SOME GOOD SWOPS BUT WE WERE WELL SATISFIED WITH WHAT WE HAD. WE HAD NO PEANUT BUTTER TO TRADE THIS WEEK. KEPT A PARTICULARLY GOOD EYE ON THE "MARKETS" TO-DAY. ALL TOLD THE DAY WAS A BUSY ONE. AT NIGHT WENT DOWN TO THE FRENCH COMPOUND WITH NED, BUT HAD NO SUCCESS. SAW THE FRENCHMAN AGAIN, WHO I MET BEFORE, BED EARLY.

28/3/45 DUTY GROUP TO-DAY, SO BUSY ORGANISING DUTIES AND DOING SAME MYSELF. CHATTED WITH TONY, WHO IS NOT WELL, SO HE DID NOT GO OUT TO WORK. DINNER LATE THROUGH DUTIES. WITH TONY IN AFTERNOON AND EVENING. HAD A "YANK" FOR COMPANY TOO. AIR-RAID DURING THE DAY, BUT NONE AT NIGHT (MOST AMAZING – ABOUT THE FIRST FREE NIGHT WE'VE HAD). SUPPER AT 8.30, THEN BED.

29/3/45 AFTER BREAKFAST WENT ROUND THE MARKETS AS PER USUAL WITH NED, THEN WENT IN WITH TONY TO GET SOME RECEIPES OFF HIM AND GIVE HIM SOME OF THOSE I HAVE (TONY STILL NO BETTER). SOUP AT 12.30, THEN SPENT THE AFTERNOON (TILL 5.00 PARADE) DISHING OUT RATIONS, PREPARING TEA AND MAKING A FUDGE WITH THE CHOCOLATE COCOA. SPENT THE EVEING WITH TONY CHATTING AND AT 8.00 CAME BACK TO MAKE THE USUAL "BREW" BEFORE RETIRING TO BED. NO AIR-RAID TO-DAY, BUT THERE WAS ONE DURING THE NIGHT (WHICH I DID NOT HEAR).

30/3/45 GOOD FRIDAY. TONY STILL OFF WORK, SO WENT ROUND TO SEE HIM ABOUT 11.00 ON COMPLETING MY USUAL JOBS ETC. DINNER AT 1.00 AND SOUP AT 2.00. TEA TOOK SOME PREPARING AND ALONG WITH CHECKING OFF THE FOOD STOCK AND WRITING UP MY DIARY AND COMPLETING WRITING OUT RECEIPES FOR TONY, I FOUND IT WAS PARADE TIME. HAD A WALK ROUND AND CHAT WITH TONY UNTIL IT

WAS TIME TO MAKE THE EVENING "BREW". WAS IN BED BEFORE THE LIGHTS WENT OUT AT 8.45.

31/3/45 LOUSY SORT OF DAY- DULL AND COLD. HAD TO VACATE THE BARRACK ALL MORNING AND AFTERNOON WHILE THEY PUT BEDS IN THE ROOM. HAD OUR MEALS AT ANY TIME - WHEN WE COULD GET ORGANISED. SOUP UP AT 10.30 – THE OLD CABBBAGE SOUP. THEY HAVE ALSO REORGANISED THE GROUPS - OURS IS NOW 9. SO I HAD EXTRA WORK TO DO ON GIVING OUT RATIONS. TONY BACK EARLY FROM WORK TO-DAY, SO WENT FOR A CHAT WITH HIM - AND GOT MY CASE AT THE SAME TIME - A "BANG-ON" JOB; TAKES 4 RED + PARCELS EASILY. MAKES A GRAND TABLE TOO. PARADE. TEA AND THEN OVER WITH TONY AGAIN. USUAL BREW. NO AIR-RAID. QUITE A CHANGE TO HAVE THE LIGHTS ON TO A REASONABLE TIME(!) – SEEMS REASONABLE TO US, ANYWAY – TILL 9.15.

1/4/45 WELL, I GUESS LAST NIGHT AT MIDNIGHT SAW MY BET WITH "CHEGGA" GO FOR A "BURTON" – THE ONE I MADE LAST SEPTEMBER. DID NOT SLEEP IN MY BUNK LAST NIGHT AS I COULD NOT GET ORGANISED IN TIME – IT NEEDED REPAIR AS A LOT OF THEM DID. HOWEVER, GOT CRACKING ON IT AFTER BREAKFAST PLUS INTERRUPTIONS FOR RATIONS ETC. HAD DINNER AT 3.15 (AFTER I HAD FINISHED AND NED & REG. HAD BEEN TO THE MATCH – ARMY v RAF & NAVY. SCORE 0-1). PREPARED TEA, THEN WENT ROUND TO TONY AND PARTNERED HIM IN A GAME OF QUOITS AGAINST ARTHUR & BILL. SCORES 15-14, 6-15, 14-15. TEA. PARADE NOT AT 6.00, SO HAVE OUR BIG MEAL JUST BEFORE. WROTE UP DIARY FOR 3 DAYS, AND GENERALLY CLEANED UP. BREW AND BED.

2/4/45 STARTED OFF A NICE DAY, BUT NOT SO GOOD LATER. A HIGH KEPT BACK THE RAIN. BREAKFAST LATE (10.45) OWING TO A LOT OF PREPARATION BEING NEEDED. GIVING OUT RATIONS ETC. UNTIL 1.15. SOUP WAS REALLY GOOD TO-DAY – CAME UP IMMEDIATELY WE HAD HAD BREAKFAST. DID SOME TRADING ON THE MARKET FOR TONY AND WROTE UP DIARY. DINNER AT 3.00 AFTER WHICH NED AND I WENT AT IT "HAMMER AND TONGS" IN AN ARGUMENT. WENT OVER TO SEE TONY AND CAME BACK FOR PARADE, BUT IT WAS CANCELLED AS IT WAS BEATING DOWN WITH RAIN. GOT DOWN TO TEA, THEN HEARD THE TAIL END OF A

SHOW BY THE AMERICAN BAND. SUPPER AND BED. CLOCKS FORWARD 1 HOUR TO-NIGHT.

3/4/45 SHOULD HAVE HAD PARCELS TO-DAY, BUT EASTER HAS COMPELLED THE ISSUE TO BE PUT OFF TILL TO-MORROW. HOWEVER, WE CAN MANAGE O.K.- FOR ANOTHER 2 OR 3 DAYS FOR THAT MATTER. RATIONS UP AFTER BREAKFAST THEN WENT ROUND FOR A CHAT TO NICK & TOM. SOUP AT 2.00 (DOUBLE RATION + SECONDS) (IN PLACE OF SPUDS) - STRINGY CARROT TYPE. PREPARED TEA AND HAD IT BEFORE 6.00 PARADE. SAW TONY FOR A WHILE, THEN CHATTED TO A "YANK" THROUGH THE WIRE TILL 8.00 – SUPPER TIME. BED 9.00. AIR-RAID.

4/4/45 PARADE AT 7.00 IN THE MORNING NOW - TOO EARLY. WE WERE SO LATE ON PARADE THAT THEY MADE US GO OUT AGAIN AT 8.00. MANAGED OUR BREW AND BISCUIT AND CHEESE FIRST THOUGH – JUST IN TIME. GOT BREAKFAST RAEDY AND PARTOOK OF SAME. NAILED UP BED A LITTLE MORE SECURELY. OUR BREAD NOW GETTING VERY LOW - HAD NO EXTRA FOR SOME TIME. USUAL DAY OF ACTIVITY - FUNNY HOW THERE ALWAYS SEEMS TO BE SOMETHING TO DO. WROTE HOME AND TO JEAN. RED + PARCELS TO –DAY (LATE).

5/4/45 THURSDAY DASHING ROUND MARKETS SWOPPING AND TRADING BOTH FOR OURSELVES AND TONY. DID QUITE A FEW DEALS. SPENT MOST OF THE AFTERNOON ON THE SAME THING. "GASH" ISSUE OF 20 CIGARETTES PER MAN (ENGLISH). GRAND TO HAVE AN ENGLISH "TAB" AGAIN. EVENING WITH TONY.

6/4/45 STILL PLENTY OF ACTIVITY ON THE MARKETS, SO MY EYES WERE "SKINNED" ALL THE TIME. CHECKED UP THE FOOD STOCK WITH MY LIST. LONG IDENTITY CHECK PARADE IN AFTERNOON – THANK GOODNESS I HAD A LOW NUMBER FOR I GOT OFF QUICKER THAN MOST – THOUGH I WAS OUT 1½ HOURS. CHATTED TO TONY AT NIGHT. GOT EXTRA BREAD AND SO DID NED, WHICH RELIEVES THE SITUATION JUST IN TIME. MADE A FRESH <u>EGG</u>(!!) ON THE DEAL. HAD A "WIZARD" FUDGE FOR TEA.

7/4/45 HAD THE EGG FOR BREAKFST ALONG WITH FRIED BREAD, FRIED SPAM AND FRIED ONIONS AND POTATOES. IT WAS A "WANGER" OF A MEAL. TOURED THE MARKETS AND "DISHED" UP RATIONS. WROTE UP DIARY FOR THE LAST

THREE DAYS. WENT TO SEE "TONY" AFTER MID-DAY SNACK, THEN WENT DOWN TO THE FRENCH AND SERBS COMPOUND WITH NED FOR TRADING PURPOSES. NOT VERY SUCCESSFUL - ONLY GOT ONIONS. HOWEVER, NED AND I BOTH GOT LOAVES FROM OUR "CONTACTS" LATER.
SAW TONY AT NIGHT AND HAD A GAME FOR "HOUSY-HOUSY" ALONG WITH REG - BUT NEVER SMELT A WINNER. LIGHTS OUT AT 9.00 - BED. "GASH" ISSUE OF CIGARETTES OF 65 PER MAN! BOY, ARE WE DOING WELL FOR CIGS – THE TROUBLE IS THEY HAVE NO VALUE ON THE MARKET OR ANYWHERE. HOWEVER, WE PUT (OUR COMBINE) 25 A PIECE INTO THE "POOL" (40 A WEEK WE ALWAYS PUT IN, ONCE 60 AND THIS WEEK 65). WE GET BREAD, ONIONS, GERMAN COFFEE (TO SAVE AMERICAN FOR TRADING) AND ANY OTHER FOOD THAT MIGHT BE GOING AT A DECENT PRICE e.g. FLOUR, POTATOES, CHOCOLATE, COCOA ETC. (1/10 OF A LOAF!!)
8/4/45 LOVELY DAY, BUT QUITE A COLD WIND. "McGINTY" KEPT US ON PARADE THIS MORNING BECAUSE SOMEONE TOLD HIM TO STOP HIS WINGEING. BREAKFAST, SOUP (WIZARD, BUT NOT MUCH OF IT), RATION ISSUING ETC. DINNER, THEN PREPARED TEA. HAD A GOOD "BATH" IN COLD WATER – BEST POSSIBLE. GOT RID OF SOME LICE BY HAVING A "SQUARE SEARCH" – HUNTED IN MY JACKET, TROUSERS ETC. TEA – WITH A FUDGE ("BANG-ON") – ONLY PARADE HURRIED US TOO MUCH, BLAST IT. SAW TONY AT NIGHT - TOOK IN 160 FAGS. GOT SOME SPUDS. SUPPER, AND BED - WORRIED ABOUT THE LICE.
9/4/45 "SQUARE" SEARCHED AGAIN AFTER BREAKFAST FINDING MORE. CLEARED UP BOX OF FOODSTUFFS AND GENERALLY TIDIED UP. SOUP LATE AND DINNER LATE. MADE A BREAD PUDDING FOR NIGHT, BOILING IT UP AT DINNER TIME. ANOTHER SEARCH IN AFTERNOON THEN TEA (ANOTHER RUSH BEFORE PARADE). AT NIGHT WROTE UP DIARY AND "DISHED" OUT SOME RED + STUFF. JIM WON A BLANKET AND I GOT SOME SHAVING SOAP. WENT IN TO SEE TONY BEFORE SUPPER AND BED.
10/4/45 PARCLES UP STRAIGHT AFTER BREAKFAST AND RATIONS - AT 10.30 WENT TO BE DE-LOUSED. IT TOOK FROM 11.00 TILL 3.30, BUT FELT LOVELY AFTERWARDS -FRESH AS A DAISY, BUT HUNGRY. PREPARED AND HAD TEA BEFORE

PARADE. SAW TONY, THEN HAD AN INOCULATION. WROTE UP DIARY. WENT IN TO TONY AGAIN RE-DEALS. SUPPER AND BED.

<u>11/4/45</u> MUM'S BIRTHDAY TO-DAY. GOD BLESS YOU, MUM. STRONG RUMOURS THAT WE'RE MOVING TO-DAY, BUT LATER SQUASHED BY M.OF C. DASHED AROUND THE MARKETS TRADING FOR 2 HOURS, THEN PREPARED A BREAD PUDDING. MID-DAY SNACK (EARLY FOR A CHANGE -1.00). TRADING AGAIN AFTER AND LISTENED TO PART OF AN OUTDOOR VARIETY SHOW. PRETTY GOOD. PREPARED TEA, THEN CLEANED UP FOOD BOXES ETC. SAW TONY AND CHATTED AND DISCUSSED DEALINGS AND MOVING. THEN CAME THE NEWS SOME OF OUR CHAPS WERE LEAVING EARLY TO-MORROW MORNING. HAD SUPPER, THEN WENT ROUND TO SAY CHEERIO TO GEOF, JOE, GEORGE, MICK, "PORKY", ROY AND PENNY – PALS - AND NICK, TOM AND BOB OF MY CREW. HAD QUITE A LONG CHAT WITH THE LAST THREE, THEN RETURNED TO BED WELL SATISFIED WITH THE ARRANGEMENTS I HAD MADE WITH THEM. TIRED TO-NIGHT. GRAND DAY.

<u>12/4/45</u> WENT ROUND TO SEE THE BOYS AFTER PARADE, THEN HAD BREAKFAST. WROTE UP DIARY, GAVE OUT RATIONS, CLEANED UP, TOURED MARKETS AND KEPT MY EYES ON THE BOYS WHO ARE LEAVING. CHATTED WITH NICK, TOM AND BOB AGAIN JUST BEFORE THEY WENT. CAME BACK TO PREPARE BREAD PUDDING, THEN HAD SOUP AND DINNER – TIME NOW 3.00! WALKED ROUND AND SAW ARTHUR. PREPARED TEA (SPAM FRIED, FRIED BREAD AND "WHISPERING GRASS" AND THEN THE BREAD PUDDING AND KLIM CREAM – WIZARD!). PARADE, CLEARED UP TEA AND WROTE UP DIARY. SAW TONY FOR A CHAT, SUPPER AND BED. 40 CIGS. ISSUED.

<u>13/4/45</u> FRIDAY THE 13TH AND THE NEWS BECOMES UNBELIEVABLE. THE BOYS WHO WENT AWAY YESTERDAY RETUNED TO-NIGHT AS THEY CANNOT GET AWAY OWING TO OUR RAPID ADVANCE. EVERYBODY ALL EXCITED. THE DAY PASSED MUCH THE SAME AS USUAL, BUT PLAYED VOLLEY-BALL AT NIGHT. LOVELY DAY. THUNDER BOLTS (YANK FIGHTERS) SHOT UP NEARBY 'DROME – MOST OF THE LADS SAW THEM PLAINLY AND THE BOMB EXPLOSIONS. "GASH" CLOTHING ISSUE, BUT I DIDN'T WIN ANYTHING IN

THE CUT. CHATTED TO ART, BILL AND MAC, LIGHTS ON LATE FOR THE BOYS RETURNING. HAD A FUDGE FOR TEA - IT WAS BETTER THAN EVER. I FEEL MARVELOUS TO-NIGHT. WROTE UP DIARY. RUMOURS GOING AROUND BY THE DOZEN. SERBS AND SOME RUSSIANS MOVED OUT TO-DAY. THE LADS DIDN'T RETURN AFTER ALL.

14/4/45 WELL, PETER, IT'S YOUR BIRTHDAY TO-DAY AND I'M THINKING OF YOU. I SHALL SEE THAT YOU HAVE A DAMN GOOD TIME WITH ME AS SOON AS I RETURN, WHICH WILL NOW BE VERY SOON. 1 OF OUR LADS SHOT DEAD AND ANOTHER SERIOUSLY WOUNDED (DIED THIS MORNING) WHILE ATTEMPTING TO ESCAPE LAST NIGHT. ANOTHER CHAP GOT BACK IN TIME. IT SEEMS SO STUPID TO MAKE AN ATTEMPT NOW, WHEN WE HAVE ONLY A FEW MORE DAYS TO WAIT OR A WEEK OR TWO AT THE MOST. RATIONS AFTER BREAKFAST (BEETROOT INSTEAD OF SPUDS - NICE CHANGE). WE HAVE RAW SPUDS, SO REG AND I GOT WEAVING ON BOILING THEM. DINNER. MESSED AROUND PREPARING TEA, WALKING ROUND AND CHATTING TO NICK ETC. WHO HAVE JUST RETURNED FROM THE STATION. THE'VE HAD A DAMN GOOD TIME FROM ALL ACCOUNTS. TEA. PARADE. CHATTED TO TONY TILL SUPPER TIME (WITH JOCK AND HIS YANKEE PALS), THEN WENT TO BED EARLY - MUCH EARLIER THAN LAST NIGHT. GOT UP LATER TO SEE A "WIZARD" AIR-RAID ON POTSDAM. PHEW! DID IT TAKE A BEATING.

15/4/45 USUAL DAY OF PREPARING MEALS, GIVING OUT RATIONS INCLUDING A "GASH" ISSUE OF CHOCOLATE AND SWEETS. BOUGHT A STEAK TO-DAY (FOR A "D" BAR AND 60 CIGS) AND HAD IT FOR TEA ALONG WITH CHIPS, FRIED ONIONS AND FRIED BEETROOT, THEN A "FUDGE" TO ROUND IT OFF. IT WAS A GRAND MEAL. HAD IT QUITE A WHILE AFTER PARADE AS OUR BLOWER BROKE DOWN. HOWEVER, REG WAS ABLE TO FIX IT. TEA AT 7.00, AND HAD SUPPER PRETTY SOON AFTER I HAD CLEARED UP. HAD A CHAT WITH TONY FOR A WHILE, THEN BED WITH THE AID OF MY LIGHT (9.45).

16/4/45 ANOTHER GRAND DAY - WARM TOO. BREAKFAST AT 10.00 DUE TO 2 PARADES AS McGINTY DID NOT SHOW UP AT 7.00. RATIONS, SOUP, ROUND THE MARKETS AND PREPARED BREAD PUDDING UNTIL DINNER AT 3.00!! WROTE UP DIARY AND PREPARED TEA. HAD TEA WELL AFTER PARADE AS

THE'RE WAS SO MUCH TO PREPARE. FINISHED ABOUT 7.30! SAW TONY, THEN HAD SUPPER AND BED. WOKE UP DUE TO A LOT OF NOISE TO FIND EVERYONE GOING OUT TO WATCH AN AIR-RAID (ON POTSDAM - 30 MILES AWAY). I GOT UP AND WENT OUT TO SEE FLARES, EXPLOSIONS AND ONE BIG RED GLOW FROM FIRES.

17/4/45 GROUP DUTY DAY (NOW 20 IN A GROUP - 10 ON TO-DAY AND 10 TO-MORROW). I DID MY TURN TO-DAY. BUSY ORGANISING DUTIES, DOING FATIGUES, DISHING OUT RATIONS AND PARCELS CAME UP TOO. KEPT A STRICT WATCH ON THE MARKETS DURING AFTERNOON AND SAW TONY. TEA, THEN WENT IN WITH TONY AND CO. TILL SUPPER. HEAVY THUNDER-STORM - BEEN COMING UP ALL DAY. SUPPER. BED FAIRLY EARLY. KNEW NO MORE.

18/4/45 ROSE EARLY AND ORGANISED THE 2ND LOT OF DUTIES. USUAL MORNING AND DINNER AT 3.00 AFTER PREPARING A STEAK FOR LATER (PRICE: D BAR OF CHOCOLATE AND 40 FAGS). CHATTED AS USUAL FOR SOMETIME AFTER DINNER, WROTE UP DIARY, MESSED AROUND AND PREPARED TEA. THE STEAK WAS "WIZARD" – MORE TENDER THAN THE LAST. ROUNDED TEA OFF WITH A FUDGE, THEN CHATTED ABOUT VARIOUS TYPES OF TOFFEE AND CHOCOLATE. TONIES AFTER PARADE AND AT 8.15 CAME IN FOR SUPPER AND SO TO BED AFTERWARDS. PLENTY OF WILD RUMOURS FLOATING AROUND AGAIN. THERE HAS BEEN A HIGH PITCH OF EXPECTANCY HERE FOR THE PAST 2 DAYS THAT THE ALLIES WILL BE HERE ANYTIME. WE'RE JUST SORT OF LIVING FROM DAY-TO-DAY FOR THEM. IT'S DISAPPOINTING THAT THERE IS STILL NO SIGN OF THEM COMING. HOWEVER, THERE IS QUITE A LOT OF AIR ACTIVITY. 160 LADS ARRIVED HERE FROM LAMSDORF TO-NIGHT, HAVING BEEN ON THE ROAD FOR 3 MONTHS. GOD HELP THEM - WHAT A HELL OF AN ORDEAL THEY MUST HAVE BEEN THROUGH. THEY LOOK TO BE IN VERY POOR HEALTH AND WERE GASPING FOR FOOD AND FAGS. MANY OF THEM DIED ON THE WAY.

19/4/45 HAD A COLLECTION OF CIGS FOR THE BOYS FROM LAMSDORF. MARKET CRAWLING AGAIN AND SAW TONY. DOUBLE SOUP (HAD NO SPUDS FOR 3 OR 4 DAYS – BEETROOT YESTERDAY). DINNER AT 1.30, THEN REPAIRED SLIPPERS AND CIG CASE, WHICH I BOUGHT YESTERDAY FOR 40 CIGS. TEA,

THEN A LONG PARADE THE SAME AS THIS MORNING. THE GERMAN DUNDERHEADS! WITH TONY ALL NIGHT TILL ABOUT 10.30, TALKING OF IRELAND ETC., EXCEPT TO GET SUPPER AT 8.30. HAD A BREW ETC. WITH TONY TOO. A LITTLE AIR ACTIVITY.

20/4/45 PARADES GETTING LONGER. BREAKFAST. RATIONS. SOUP. TRADING, PREPARING BREAD PUDDING. DINNER 2.30. LAY OUT IN THE SUN FOR AN HOUR WRITING UP DIARY, FIGURING OUT PAY, WROTE HOME AND TO JEAN. TEA AND AGAIN A LONG PARADE. WENT TO SEE TONY AND THEN NORMAN DELAYEN RE-CELEBRATION ON RETURN. SUPPER. BED EARLY.

21/4/45 NO PARADE THIS MORNING. MANY WILD RUMOURS FLYING AROUND AND PLENTY OF EXCITEMENT. PLENTY OF GUNFIRE IN THE DISTANCE. AFTER BREAKFAST (ABOUT 10.30) THINGS BEGAN TO REACH A CLIMAX. ALL THE JERRIES CLEARING OUT – SEEM TO BE IN A HURRY TOO. RUSSIAN GUNCREW CAME IN CAPTURED JUST OUTSIDE LUCKENWALDE! (SUPPOSED TO BE AN ADVANCE PATROL). RUSSIANS GOING EVERYWHERE. REPORTS SAY THE RUSSIANS WILL BE HERE TO-NIGHT. PREPARED MEALS ETC. IN AFTERNOON – GOING A LITTLE MORE RASH. MORE ACTIVITY, GUNFIRE ETC. SLEPT BESIDE MY BOX AS HAVE LOST THE LOCK AND KEY! SPENT NIGHT CHATTING WITH TONY. AN UNIDENTIFIED AIRCRAFT STRAFED THE CAMP ABOUT 10.00 AND SCARED HELL OUT OF US. HAD A JOB TO GET TO SLEEP AFTER THAT – NERVES ALL TO HELL, I GUESS, WITH WAITING, SUSPENSE AND ACTIVITY. ALL OF US ARE THE SAME.

22/4/45 HARDLY A "JERRY" TO BE SEEN ANYWHERE. ALL NATIONALITIES OF PRISONERS WALKING AROUND AS THEY WISH – SERBS, NORWEGIANS, FRENCH, RUSSIANS, AMERICANS, POLES, ITALIANS AND ENGLISH – ALL EXPECTING BIG THINGS TO HAPPEN ANY MINUTE. AND THEY DID HAPPEN AFTER BREAKFAST (ABOUT 11.00). RUSSIANS WITH AMERICAN WAGGONS CAME STREAMING THROUGH – IT WAS A GREAT SIGHT WITH EVERYONE GOING ALMOST HYSTERICAL. FOR A SECOND TIME I WAS IN TEARS OF HAPPINESS SINCE I BECAME A PRISONER – I KNOW OF A THIRD YET TO COME – MY ARRIVAL HOME. OH BOY OH BOY! PLENTY OF EXCITEMENT ALL DAY AS A "JERRY" POCKET OF

RESISTANCE HELD OUT ALL DAY IN A WOOD JUST NEXT TO THE CAMP. F.W.190s DID PLENTY OF DIVE-BOMBING. RUSSIAN PRISONERS RELEASED MOVED OUT, SO NED AND I WENT DOWN TO SEE WHAT WE COULD GET – GOT SPUDS (SACK FULL), RHUBARB, AND A CABBAGE WITH STOOLS, STEW POTS, MIRRORS, COFFEE POT ETC. SPENT THE REST OF THE DAY COOKING THE SPUDS, RHUBARB, CABBAGE AND BREAD PUDDING. ¼ OF A PARCEL PER MAN CAME UP JUST BEFORE TEA AND SOME "GASH" FOOD, CIGS. AND OTHER REQUIREMENTS. HAD TEA JUST BEFORE THE WING COMMANDER'S PARADE AT 5.45. HAD A SUPER-DUPER TEA:- FRIED SPAM, MASHED POTATOES (NO SHORTAGE), CREAMED MEAT & VEG. WITH BREAD AND BUTTER, BREAD PUDDING, STEWED RHUBARB AND CREAM. BREAD, BUTTER, JAM, CHEESE, COFFEE, ½ BAR CHOCOLATE (THIS REALLY FILLED ME). SAW TONY FOR A WHILE AFTERWARDS, PREPARED SUPPER AND THEN BED. TOO EXCITED TO GET TO SLEEP EARLY, BUT DID EVENTUALLY. HEARD MACHINE GUN FIRE SEVERAL TIMES DURING THE NIGHT. SLEPT ON BED (FOUND LOCK TO-DAY). MORE COMFY ON FLOOR!

<u>23/4/45 MONDAY</u> NO MORNING PARADE, SO LAY IN UNTIL 8.00. WIZARD. I ROSE THEN, AND GOT THE OTHERS A "BREW" IN BED. USING OUR AMERICAN COFFEE WE'VE SAVED. PREPARED BREAKFAST – MORE THAN USUAL. WENT ROUND FOR PARTICULARS, CLEARED UP, PREPARED DINNER AND HAD IT – MORE LIKE A NORMAL DINNER. PARADED AT 2.30. WROTE UP DIARY AND PREPARED TEA INCLUDING A "FUDGE". WENT ROUND TO SEE TONY EARLIER ON BUT HE'S GONE ALTOGETHER - GOD KNOWS WHERE. A RUSSIAN PRESS PHOTOGRAPHER CAME ROUND TO TAKE PHOTOGRAPHS. PRATICALLY NO ACTIVITY AROUND HERE NOW AT ALL, THANK GOODNESS. HAD TO GO AROUND GROUP AGAIN FOR PARTICS. REGARDING CLOTHING, BLANKETS ETC. HAD TEA AT 6.00, THEN HAD A WALK ROUND BEFORE SUPPER AT 8.30. BED IMMEDIATELY AFTER, BUT COULD NOT GET TO SLEEP. HAD AIRCRAFT OVER LOW, WHICH CAUSED SOME EXCITEMENT-THEY WERE FIRED ON BY THE RUSSIANS. ALSO HAD A SIMILAR INCIDENT DURING THE NIGHT ONLY THEY DROPPED SOME BOMBS. DID NOT WAKE UP UNTIL AFTER IT WAS OVER - IT APPARENTLY MADE MANY OF THE BLOKES MOVE PRETTY QUICK.

24/4/45 EVERYBODY GETTING "CHEESED" NOW, WAITING TO BE MOVED. NEWS COMES UP REGULARLY - VERY GOOD. RATIONS TO-DAY (1/8TH LOAF – SMALLER; DAMN GOOD SOUP, THOUGH NOT A LOT; ABOUT 6 SPUDS; PURE BUTTER-ABOUT 1½ oz; FLOUR), STILL TUCKING WELL INTO OUR RED+ PARCEL SUPPLIES. SPENT ALL DAY GIVING OUT RATIONS, PREPARING MEALS AND COOKING, SAW TONY FOR A FEW MINUTES (HE HAS ONLY BEEN IN LUCKENWALDE). GET UP LATER (NO PARADES TO-DAY) NOW, THAT'S WHY MY TIME WAS ALL FILLED IN. OUR FOOD RATIONS WOULD BE GREATER IF IT WAS NOT FOR THE FACT THAT WE HAD TO GIVE THE FRENCH SOME. GASH ISSUES OF TOILET PAPER(!), "ELEGANTES", CLOTHING AND ODDS & SODS. WE GOT A ¼ OF A CANADIAN PARCEL PER MAN – OUR COMBINE GOT A COMPLETE UNPUNCTURED ONE. WE ALWAYS WANTED A CANADIAN PARCEL. SHORTAGE OF RUMOURS TO-DAY. BED EARLY.

25/4/45 BUSY ALL MORNING WITH THE USUAL (RATIONS, GASH ISSUES ETC. BY THE DOZEN – I'M ALL FOR IT!), AFTER GETTING UP ABOUT 8.30 - JIM GOT THE EARLY MORNING BREW. SAW TONY IN THE AFTERNOON THEN PREPARED BREAD PUDDING. TEA AT 5.30 AND AT NIGHT WENT FOR A WALK ROUND WITH NED, GOING A LITTLE WAY ALONG THE ROAD OUT OF CAMP. HAD AN EXHILARATING FEELING BEING OUT OF BARBED WIRE ONCE AGAIN. MET A COUPLE OF SERBS AND WE CHATTED TO THEM AS BEST WE COULD IN GERMAN. SUPPER IN THE DARK, THEN BED. PUT CLOCKS FORWARD AN HOUR TO CONFORM TO RUSSIAN TIME.

26/4/45 ROSE AERLY AND MADE THE "BREW" BEFORE PREPARING BREAKFAST. MORNING FILLED IN AGAIN BEFORE I REALISED IT. WIZARD SOUP TO-DAY (¾MEAT) ¼ LOAF PER MAN TOO WITH SUGAR, PUDDING POWDERS AND MEAT IN ADDITION. MORE "GASH" ISSUES INCLUDING 124 CIGS PER MAN (NOW HAVE OVER 400 MYSELF). HAD A GOOD WASH AND SHOWER UNDER TAPS; AND GENERALLY CLEANED UP. TEA AT 5.00 AND THEN WENT TO SEE OUR SERBIAN FRIENDS WITH WHOM WE HAD A VERY STRONG BREW OF COFFEE WITH 2½ SPOONFULS OF SUGAR IN A VERY SMALL CUP!! IT WAS VERY GOOD, THOUGH. THEY GAVE US A TINFUL OF SUGAR, SO WE GAVE THEM SOME CIGARETTES.

BACK FOR SUPPER, THEN STROLLED AROUND AGAIN FOR A SHORT WHILE WITH NED BEFORE RETIRING.

27/4/45 HAD BREAKFAST EARLY AND THEN WENT TO MEET OUR SERBIAN FRIENDS TO GO TO LUCKENWALDE. PUT IT OFF TILL 12.00 AND RETURNED TO GET SOUP AND DISH OUT A "GASH" ISSUE OF SWEETS AND CHOCOLATE (FROM A COMPLETE PERSONAL PARCEL). RETURNED ABOUT 12.30 AND THEY HAD GONE, SO WENT DOWN WITH FOUR OTHERS. HUNG AROUND WITH THEM IN SOME SERBIAN QUARTERS, THEN THEY WENT ROUND SOME SHELLED HOUSES, SO NED AND I, "CHEESED" OFF BY THIS TIME, WENT OFF ON OUR OWN. THEN NED STARTED HELPING A DRUNK (OUT OF CONTROL – IRISH!), SO I BEETLED OFF ON MY OWN. MET UP WITH ANOTHER CHAP AND WE WENT ROUND SOME HOUSES IN A WOOD AND MANAGED TO GET AN EGG APIECE, SOME ONIONS AND RHUBARB FOR SOAP AND CIGARETTES, WE WERE AFTER A HEN APIECE, BUT NO ONE WOULD PLAY. BACK TO CAMP AT 5.00 TO GET DOWN TO TEA, AND AFTER BEING SATISFIED, CLEARED UP AND WROTE UP DIARY. GAVE OUT RATIONS, WHICH WERE LATE TO-DAY, THEN HAD SUPPER, SHORT WALK ROUND AND AN ARGUMENT WITH "NED" RE "THE FIGHT PUT UP BY THE GERMANS" THEN BED. GOSH! I WAS TIRED AND I HAD A LOVELY NIGHTS SLEEP! – BEST YET. (ONLY GOT UP ONCE!). REALLY ENJOYABLE DAY. "YANKS" ARRIVED IN LUCKENWALDE TO-NIGHT – PLENTY OF CHEERING WHEN THE OFFICER TOLD US.

28/4/45 ROSE AT 8.00 TO WASH ETC. AND PREPARE BREAKFAST BEFORE 9.00 PARADE (TO BE HELD DAILY FROM NOW ON TO DETERMINE THE RATION STRENGTH). PREPARED BREAD PUDDING FOR TEA, CLEANED UP AND MESSED AROUND IN GENERAL. DINNER AT 2.30, THEN SWEPT UP AND WROTE UP DIARY TO-DATE. PREPARED TEA AND MESSED AROUND WAITING FOR REG TO COME BACK FROM FATIGUES. TEA AT 7.00. WENT ROUND TO SEE NICK, BOB AND TOM LATER, RETURNING FOR SUPPER AT 9.00. RUSSIAN REPATRIATION OFFICER ARRIVED TO-NIGHT WITH 50 FOOD WAGONS – GOOD NEWS. WE ALL HOPE HE'S HERE TO GET US OUT OF HERE IN THE NEXT FEW DAYS. MANY OF THE LADS ARE VERY "CHEESED" AND THE ARMY BOYS ARE THREATENING TO MARCH OUT TO MEET THE "YANKS".

29/4/45 ROSE AT 8.00 TO PREPARE BREAKFAST BEFORE 9.00 PARADE, WHICH WAS "SCRUBBED" (IN THE FUTURE TOO!) – DAMN GOOD JOB. AFTER MEAL (10.30) COOKED SPUDS, PANCAKES AND MADE A BLAMONGE. PREPARED DINNER AND MADE A FUDGE. DINNER WAS AT 2.15 TILL 2.45, CLAENED UP AND WROTE UP DIARY AND IT WAS TIME TO PREPARE TEA. THE TEA FILLED THE FOUR OF US. AFTER CLEANING UP, NED AND I WENT ROUND TO SEE OUR SERBIAN FRIENDS WITH WHOM WE REMAINED TALKING UNTIL 9.20 – QUITE A STRAIN TALKING IN GERMAN ABOUT ALL THINGS AND TRYING TO UNDERSTAND ONE ANOTHER. HAD TWO "WIZARD" PANCAKES APIECE ALONG WITH A SMALL CUP OF SUGARY COFFEE (NIX MILK). SUPPER, THEN BED. JIM BROUGHT IN SOME GERMAN SAUSAGE, CHEESE AND CIGARS!

30/4/45 MICKEY'S BIRHTDAY TO-DAY. MANY HAPPY RETURNS WHEREEVER YOU MAY BE, MICK. ROSE LATE TO-DAY, SO DID NOT HAVE BREAKFAST TILL 10.30. HAD A GOOD ONE THOUGH, WITH A CIGAR AFTERWARDS. SOUP AT 11.30, GIVING OUT RATIONS AFTERWARDS, GASH ISSUE DISTRIBUTION, MAKING AND COOKING PANCAKES AND BREAD PUDDING, COOKING SPUDS AND ORGANISING GROUP FOR DUTIES (WE ARE DUTY BARRACK). DINNER AT 2.15. PREPARED TEA AND PUTTING AWAY THE STUFF NED BROUGHT IN FROM HIS "FORRAGE" ABROAD. SWEPT UP AND WROTE UP DIARY. BY THE WAY, I HEARD THE 6.00 NEWS (NOT FOR THE FIRST TIME HOWEVER). IT IS 7.00 TO US ACTUALLY AS WE NOW GO BY RUSSIAN TIME – ONE HOUR AHEAD. SUPPER AT 9.00 AND BED SOON AFTERWARDS – JUST BEAT THE LIGHTS OUT. LIGHTS OUT AT 10.30. SOME "YANKS" LEFT FOR THE ADOLF HITLER CAMP – ADVANCE PARTY. SNOW IN SOUTHERN ENGLAND!

1/5/45 STILL NO NEWS OF GETTING HOME AND ARE WE GETTING "CHEESED". SEEMS THAT WE WILL BE HERE SOMETIME YET AS THE ARE PREPARING THE NEW CAMP FOR US – IT CERTAINLY APPEARS TO BE A "WIZARD" CAMP, BUT TO HELL WITH IT – WE WANT TO GET HOME. BREAKFAST 11.15 AS WE WAITED FOR REG TO COME OFF GUARD DUTIES. HOWEVER, WE COULD WAIT NO LONGER, SOUP 12.00 (DOUBLE HELPING OF REALLY THICK PEA SOUP) AND THEN AT 2.00 WE GOT A DOUBLE LOT OF BARLEY, SO WE DID NOT

PREPARE A DINNER. WENT ROUND TO SEE "SPUDDER" HARRISON – HAD TO LOOK FOR HIM FIRST. HAD A SHORT CHAT, THEN RETURNED TO PREPARE TEA. TEA AT 5.30. RATIONS UP AT THE SAME TIME - TO BE AWKWARD. $1/5^{TH}$ LOAF, 1/10 BLOCK MARGARINE, $1/3^{RD}$ TIN CHEESE, RAW SPUDS AND A GOOD LOT OF FLOUR TO-DAY, AS WELL AS TWO LOTS OF SOUP! CERTAINLY THE FOOD SITUATION IS EXCELLENT TO WHAT IT WAS. OUT RED CROSS FOOD IS LASTING US VERY WELL – STILL HAVE A GOOD BIT PLUS A GOOD DEAL OF OTHER STUFF WE'VE SCROUNGED. WROTE UP DIARY, THEN HAD A SHORT CHAT TO TONY. SUPPER AT 9.00. WENT TO HEAR THE 9.00 NEWS AT 10.00 AND THEN RETURNED TO BED. IT HAD BEEN A GRAND DAY. PLENTY OF GUNFIRE STILL IN THIS VICINITY. LUCKENWALDE IS SAID TO BE PRETTY "HOT" – A GOOD DEAL OF FIGHTING GOING ON – RUSSIANS DRUNK, AS IT IS A DAY OF CELEBRATION FOR THEM – MAY DAY.

<u>2/5/45</u> SLEPT IN UNTIL 9.30. BREAKFAST AT 11.00 AND SOUP AT THE SAME TIME. GOSH, I WAS FULL. MADE SOME CAKES AND FLAP JACKS WITH SOME OF THE FLOUR WE HAVE, THEN BAKED (OR RATHER TOASTED THEM) WITH OUR "BLOWER". HELL, I GOT RATHER CHEESED AFTER A COUPLE OF HOURS – THEY TOOK AT LEAST 3 HOURS WORK. HAD A BREW AND THEN PREPARED TEA. FINISHED TEA AT 6.30, THEN HAD A WALK ROUND AND WATCHED ALL THE RUSSSIAN TROOPS AND TRANSPORTS GOING BY ON THE TOP ROAD IN ONE CONTINUOUS STREAM. CALLED IN TO SEE NORMAN DELAYEN AND HAD A "SNOOP" ROUND OUR NEW ITALIAN NEIGHBOURS. DIRTY MOB! SUPPER. HEARD 9.00 NEWS AT 10.00, THEN BED.

<u>3/5/45</u> ROSE EARLY (WE CALL 8.00 EARLY NOW) AND HAD BREAKFAST BEFORE 10.00 PARADE. I REPORTED SICK BEFORE THE PARADE AND WAS TOLD I HAD A TOUCH OF IMPERTIGO – BLAST IT. TREATMENT TWICE A DAY FOR 3 DAYS, THEN HAVE TO SEE THE M.O. AGAIN. PARADED, THEN CAME BACK TO PREPARE A BREAD PUDDING FOR TO-NIGHT. HAD SOUP AND GAVE OUT SPUDS. DINNER AT 1.30 AND HEARD NEWS AT 2.00 WANDERED AROUND, CLEARED UP, WROTE UP DAIRY, AND THEN PREPARED TEA. DID SOME COOKING WITH REG ON SYD'S BLOWER. HAD A CHAT WITH ART. TREATMENT AT 4.30 AND ON RETURN, WE GOT DOWN TO

TEA. WALKED ROUND WITH ART, THEN LISTENED TO 6.00 NEWS (AT 7.00). WENT DOWN TO THE MAIN GATE TO SEE THE FIRST "YANK" TO ARRIVE (4 OF THEM) – AMERICAN WAR CORRESPONDENTS. CAME BACK TO MAKE SOME PANCAKES FOR SUPPER, WHICH WE HAD SOMEWHAT EARLIER THAN RECENTLY (9.00). CLEARED UP AND THEN QUICKLY WROTE A POSTCARD TO HOME AND ONE TO JEAN. TOOK THEM TO THE AMERICAN CORRESPONDANT TO POST FOR US ON HIS RETURN TO-NIGHT. HE WILL BE IN LONDON TO-MORROW NIGHT (LUCKY BLOKE). HOPE HE POSTS THE LETTERS IN LONDON, IN WHICH CASE THEY SHOULD BE HOME IN THREE DAYS. STRONG RUMOURS GOING AROUND WE'RE LEAVING TO-MORROW, BUT I DOUBT IT. SHOULD BE SOON, THOUGH, NOW THAT THIS AREA HAS BEEN FINALLY CLEARED UP. THE NEWS IS GREAT, BUT NOT THE BEST FOR US – THE BEST FOR US? – YES, GOING HOME TO-MORROW AND FLYING BACK. ROLL ON DAYS AND LETS GET HOME. SIGNED. <u>ALL!</u>
<u>4/5/45</u> ROSE LATE (9.45). HAD SOME GOOD ENGLISH PORRIDGE FOR BREAKFAST, WHICH WE FINISHED AT 11.00. TREATMENT. WROTE UP DIARY, CLEARED UP, SOUP AND GAVE OUT SPUDS. HAD A WANDER ROUND, THEN WENT TO SEE NICK AND CROWD. DECIDED TO LEAVE WITH THEM TO-MORROW MORNING AND GET TO THE YANKS ON FOOT. WALKED ROUND AND FINDING IT WAS THEN 2.00 CAME IN AND HAD DINNER. CLEARED UP AND STARTED PRELIMINARY PACKING. MORE "YANKS" HAVE ARRIVED THIS AFTERNOON AND IT HAS BEEN OFFICIALLY STATED WE MUST BE PREPARED TO MOVE ANYTIME FROM NOW ON AND WE'LL ALL BE GONE IN 2 OR 3 DAYS. GREAT NEWS. CANCELLED OUR ARRANGMENTS TO GO TO-MORROW. MANY RUMOURS GOING AROUND – WE'RE GOING 100 MILES BY ROAD, THEN FYLING TO NORMANDY, THEN TO ENGLAND. ENGLAND IN A WEEK – HOME IN 10 DAYS. OH BOY. OH BOY. PREPARD A WHOPPING GREAT STEW FOR TEA ALONG WITH A "FUDGE". ALL OF US F.T.B AFTERWARDS. LISTENED TO THE 6.00 NEWS AND HEARD WE HAD BEEN OFFICIALLY REPORTED LIBERATED – AFTER 10 DAYS. IT SOUNDED GOOD OVER THE WIRELESS. BACK TO GIVE OUT RATIONS AND CHAT TO MAC AND ART. COOKED PANCAKES AND GOT STUCK INTO THEM FOR SUPPER AT 9.00. OUR BARRACK CUT SECOND TO GO, SO WE HAVE TO STAND-BY

TO-MORROW MORNING ONWARDS. BED AT 10.30, BUT COULD NOT SLEEP FOR A LONG TIME – LAY IN BED LISTENING TO "GERALDINE" PLAYING THE PIANO.

5/5/45 ROSE AT 9.00 AND PREPARED AND ATE A GOOD BREAKFAST. HAD M&V WITH MASHED POTATOES (2 TINS); CANADIAN BISCUITS, SOAKED AND FRIED AND EATEN AS A PANCAKE, BREAD AND BUTTER; BISCUITS AND CHEESE; CAKE. I WAS FEELING PRETTY TIGHT AFTERWARDS. CHATTED WITH MAC AND ART AND THEN WENT OVER TO SEE THE AMERICAN AMBULANCES JUST ARRIVED TO TAKE AWAY THE SICK. EVERYONE WAITING EAGERLY FOR THE MAIN FORCE TO ARRIVE – BEEN EXPECTED SINCE LAST NIGHT. JUST HEARD THEY'RE HERE – 3.00. SEEMS AS THOUGH IT WAS A FALSE ALARM. IT WAS, ALL RIGHT. PREPARED A BIG TEA, WHICH I THOROUGHLY ENJOYED. AT NIGHT JUST SORT OF HUNG AROUND EXPECTANTLY AND SORTED OUT A FEW THINGS. WENT TO BED AT 11.00, BUT IT WAS SOMETIME BEFORE I GOT TO SLEEP.

6/5/45 LORRIES DEFINITELY COMING FOR US TO-DAY. AFTER BREAKFAST (WHICH WAS LATE, AS WE SLEPT IN), DIVIDED UP OUR REMAINING FOOD, THEN COOKED SPUDS, MADE PANCAKES AND BISCUITS WITH FLOUR ETC. FOR THE JOURNEY. PREPARED TEA AFTER THIS, SOUP PROVIDING US WITH OUR DINNER. LORRIES ARRIVED IN THE AFTERNOON (25 WITH ANOTHER 90 FOLLOWING). PACKED MY KIT AFTER TEA – WHAT A PANIC, THOUGH, AS WE'RE ONLY ABLE TO TAKE THE EQUIVALENT OF A RED CROSS BOX OF GOODS AND CHATTELS. INCLUDING FOOD AND EVERYTHING. OH! A HITCH. EVERYONE MUST REGISTER BEFORE THEY LEAVE AND THE RUSSIANS HAVE NOT YET RECEIVED PERMISSION FROM HIGHER AUTHORITY TO LET US GO, SO WE MUST WAIT UNTIL THEY DO. WHAT GOD DAMN RED TAPE! BY HELL, AFTER ALL THIS TIME WAITING THEY'RE GOING TO HOLD US BACK AND ALSO COMMENCE REGISTERING EVERYONE. HOWEVER, ⅔ OF THE 25 AMERICAN LORRIES LEFT FULL OF YANKS. DON'T KNOW WHAT HAPPENED TO THE OTHER ⅓. (LEARNT THEY RETURNED EMPTY). STAYED UP TILL LATE LISTENING TO THE RADIO. BED AT MIDNIGHT. REGISTRATION GOING ON UNTIL EARLY HOURS, BUT TOO LONG A QUEUE TO BOTHER.

7/5/45 HELL OF A LOT OF RUMOURS AROUND WITH CHAPS GOING OFF ALL DAY TO THE LORRIES, BUT NO ONE GETTING AWAY. I SPENT MOST OF THE DAY COOKING FLOUR ETC. AND KEEPING PACKED. WENT ROUND TO SEE NICK. CHATTED. JOINED MAC, ART AND BILL IN COMBINE – GOT THOROUGHLY FED UP WITH NED (AND ALWAYS WAS WITH JIM). HEARD NEWS, BUT WAS TO "CHEESED" TO FEEL TO ELATED & EXCITED. BED FAIRLY EARLY. NICK ETC. GONE DOWN TO SLEEP IN LORRIES!

8/5/45 ROSE FAIRLY EARLY TO GET BREAKFAST AND PACK. SOON AFTER AN ORDER CAME THROUGH TO GO DOWN TO LORRIES NEAR VILLAGE, SO THERE WAS AN IMMEDIATE RUSH. LATER LORRIES CAME TO CAMP AND SO RODE BACK ON FOOTBOARD. OFFICIALLY TOLD LORRIES WILL RETURN EMPTY – NEARLY A RIOT – RUSSIAN GUARDS TURNED OUT WITH "TOMMY" GUNS – TRUCKS BOARDED AGAIN – RUSSIANS WERE CURSED OPENLY. HOWEVER, EVENTUALLY WE SAW THEM LEAVE EMPTY AND THERE WAS MANY A MISERABLE FACE TO BE SEEN AND NOT A GOOD WORD FOR THE RUSSIANS – ME INLCUDED, DAMN THEM. SHOTS GOING OFF MOST OF DAY – WARNING SHOTS BY RUSSIANS TO OUR CHAPS WHO ARE TRYING TO MAKE IT ON FOOT AND CATCH THE LORRIES TOO, IF POSSIBLE. RETURNED TO FIND OUR BARRACKS RANSACKED (BY FRENCH & ITALIANS). GOT SORTED OUT AGAIN, CLEANED UP AND RE-ORGANISED IN AN EVACUATED BED. LOVELY DAY, SO LAY IN SUN FOR WHILE. COOKED, GAVE OUT RATIONS ETC. PLAYED WITH RADIO. HEARD THE KING AND CHURCHILL. BED 11.00

9/5/45 "BROWNED OFF" – TO THE EYEBROWS. HAD BREAKFAST IN BED – THANKS TO MAC. TREATMENT, RATIONS, DUTY GROUP, SO ORGANISED DUTIES, WASHED TOWEL, PREPARED DINNER ALONG WITH SOUP. READ AND MESSED AROUND IN AFTERNOON. PREPARED TEA AND HAD A GOOD ONE. CHATTED AND THEN WROTE UP DIARY. SUPPER AFTER A SHORT WALK ROUND. BED EARLY, AS SO FED UP.

10/5/45 DID NOT GET UP UNTIL 10.00, HAVING BREAKFAST IN BED AGAIN. READ FOR A WHILE, RATIONS AND WASHED UP ETC. GOT DINNER READY TO CO-INCIDE WITH SOUP. READ MY LETTERS OVER AND MADE MYSELF HOME-SICK; WAS UNABLE TO HOLD BACK A FEW TEARS. READ IN SUN

(MARVELELOUS DAY). WANDERED BARRACKS TALKING TO THOSE I KNOW WHO HAVE NOT LEFT (NOT MANY NOW). HAVE FELT REALLY MISERABLE THESE LAST TWO DAYS. TEA AND SOON AFTERWARDS COMMENCED TO PREPARE A BIG EARLY SUPPER. HAD A SHORT WALK AFTER WITH BILL AND ART, THEN RETURNED TO HEAR THE NEWS AT 10.00. HAD A LAST BREW, WROTE UP DIARY AND BED. VERY LITTLE NEWS TO-DAY AND NO RUMOURS. ON THE NEWS 10,000 PRISONERS TAKEN BACK TO ENGLAND BY AIR AND HERE WE STILL ARE. WE NOW JUST LIVE ON THE RATIONS SUPPLIED: TO-DAYS? 1/3 LOAF, POWDERED CHEESE, ½ TUBE CHEESE, LITTLE SUGAR, SPUDS, SOUP, PER MAN. FACE NOT CLEARED UP YET. WONDERED IN BED HOW NICK, TOM, BOB, NORMAN DELAYEN AND OTHERS ARE GETTING ON. GAVE TWO SLICES OF BREAD AT TEA-TIME TO TWO HUNGRY LITTLE GERMAN CHILDREN. THEY WERE SO GLAD OF IT AND IT REALLY TOUCHED MY HEART.

<u>11/5/45</u> GOT UP LATE, 10.30, SO THAT THE DAY WOULD BE SHORTER. BREAKFAST. TRETMENT. RATIONS. SOUP. DINNER. WENT DOWN TO LAKE WITH MAC AND AFTER MUCH HESITATION, FINALLY WENT IN FOR A SHORT SWIM. SUNBATHED. TEA AT 6.00. READ. PREPARED SUPPER FOR 8.30. WALKED ROUND AFTERWARDS AND HEARD NEWS. LATE SNACK WITH BREW, THEN BED TO READ FOR A WHILE. QUIET DAY.

<u>12/5/45</u> (SATURDAY) JOAN'S 21ST BIRTHDAY. MANY HAPPY RETURNS OF THE DAY, JOAN, AND THE VERY BEST OF LUCK TO YOU ON YOUR COMING OF AGE. GOT UP AT 9.30 AGAIN AND WENT TO SEE THE M.O. RE FACE. GRADUALLY CLEARING UP, BUT MUST HAVE AN IMMEDIATE INJECTION FOR VITAMIN C. HAD IT (IN THE POSTERIOR) – 2 MORE TO COME. BREAKFAST. READ. RATIONS. SOUP. DINNER. THE 4 OF US WENT TO THE LAKE AGAIN – READ AND SLEPT IN SUN. MARVELOUS WEATHER NOW – NO CLOTHING REQUIRED. RETURNED FOR TEA AT 5.30, THEN SAW BELGIAN AND DUTCH CIVILIAN (EX) FORCED LABOUR POUR IN, AS THEY DID YESTERDAY. HAD TO MOVE OUT OF BARRACK TO THE TRUPPENLAGER (BETTER QUARTERS AND THEY WANT OURS FOR THE CIVILIANS, INCLUDING WOMEN). HAD SUPPER FIRST, THEN MOVED. NOT MUCH ROOM IN THE NEW ROOM FOR 11, SO THE 4 OF US SLEPT ON THE LAWN IN THE OPEN.

IT WAS GRAND. BED AT 12.00 AND LAY TALKING TILL WHAT MUST HAVE BEEN NEARLY 2.00. RUMOUR – OFF TO-MORROW. NEVER!! – POSSIBLE!

13/5/45 IN BED TILL 10.00. SHOWER. BREAKFAST. PANICED FOR MY GREATCOAT & JACKET. HERE ALL THE TIME – THOUGHT THE "ITI'S" HAD GOT IT. WROTE UP DIARY AND READ IN SUN, TILL SOUP CAME UP. CONTINUED READING AND SLEPT FOR A SHORT WHILE LATER. TEA, ART AND I GOING FOR A BUCKET FULL OF ALREADY BREWED COFFEE FROM THE COOKHOUSE. WALKED ROUND WITH ART TO SEE THE DUTCH REFUGEES COMING IN. WHAT A TERRIBLE SIGHT. SUPPER. LISTENED TO MR CHURCHILL'S "REVIEW OF THE WAR". CLEANED UP AND THEN TO BED – GRAND DAY (AND NIGHT) SO SLEPT IN OPEN AGAIN.

14/5/45 STILL NO SIGN OF A MOVE! MUST BE A BUNCH OF THE "FORGOTTEN". ROSE EARLY (9.30) FOR A RATION STRENGTH PARADE – JUST SOME "BULL". AFTER WENT FOR TREATMENT (2ND INJECTION). BREAKFAST. PREPATED BEDS IN ROOM (AND LOCKERS) IN CASE OF BAD WEATHER. SOUP AND DINNER. FATIGUES – CLEARING UP COMPOUND. SHOWER. PREPARED TEA WITH ART. AFTER TEA WENT FOR A SHORT WALK ROUND. PREPARED SUPPER AND SAW TO OUR 4/7THS OF A PARCEL (A SMALLER EDITION OF THE AMERICAN RED + NO 10 PARCEL). 4/7THS IS NOT MUCH FOR 4 MEN. WROTE UP DIARY AND PREPARED BEDS THEN RETIRED TO READ UNTIL PRETTY LATE.

15/5/45 PARADE. TREATMENT. BREAKFAST. READ. "THIS ABOVE ALL" (CONTINUING) SOUP. GOT DINNER. READ AGAIN. RATIONS BECOMING BAD AGAIN, EXCEPT BREAD (STILL1/3). ALL WE GOT WAS BREAD, CHEESE (3 TO A TUBE). POTATOES AND SOUP! NOT SUFFICIENT. "MOOCHED" AROUND BEFORE PREPARING TEA AND GETTING STUCK IN – TO WHAT THERE WAS. WENT UP TO THE VORLAGER WITH "ART" – OUR USUAL BEFORE SUPPER WALK. COOKED SUPPER (A TREAT- HAD OUR SPAM, WITH ONIONS, POTATOES, ONION GRAVY AND TOAST). HEARD NEWS, THEN BED. FEELING HEAVY IN THE HEAD. THIS IMPERTIGO NOT SEEMING TO GET MUCH BETTER – BLAST IT. GRAND DAY AGAIN.

16/5/45 ROSE AT 9.30 TO GO ON PARADE, BILL GETTING US BREAKFAST IN BED. WENT FOR TREATMENT AND MY THIRD AND FINAL INJECTION. READ ON RETURN AND GAVE OUT

RATIONS (POTATOES, 1/3 LOAF AND SPOONFUL OF SUGAR). SOUP AND DINNER. FINISHED READING "THIS ABOVE ALL". ON NOTICEBOARD THAT WE WILL DEFINITELY BE OUT OF HERE BY THE END OF THE MONTH – GOD, I HOPE SO! APPARENTLY WE ARE THE FIRST CAMP ON THE REPATRIATION LIST COMING UNDER RUSSIAN CONTROL. I HOPE THAT IS NOT SOMETHING JUST TOLD US TO KEEP OUR SPIRITS UP. IT WOULD NOT BE SO BAD HERE, GIVEN A REASONABLE AMOUNT OF FOOD. FELL ASLEEP TILL TEA TIME, THEN HAD A BLOMONGE AND 2 SLICES OF BREAD FOR TEA. USUAL WALK WITH "ART", THEN SAT FOR A CHAT NEAR THE MAIN GATE. RETURNED FOR SUPPER. BED SOON AFTERWARDS.

17/5/45 ROSE EARLY AND GOT THE COFFEE. WASHED, THEN WENT TO SEE THE M.O. OF THE (NOW) CIVILIAN REVIER. ANOTHER 3 VITAMIN C INJECTIONS PLUS 7 MORE DAYS CRYSTAL VIOLET TREATMENT. SEEMS A LITTLE BETTER TO-DAY. BREAKFAST (2 SLICES OF TOAST!!). WENT UP TO THE REVIER AGAIN FOR A HAIRCUT. GAVE OUT RATIONS. PREPARED DINNER AND HAD SOUP (LOUSY – PRACTICALLY WATER). GOT SECONDS. NO SPUDS TO-DAY. READ "CAPPY RICKS", THEN WENT TO SLEEP FOR ABOUT 2 HOURS IN THE SUN UNTIL THEY TOLD ME TEA WAS READY. LAY IN SUN AGAIN, READING AND TALKING. THOUGHT AND TALKED OF WHAT THE BOYS WOULD BE DOING WHO GOT AWAY FROM HERE AND WOULD NOW BE IN ENGALND – PROBABLY HOME. MADE MYSELF THOROUGHLY MISERABLE. SUPPER. LISTENED TO RADIO (TOMMY HANDLEY) AND NEWS. WROTE UP DIARY, THEN WENT TO BED TO READ FOR A WHILE.

18/5/45 ROSE FOR PARADE. BREAKFAST. TREATMENT, READ. SOUP AND DINNER. READ AND SLEPT TILL TEA. WENT FOR A WALK AND "SCROUNGE" WITH "ART" (OBTAINED SOME DRY PEAS). GOT SOME COAL TOO. PREPARED SUPPER AND GOT DOWN TO IT (WHAT THERE WAS)! HEARD NEWS. READ AGAIN WHEN GOT IN BED. "CAPPY RICKS" I GOT THROUGH TO-DAY.

19/5/45 "BROWNED OFF" TRULY. NO RUMOURS – NOTHING - LOOKS AS THOUGH WE'LL HAVE TO SETTLE HERE. NO SIGNS OF ANY MORE FOOD COMING UP EITHER. SLEPT IN TILL PARADE, AFTER WHICH HAD BREAKFAST. WENT UP FOR TREATMENT WITH "ART" BUT TOO LATE. READ NOTICES,

THEN RETURNED. WENT OUT ILLEGALLY GETTING SOME NEWLY SOWN POTATOES. SOUP AND DINNER. BILL, ART AND I WENT OUT AGAIN (WITH A SACK THIS TIME) FOR MORE SPUDS. GOT THE SACK NEARLY FULL WHEN WE GOT THE CHASE - I HOPE WE HAVE ENOUGH TO LAST US UNTIL WE GET OUT OF HERE - GOT ABOUT 5 OR 6 DAYS SUPPLY. GOING FAIRLY HEAVY AS WE ARE SURE TO. BOILED SOME SPUDS, THEN WENT FOR TREATMENT. TEA, WROTE UP DIARY, DID SOME WASHING, THEN PREPARED IRISH STEW FOR SUPPER WITH "ART". CLEANED UP A LITTLE AND THEN GOT DOWN TO THE STEW. DAMN GOOD. AFTER RAY CAME ROUND AND TOLD US THAT WE WERE PROBABLY LEAVING IN THE MORNING AND THAT THE "RETURN TO CAMP" SIREN WAS GOING. IT DID AND THEN THE EXCITEMENT. WE HAD ANOTHER BREW AND MORE SPUDS, IN ADDITION COOKED SOME MORE FOR BREAKFAST TO-MORROW. DID SOME PACKING AND THEN BED, NOT FEELING TOO WELL NOR IN TO GOOD A HUMOUR.

20/5/45 ROSE SOON AFTER 9.00 AND GOT BREAKFAST ETC. PARADE. RATIONS. SOUP – ALL BY 11.00. SEEMS DEFINATE WE'RE GOING NOW. SIRENS SOUNDED AGAIN. GATHERED AGAIN AT 12.00 AND SOON AFTERWARDS THE TRUCKS CAME DOWN FOR US. MUCH EXCITEMENT AND REJOICING NOW. BOARDED WAGONS AND AS MIGHT BE EXPECTED THERE WAS A LOT OF WAITING IN THE TRUCKS BEFORE WE ACTUALLY HIT THE TRAIL. AND WHAT A TRAIL! ONLY 50KMS TO DO, BUT THE GOING WAS REALLY HARD. CONTINUOUSLY COMING ACROSS BLOWN UP BRIDGES, ROAD BLOCKS ETC. SOME OF WHICH WERE VERY DIFICULT TO OVERCOME, NECESSITATING IN SOME CASES, THE TRUCKS HAVING TO GO DOWN (AND UP) STEEP GULLIES ON NOTHING BUT A TRACK WITH TREES ON EITHER SIDE ALLOWING ONLY ENOUGH ROOM FOR THE TRUCKS TO PASS THROUGH. THOSE DRIVERS DID A GOOD JOB. FREQUENT LONG STOPS WERE NECESSARY IN ADDITION TO REFORM THE CONVOY. WE HAD A TYRE BURST ONCE AND ANOTHER TIME A BIG STONE LODGED BETWEEN THE DOUBLE WHEELS IN REAR (WHICH, BY THE WAY) MADE US INSTEAD OF 7TH ABOUT 27TH! I WAS PEEVED ABOUT THAT. THE JOURNEY TOOK US ABOUT 5½ HOURS, REACHING THE ELBE NEAR WITTENBERG ABOUT 7.00. WAITED AWHILE, THEN WALKED OVER PONTOON

BRIDGE TO OPPOSITE BANK AND THEN I HEAVED A BIG SIGH OF RELIEF. OUT OF RUSSIAN HANDS AT LAST – THANK GOD. BY THE WAY, SAW A LOT OF FOREST FIRES, DAMAGE AND RAVAGES FOR WAR ON THE JOURNEY INCLUDING AN EMACIATED BODY OF A MAN BY THE ROADSIDE. LONG WAIT IN TRUCKS ON OTHER BANK BEFORE WE MOVED OFF ABOUT 9.00 (10.00 RUSSIAN TIME). MADE STEADY PROGRESS DOING APPROX. 40 MILES (60 KMS) IN 2½ HOURS, ARRIVING AT HALLE/LEIPZIG AERODROMES ABOUT 11.30. WAITING AROUND MOST OF TIME FROM THEN UNTIL 2.00A.M. QUEUEING – FILLED IN ONE FORM; FORMED INTO GROUPS OF 25! (I WAS MADE A GROUP LEADER – ALWAYS MANAGING TO DROP FOR THESE DUTIES NOWADAYS!); ALLOCATED OUR BILLETS; HAD A DAMN GOOD MEAL PLUS SOME CIGARETTES (INCIDENTALLY, HAD NOTHING TO EAT SINCE 1.00 WHEN I ATE MY LAST 2 PIECES OF BREAD - ALL I HAD FROM YESTERDAYS AND THIS MORNING RATIONS). COLLECTED BLANKETS AND THEN TO BED AND WAS I GLAD TO GET IN. I WAS DOD-TIRED AND IN ADDITION FELT NONE TOO WELL. HAD BEEN FEELING COLD ALL DAY. HAD TO WEAR MY GREATCOAT ALL THE TIME ALTHOUGH THE SUN WAS BLAZING ALL DAY – MOST OF THE CHAPS WERE TOO HOT EVEN WITHOUT ONE!! HOWEVER, I WAS REALLY A HAPPY MAN TO-NIGHT FOR I REALLY FEEL NOW MY P.O.W. DAYS ARE OVER.

21/5/45 MONDAY ROSE AT 6.00A.M. FOR BREAKFAST, A DAMN HARD JOB FOR MOST OF US, BUT THE BREAKFAST REALLY MADE IT WORHTWHILE. LAY IN BED AFTERWARDS TRYING TO SLEEP, BUT WAS UNSECCESSFUL. CHATTED AND HAD A LOOK ROUND BEFORE DINNER AT 12.00. WENT FOR TREATMENT AFTERWARDS FOR THE IMPERTIGO – 2 HOURS TREATMENT, BUT IT WAS REALLY WORTH IT – IT FEELS 100% BETTER ALREADY. RACED AROUND THEN WITH THE RED CROSS CHITS FOR CIGS, CHOC, TEETH AND SHAVING REQUIREMENTS. WALKED DOWN TO THE RED CROSS CLUB TO COLLECT ARTS, BILLS AND MINE (LOST MAC, INCIDENTALLY, AS HE WAS ON A DIFFERENT TRUCK TO US FROM THE OUTSET AND AT THE ELBE WAS PROBABLY IN THE SMALL CONVOY THAT LEFT A GOOD WHILE BEFORE THE MAIN ONE. IF ONLY WE HAD KEPT OUR POSITION IN THE RUSSIAN CONVOY WE WOULD HAVE BEEN IN THAT

SMALL CONVOY TOO). TEA (LAST MEAL). WENT TO CINEMA, BUT SO FULL WE COULD NOT SEE PROPERLY, SO EVENTUALLY CAME BACK TO BILLET. MESSED AROUND, TALKED AND READ. LATE ON RATION PACKET SOUP FOUND IN BILLET. GOOD. READ AND WROTE UP DIARY. SLEEP EVENTUALLY SOMETIME AFTER MIDNIGHT. OH! IT'S GRAND TO BE EATING GOOD FOOD AGAIN AND I FEEL TRULY GREAT – FULL AND ELATED. NO LONGER DO I HAVE ANY "KRIEGY" FEELING. A TRULY GRAND DAY.

22/5/45 WAS ROUSED SUDDENLY BEING TOLD ALL WERE GONE FOR "CHOW" – TIME 6.30! GOT OUTSIDE AND IT WAS 5.30! HOWEVER, WE GOT THERE DEAD ON 6.00 AND WHAT A MARVELOUS BREAKFAST - CEREAL, POWDERED EGG, PURE WHITE BREAD AND MARMALADE. COFFEE. TRULY DELICIOUS. WROTE UP DIARY, READ AND LAY DOWN UNTIL DINNER AT 12.00. GAVE OUT CIGARETTE RATIONS ETC, THEN WENT FOR A WALK ROUND. RETURNED TO REST UNTIL TEA AT 6.00. WENT TO THE CINEMA IMMEDIATELY AFTERWARDS, BUT CAME OUT AGAIN AFTER A WHILE AS IT WAS TOO CROWDED AND UNCOMFORTABLE. LISTENED TO ONE OF THE CHAPS RELATING HIS POW EXPERIENCES - AN IRISHMAN. IT WAS VERY INTERESTING. TALKED UNTIL 1.30. SLEEP.

23/5/45 UP JUST BEFORE 5.00, AS WE HAD TO DO FATIGUES, ONE GROUP, IN THE COOKHOUSE FROM 5.00 – 2.00AM. COULD NOT EAT ANOTHER THING WHEN I CAME AWAY – HAD BEEN EATING ALL MORNING. GOT SOME "BUCKSHEE" FOOD TO BRING AWAY TOO. GAVE OUT RATIONS, THEN WENT TO SLEEP UNTIL TEA. RETURNED TO BILLET AND BED AND I DID NOT GET UP AGAIN TO-NIGHT. LAY LISTENING TO "KRIEGY" TALES AND HAD A "BREW" AND SNACK ABOUT 10.00PM BEFORE GOING TO SLEEP. LOT OF NEW CHAPS ARRIVED FROM 4B.

24/5/45 BREAKFAST AT 6.00, THEN RETURNED TO BED UNTIL DINNER-TIME AT 12.00 – SLEEPING ALL THE TIME. DINNER. GAVE OUT RATIONS. WROTE UP DIARY. WENT TO THE CINEMA TO SEE "HAVING A WONDERFUL CRIME". NOT TO BAD. WENT FOR TREATMENT WHEN I CAME OUT. TEA. LAY IN BED AWHILE, THEN HAD A WALK ROUND WITH BILL LOOKING OVER THE VARIOUS WRECKED GERMAN KITES. CINEMA AGAIN TO SEE QUITE A GOOD MUSICAL SHOW.

RETURNED ABOUT 11.00 AND MADE A BREW OF TEA. LISTENED TO PADDY AGAIN. BED AT 1.00.

25/5/45 UP FOR BREAKFAST AS USUAL. FATIGUES - SWILLING DOWN FRONT OF MESS HALL, FOR WHICH WE GOT EXTRA RATIONS. GAVE OUT ORDINARY RATIONS, THEN PACKED. DINNER. FLEW TO BRUSSELS – PLENTY OF WAITING BEFORE HAND, THOUGH GOOD TRIP. DETAILS FOR LOG – BOOK

    25/5/45 DAKOTA 16.45 1.45 HRS
        HALLE/LEIPZIG - BRUSSELS.

DE-LOUSED, ATE, KITTED, QUESTIONED ETC. THEN TO BILLETS. HAD A PINT OF BEER IN CANTEEN, THEN WENT TO SEE FILMS AND MORE DRINKS IN THE DRY CANTEEN. I FEEL GRAND NOW – CLEAN, FULL, SMOKING WELL, GRAND BED, PLENTY OF CHOCOLATE. BED ABOUT 2.30.

26/5/45 MESSED AROUND IN CANTEEN – READING, EATING, DRINKING, GETTING MORE RATIONS, CHATING ETC. TILL DINNER. GROUP WAS CALLED OUT AFTERWARDS, SO TAKEN TO DROME AND FLOWN TO OAKLEY, ENGALND. WIZARD TRIP. LOG BOOK DETAILS.

    26/5/45 LANCASTER K P/O WHITE 16.00 2 HRS
        BRUSSELS – BEACH HD – OAKLEY

MEAL AT OAKLEY – WHERE BY THE WAY, WE HAD A GRAND RECEPTION FROM A.T.S, WAAFS ETC. TRANSPORT TO BICESTER. MEAL, THEN TO BILLETS. RETURNED TO SGTS MESS FOR A PINT AND PHONED UP HOME, THROUGH MRS H JERSING. HAD AT LEAST ½ HOUR CHAT. WIZARD. BACK TO BILLET WITH BILL (MY OLD ENGINEER) AND BED – ABOUT 12.00. TIRED.

27/5/45 UP 8.00. BREAKFAST, PARADE AT 10.30 AFTER READING PAPERS TO TAKE TRAIN TO COSFORD FROM BICESTER. THERE WE GOT DINNER, BILLETS, NEW KIT, MEDICAL, INTERROGATION, 1250'S, X-RAY, TAILORING ETC. TEA AT 8.30, THEN NAAFI FOR RATIONS AND A DRINK. COLLECTED OUR BATTLEDRESS TUNICS, THEN BACK TO BILLET TO SORT OUT GEAR AND PACK FOR LEAVING TO-MORROW MORNING. BED. TIRED.

28/5/45 BREAKFAST 8.00. PACKED AND COLLECTED OUR LEAVE PASSES. WENT TO NAAFI FOR CUP OF TEA BEFORE GETTING TRANSPORT TO STATION. CAUGHT 11.30A.M. TRAIN AND GOT INTO N/C CENTRAL STATION AT 9.03P.M. AFTER HAVING A MEAL IN YORK AS HAD AN HOUR TO WAIT FOR

THE CONNECTION (NEARLY MISSED IT INCIDENTALLY). TOLD DAD TRAIN ARRIVED AT 10.03 (WAS TOLD WRONG AT BIRMINGHAM), SO WAITED FOR THEM COMING AT THE STATION. TALKED AND ATE UNTIL 3.00A.M! HOW MARVELOUS IT FEELS TO BE BACK HOME. NOW TO SETTLE DOWN TO 6 WEEKS OF HEAVEN.

AMEN.

That concludes Tom's day to day diary. The two books were also crammed with many other notes/facts/camp songs/musings etc. Here are some of them.

OCCUPANTS OF 42/12 BARRACK 42 ROOM 12
ROOM AREA 15' X 22'

LEYLAND	O'LEARY	F/S (CAN)
GEORGE	THOMSON	SGT
NORMAN	BRUCE	W/O (CAN)
TOM	GLENN	P/S
JOE	LUDWIG	SGT (CAN)
HARRY	MATE	F/S
"KNOBBY"	CALRKE	SGT
GEOF	FLAY	F/S (N.Z)
JACK	LINDSAY	F/S (AUS)
VIC	POPPA	W/O (CAN)
LES	KELLY	F/S
MICK	FORD	SGT (CAN)
REG	DALE	SGT
JIM	BUTLER	L.A.C.

<u>LATE ARRIVALS IN 42/12</u>
SGT "LOFTY" LEE
SGT GORDON WEEDON
SGT ROY GREEN (AUS)
SGT GEORGE KELLY (IN "KNOBBY'S" PLACE)

DIVISION 1
<u>LEADER:</u>   PARRY -JONES
<u>WELFARE MAN:</u> McGRAW
MESSING REP: BETHEL

CAMP PERSONALITIES
<u>The Man of Confidence</u>
RICHARD ARTHUR GREENE was born at Akron, Ohio on July 27th 1918. It appears that he has done everything in civilian life. He entered the R.C.A.F. in 1940 and has been a prisoner of war for over two years.
<u>The Camp-Leader</u>
PETER ANGUS THOMSON, was born in South Perth, Western Australia, on February 4th 1916. After finishing his schooling, he followed the trade of his country and became a farmer. His sport is cricket, but since meeting the Canadian boys he has become a convert to the ball game. Cricket, however, remains his first love.

The Deputy Camp-Leader
KENNETH ALBERT LANE was born at Worle, Weston-Super-Mare on January 18th 1921. He first became apprenticed to an ironmonger, but forsook this work to take up football, playing first for Cardiff City reserves and then Bristol City reserves. In 1938 he toured Denmark with a West of England Y.M.C.A. representative football team. He joined the R.A.F. in 1941 and won the D.F.C. in March this year.

The Sports Leader
NOEL WILLIAM WRAY, was born at Knutsworth, Cheshire on December 26th 1913. He was a driver-salesman before being called up for service in the R.A.F. He is married and has two children. Very keen on boxing, having fought in Manchester, Liverpool and London. In 1942, he won the Duke of Portland Cup in the Northern Area Lightweight Championship (R.A.F.).

The Camp Adjutant
JOHN JOESEPH WALKTY was born on March 5th 1918 at Winnipeg, Manitoba. He was a machinist in civilian life and joined the R.A.F. as a navigator on Feb 2 1942. He is married. His favourite sports are swimming and tennis.

The Chief Medical Orderly
GEORGE JAMES KING, born Oct. 16th 1921 at Bromley, Kent. Civilian occupation, slaughterman. Sports, shooting. Joined the R.A.F. in October 1942 as a W/Op. A.G. Hobby is nursing.

ODDS AND ENDS

IN THE BAD OLD DAYS
BEFORE THE WAR
THEY MADE ME WORK
WHICH WAS A BORE

BUT NOW I AM AN AIRMAN BRAVE
I NEVER WASH AND SELDOM SHAVE
I SLACK ABOUT AND SLEEP ALL DAY
FOR WHICH I GET ENORMOUS PAY!!

NAMES APPLIED TO HUTS IN CAMP

"HOLIDAY INN"	"THE LEAGUE OF NATIONS"
"HALFWAY HOUSE"	"THE FLEECE INN"
"KREM-LYNN"	"THE WANDER INN"
"SELDOM INN"	"OPS RETREAT"
"DEWDROP INN"	"BITCHERS INN"
"RANCHO DIABLO"	"KEYHOLE KENNEDYS"
"CRAZY KOTTAGE"	"BRIDGE INN"
"CLUELESS CABIN"	"THE GOTSUM INN"
"THE RUSHIN INN"	"DIM VIEW"
"THE JOE STAL INN"	"UTILITY VILLA"
"KARY'S KENNEL"	"ALL WAYS INN"
"FINGER INN"	"NEVER INN"
"MACS DOSS HOUSE"	"STIRLING"
"THE HUNGRY SIX"	"ELLINSIDE"
"ASTON VILLA"	"39 STEPS" (BARBERS)
"BOOZERS GLOOM"	"HOME SWEET HOME"
"GREMLINS GROTTO"	"TUNNEL INN"
"WHO'S INN"	

From a Diary......................Sat. June 10th 1944

Last Tuesday night, with the invasion 24 hours old, things started to happen here. Some Germans on the Censorship staff received their tickets to move. One said Good-bye to an Englishman, grinned and said, "Well, I'll be in England before you".

Then last night an army marched past and into the dark. Arclights lit up a word on their serried faces. War....... They walked with conscious import and in silence. No singing. No manoeuvre, this, no going out to take shots at a target towed by an old but useful Junkers, nor to storm the group of buildings that so many trainees have taken and retaken up there on the hill. Between the columns rumbled horse-drawn supplies. Only a double lattice of wire separated them from us, in our shadowed hut doorway; full equipment, jack boots echoing along macadam, clank of slung helmets and respirator cylinders. They looked grim and efficient and we know its going to be quite a fight. These reserves leaving their rural centre of Bankau, Upper Silesia, are a segment in the action-pattern of military Germany at the day and hour. They are hiking to history.............

Bill Strutton
South Australia.

ANZAC DAY

A.N.Z.A.C was the official abbreviation of the Australian and New Zealand Army Corps during action at the Dardanelles.

The portion of the coast allotted to the A.N.Z.A.C. became known as ANZAC COVE and members of the A.N.Z.A.C. as "ANZACS".

This historic campaign marked the first occasion in which Australian and New Zealand had combined forces in the field, and the baptism of fire for Australian and New Zealand troops in the Great War.

The day of the landing on Gallipoli, 25th April 1915, has since been known as "ANZAC DAY" and is commemorated annually throughout Australia and New Zealand as the day of Remembrance for those who fell in the Great War.

On Anzac Day, 1919, The Rector of Abany, Western Australia, conducted a ceremony at dawn. It was attended by returned Australian soldiers, Sailors and Airmen, and widows or near relatives of men who fell in the Great War. They assembled at the Local War Memorial and stood in silence awaiting the breaking of dawn when the "Last Post" was sounded, two minutes silence observed and "Reville" sounded. This little ceremony was the forerunner of ANZAC DAWN SERVICES, which are conducted annually.

FASHION NOTE

A NAVAL CAP

A smart naval cap, complete with lustrous gold Crown and Anchor and glossy peak has been seen about camp lately. Among sober blue and khaki headgear it attracted much attention and admiring comments.

Owner is Petty Officer Wilkins, R.N. and the camp is a substitute for the one he left on board ship the last time he came ashore.

It happened this way. In January 1940 the submarine "Starfish" was cruising off Heligoland when a German destroyer and minesweeper appeared. The Starfish dived into 80 feet of water and lay on the bottom, but the German craft had spotted her and after trying all day, finally depth-charged her.

The batteries started gassing and filled the hull with choking chlorine. Then the stern floated up until it broke the surface. It was then that Wilkins forgot his cap.

Later he found that Army field service caps were ill suited to seafaring heads, and commenced collecting for a new naval covering. First he obtained a beret of the correct blue from a French officer, then a cap band from a Dutch officer and the shiny covering of a guitar case made the peak.

An Australian airman supplied the Gold Crown and another naval man donated the anchor. Guitar strings woven into a rope completed the cap badge, and the buttons of a Fleet Air Arm officer made the proper attachment for the patent leather chin-strap.
From "TIME"
Stalag 383, Hohenfels, Germany

WITHOUT COMMENT!

Reply received by a P.O.W. to a letter of thanks to a woman donor of a pair of socks-----------------------"I am disappointed that a prisoner of was has got them. I thought they would go to a real soldier........"
<u>Action taken</u> – Remittance of two shillings from credits to Bella Bigheart.

HEARD TO REMARK!

"Sorry, I can't even roll my own from the butts of the butts I rolled from the butts of my last cigarette parcel"

A COMMON OCCURRENCE!

<u>1ST GEFANG</u> "Hello, old man, where have I seen you before?"

2nd GEFANG "Dunno, where?"

1st GEFANG "I.T.W., O.T.U., Gloucester, Conversion Unit?"

2nd GEFANG "Don't remember you there".

1st GEFANG "Oh! I know, down at the pump the other afternoon".

PERJUDICE!

A CAMP SOCCER MATCH WAS IN PROGRESS AND ONE OF THE OPPOSING FORWARDS TOOK A SHOT AT GOAL, WHICH WENT WELL WIDE. SPECTATOR (WITH SCORN): "MUST BE A BOMB-AIMER!"

A WARNING

A WISE OLD OWL SAT IN AN OAK;
THE MORE HE HEARD, THE LESS HE SPOKE;
THE LESS HE SPOKE, THE MORE HE HEARD;
OH! AIRMEN, BE WISE LIKE THIS OLD BIRD.

VERY COMPLIMENTRAY!

"IF YOUR BRAINS WERE MADE OF DYNAMITE, YOU
WOULDN'T HAVE ENOUGH TO BLOW YOUR NOSE!"

THE SHOOTING OF DAN McGREW

A BUNCH OF THE BOYS WERE WHOOPING IT UP IN THE
MALAMITE SALOON;
THE KID THAT HANDLES THE MUSIC BOX WAS HITTING A
RAG-TIME TUNE;
BACK OF THE BAR, IN A SOLO GAME, SAT DANGEROUS DAN
McGREW;
AND WATCHING HIS LUCK WAS HIS LIGHT-O-LOVE, THE
LADY THAT'S KNOWN AS LOU.
WHEN OUT OF THE NIGHT, WHICH WAS FIFTY BELOW, AND
INTO THE DIN AND THE GLARE,
THERE STUMBLED A MINER FRESH FROM THE CREEKS, DOG-
DIRTY AND LOADED FOR BEER.
HE LOOKED LIKE A MAN WITH A FOOT IN THE GRAVE, AND
WITH SCARCELY THE STRENGTH OF A LOUSE.
YET HE TILTED A POKE OF DUST ON THE BAR, AND HE
CALLED FOR DRINKS ON THE HOUSE.
THERE WAS NONE COULD PLACE THE STRANGER'S FACE,
THO'WE SEARCHED OURSELVES FOR A CLUE;
BUT WE DRUNK HIS HEALTH, AND THE LAST TO DRINK WAS
DANGEROUS DAN McGREW.
THERE'S MEN THAT SOMEHOW JUST GRIP YOUR EYES, AND
HOLD THEM LIKE A SPELL;
AND SUCH WAS HE, AND HE LOOKED TO ME LIKE A MAN
WHO HAS LIVED IN HELL;
WITH A FACE MOST PALE , AND THE DREARY STARE OF A
DOG WHOSE DAY IS DONE,

AS HE WATERED THE GREEN STUFF IN HIS GLASS, AND THE DROPS FELL ONE BY ONE.
THEN I GOT TO FIGGERING WHO HE WAS, AND WONDERING WHAT HE'D DO,
AND I TURNED MY HEAD – AND THERE WATCHING HIM WAS THE LADY THAT'S KNOWN AS LOU.
HIS EYES WENT ROVERING ROUND THE ROOM, AND HE SEEMED IN A KNID OF DAZE,
TILL AT LAST THAT OLD PIANO FELL IN THE WAY OF HIS WANDERING GAZE.
THE RAG-TIME KID WAS HAVING A DRINK; THERE WAS NO ONE ELSE ON THE STOOL.
SO THE STRANGER STUMBLES ACROSS THE ROOM, AND FLOPS DOWN THERE LIKE A FOOL.
IN A BUCKSKIN SHIRT THAT WAS GLAZED WITH DIRT HE SAT, AND I SAW HIM SWAY;
THEN HE CLUTCHED THE KEYS WITH HIS TALON HANDS – MY GOD! BUT THAT MAN COULD PLAY!
WERE YOU EVER OUT IN THE GREAT ALONE, WHEN THE MOON WAS AWFUL CLEAR,
AND THE ICY MOUNTAINS HEMMED YOU IN WITH A SILENCE YOU MOST COULD HEAR?
WITH ONLY THE HOWL OF A TIMBER WOLF, AND YOU CAMPED THERE IN THE COLD,
A HALF-DEAD THING IN A STARK, DEAD WORLD, CLEAN MAD FOR THE MUCK CALLED GOLD;
WHILE HIGH OVERHEAD, GREEN, YELLOW AND RED, THE NORTH LIGHTS SWEPT IN BARS –
THEN YOU'VE A HUNCH WHAT THE MUSIC MEANT……..HUNGER AND NIGHT AND THE STARS.
AND HUNGER NOT OF THE BELLY KIND, THAT'S BANISHED WITH BACON AND BEANS;
BUT THE GNAWING HUNGER OF LONELY MEN FOR A HOME AND ALL THAT IT MEANS
FOR A FIRESIDE FAR FROM THE CARES THAT ARE, FOUR WALLS AND A ROOF ABOVE;
BUT OH! SO CRAMFUL OF COSY JOY, AND CROWNED WITH A WOMAN'S LOVE;
A WOMAN DEARER THAN ALL THE WORLD, AND TRUE AS HEAVEN IS TRUE –

(GOD! – HOW GHASTLY SHE LOOKS THRO' HER ROUGE – THE LADY THAT'S KNOWN AS LOU).
THEN ALL OF A SUDDEN THE MUSIC CHANGED, SO SOFT THAT YOU SCARCE COULD HEAR;
BUT YOU FLET THAT YOUR LIFE HAD BEEN LOOTED CLEAN OF ALL THAT IT ONCE HELD DEAR,
THAT SOMEONE HAD STOLEN THE WOMAN YOU LOVED;
THAT HER LOVE WAS A DEVIL'S LIE;
THAT YOUR GUTS WERE GONE, AND THE BEST FOR YOU WAS TO CRAWL AWAY AND DIE.
'TWAS THE CROWNING CRY OF A HEART'S DESPAIR AND IT THRILLED YOU THRO' AND THRO' –
"I GUESS I'LL MAKE IT A SPREAD MISERE" SAID DANGEROUS DAN McGREW.
THE MUSIC ALMOST DIED AWAY…..THEN IT BURST LIKE A PENT UP FLOOD;
AND IT SEEMED TO SAY, "REPAY, REPAY" AND MY EYES WERE BLIND WITH BLOOD.
THE THOUGHT CAME BACK OF AN ANCIENT WRONG, AND IT STUNG LIKE A FROZEN LASH,
AND THE LUST AWOKE TO KILL, TO KILL…….THEN THE MUSIC STOPPED WITH A CRASH,
AND THE STRANGER TURNED, AND HIS EYES THEY BURNT IN A MOST PECULIAR WAY;
IN A BUCKSKIN SHIRT THAT WAS GLAZED WITH DIRT HE SAT, AND I SAW HIM SWAY;
THEN HIS LIPS WENT IN, IN A KIND OF GRIN, AND HE SPOKE AND HIS VOICE WAS CLAM;
AND "BOYS", SAYS HE, "YOU DON'T KNOW ME, AND NONE OF YOU CARE A DAMN";
"BUT I WANT TO STATE, AND MY WORDS ARE STRAIGHT, AND I'LL BET MY POKE THEY'RE TRUE",
"THAT ONE OF YOU IS A HOUND OF HELL….AND THAT ONE IS DAN McGREW!.
THEN I DUCKED MY HEAD AND THE LIGHTS WENT OUT, AND TWO GUNS BLAZED IN THE DARK;
AND A WOMAN SCREAMED, AND THE LIGHTS WENT UP AND TWO MEN LAY STIFF AND STARK;
PITCHED ON HIS HEAD, AND PUMPED FULL OF LEAD WAS DANGEROUS DAN McGREW,

WHILE THE MAN FROM THE CREEKS LAY CLUTCHED TO THE BREAST OF THE LADY THAT'S KNOWN AS LOU.
THESE ARE THE SIMPLE FACTS OF THE CASE, AND I GUESS I OUGHT TO KNOW;
THEY SAY THAT THE STRANGER WAS CRAZED WITH "HOOCH", AND I'M NOT DENYING ITS SO.
I'M NOT SO WISE AS THE LAWYER GUYS, BUT STRICTLY BETWEEN US TWO –
THE WOMAN THAT KISSED HIM – AND PINCHED HIS POKE – WAS THE LADY THAT'S KNOWN AS LOU.

..................................THE END..

EXTRACT FROM POW – WOW (CAMP WEEKLY)

SOME PERTINENT QUESTIONS

1. WHY ANYONE SHOULD WANT TO ENTER THE MAN-OF-CONFIDENCE'S OFFICE OR THE ORDERLY ROOM "EXCEPT ON BUSINESS"?
2. WHY THESE TOUGH COLONIALS SHOULD WANT TO PLAY SOFTBALL INSTEAD OF BASEBALL?
3. IF ANYONE CAN SUGGEST, IN VIEW OF THE RECENT SEARCHES, A HIDING PLACE FOR 3 LANCS, 2 HALYS AND 3 SPARE "BODDS"?
4. IF A PLACE CAN BE RESERVED IN THE QUEUE AT THE GATE FOR THE RECEPTION AND DISSECTION OF NEWCOMERS?
5. WHETHER, THROUGH SOME EROR IN TRANSPORT, 700 "BODDS" WERE BROUGHT HERE BY MISTAKE AND THAT 700 CHICKENS ARE NOW LIVING IN LUXURY IN A BRAND NEW LUFT CAMP?
6. IF WE ARE ALL DEAD AND THIS IS HELL?
7. WHICH OF THE TWO TELL THEIR STORY FIRST, WHEN THE "OLD BODD" AND THE "BRAND NEW BODD" MEET AT THE GATE?
8. IF THE "HOUSEWIFE" TO BE APPLIED FOR FOR THE PURPOSE OF MENDING TORN CLOTHING, CAN ALSO COOK?
9. IF "RACKETS" FLOURISH IN HELL?

10. IF BOMBAY WAS SO NAMED AFTER A TYPE OF AIRCRAFT?
11. WHY THE RUSSIANS ARE NOT HERE YET?
12. IF THE HANGER DOORS AT LUFT 7 EVER CLOSE?
13. HOW OLD IS "THE OLD FIRM OF LYNCH AND STURGESS?

THE CITY

LOOKING UP WE SAW THIS ANCIENT LAND,
HIGH ON THE HILL IN THE SUNSETS GLOW,
LIKE A ROCK HEWN BY SOME GIANTS HAND,
OR GRANITE CRAG WORN BY THE CEASELESS FLOW
OF A MIGHTY RIVER BOUNDING FORTH;
BOUNDING ON RIVERS BED LIKE TEMPESTS WRATH.

THE MAMMOTH STRUCTURE BEFORE OUR SIGHT
WITH COLUMNS THAT ROSE, HUGH ABOVE ALL,
A HIDDEN HISTORY SEEMED TO WRITE
OF SOME DEAD NATIONS DECLINE AND FALL:
CAME THE EVENINGS STARS AND ALL AROUND
THE CITY WAS SILENT WITHOUT SOUND…………
"SAGITTARIUS"

KNOW YOUR RUSSIAN!

ENGLISH	RUSSIAN	PRONUNCIATION
BEER	ПИВО	PEEVOH
CIGARETTE	ПАПИРОСА	PAH PEE ROSSAH
I WOULD LIKE	AXOTENSSI	YAH XTYEL BEE
MATCHES	СПИЧКИ	SSPITCHKEE
PARDON ME	ИЗВИНИТЕ	ISVINYITYE
GOOD DAY	ЗАРНВСТВУЙТЕ	sDRASSTVOOYTYE

ITALY

LAND OF THE ORANGE AND THE VINE
SMILING SIGNORINAS AND EXHILARATING WINE
LAND OF MUSIC, SONG AND DANCE
MUST BE VISITED IF YOU GET THE CHANCE,
        -     THAT'S ITALY

MOUNTAINS BEAUTIFUL TO BEHOLD
BUT HELL TO CLIMB WHEN YOU'RE GETTING OLD.
THEY HAVE BUILT ROADS WHICH ARE SHOWN ON THE MAP
OVER WHICH GLIDE CARS ONLY FIT FOR SCRAP.
        -     THAT'S ITALY

THE CAPITAL OF THIS WONDERFUL LAND
IS KNOWN AS ROME AND IT SURE LOOKS GRAND
THE CHURCHES AND STATUES ARE A WORTHWHILE SIGHT
BUT THE PEOPLE LACK GUTS AND DON'T LIKE A FIGHT
        -     THAT'S ITALY

THEY FORMED AN ARMY OF A MILLION AND TEN
THE MILLION WERE GENERALS; THE OTHERS JUST MEN
THEY LIVED ON SPAGHETTI – MACARONI TOO
AND THEY SOUNDED GOOD TILL THEY HAD SOMETHING TO DO
        -     THAT'S ITALY

THEY WENT OUT TO AFRICA TO FIGHT FOR THE HUN
BUT WHEN THE BULLETS FLEW THEY COMMENCED TO RUN
AND NOW THIS LAND HAS NOTHING TO SHOW
THEIR GLORY LIES DEAD AND THEIR SPIRIT IS LOW
        -     THAT'S ITALY

SO IF YOU'RE THINKING OF TRAVELLING THIS FOREIGN LAND
YOU'LL FIND AS A SUBSTITUTE PICADDILLY AND THE STRAND
ORANGES AND WINE YOU CAN ALWAYS BUY –
AND THE BRITISH SPIRIT WILL NEVER DIE.

                       "Jean Petit"

ALL TAKEN IN GOOD PART
"If your brains were made of ink, you would not have enough to make a full stop!"

SOMEONE'S OPINION ABOUT BRIDGE!
Bridge, as we all know, can cease to be a pleasant pastime and become the vehicle of more concentrated rudeness and unpleasant back-chat than almost any other game. "SAPPER"

RECEIPE!
CAKE
¼lb bread
2pkts biscuits
¾pts raisins
1 bar chocolate (American)
3oz margarine
½ tin klim
½ tin orange juice
Condensed milk for icing
Bake in 3 relays of ¾ hr each. Designs done in currents.
Result – mixture of haggis, bread pudding and cement!
No casualties, but one knife broken cutting it!!

"TUESDAY"
The larks were singing in the still air as the dawn softened the steely blue heavens to a pearly pink. Slowly the bleary-eyed dwellers emerged from their regal quarters staggering towards the cuisine, selecting an "Elegante" from their tin-cases as they went. They noticed later risers determination upon their features, speeding post-haste for their usual morning "shower". A noticeably expectant air was prevalent, even upon the faces of the laggards. The hours in their passing brought about a great change in the dwellers attitude, and they became very impatient, their eyes all the time on one spot of the barbed wire which encircled the "holiday camp".
Then the electric atmosphere was suddenly lifted, as the eldest of vehicles, drawn by two energised skeletons, came into view, and for why? The vehicle was piled high with brown boxes.
Gestures of approval, and thoughts, were put into the words of glad simplicity, for once again the Red Cross had delivered the goods for another week.

OLD RIVALS!

NOTICE PUT ON BOARD

18.30 TO-NITE   FRIDAY 25 AUG

APES SET TO TROUNCE LUFTSTAFF
                    SPECIAL CORRESPONDENT.

WHEN THE APES GO TO BAT TO-MORROW, IT IS EXPECTED THAT GREENS GOONS WILL FOLD UP LIKE AN OPERA HAT. POP ADYS, HARD BITTEN MANAGER OF LAMONTS APES, PREDICTS SMASHING WIN. "WE'LL TEAR 'EM APART!" STATED POP IN PRESS INTERVIEW. HERE IS TO-MORROW'S LINE UP:-

"PONGO" PALMER – CAPTAIN
"LOONY" LAMONT
"MAD" SMITH
"BONGO" WHITING
"GRANDPA" DAVIS
"BLUDGER" JONES
"PODGE" PORRETT
"SLASH" CONNOR
"STINKER" CONETTI
"POP" ADYE, MANAGER
         AND WATER BOY

A MIMIC SOFT BALL GAME
APES v LUFTSTAFF

(SCANNED FROM THE DIARY)

COMPLAINTS TO GENEVA   BY "GEGANG"

WE HAVE BOTHERED YOU WITH UNIMPORTANT DETAILS,
WE'VE COMPLAINED CONCERNING NOTHING IN THE PAST,
WE'VE BEEN INCONSIDERATELY RUDE
CONCERNING LITTLE THINGS LIKE FOOD;
BUT WE'VE REALISED HOW WELL OFF WE ARE AT LAST.

THERE WAS A TIME WHEN LIGHTS WERE QUITE A QUESTION;
HOW SELFISH HUMAN NATURE SEEMS TO BE;
NOW WE REALISE, WE DON'T MIND,
IF A FEW OF US GO BLIND
IN ANY CASE, WHAT IS THERE HERE FOR US TO SEE?

THE OTHER DAY A COUPLE DIED FROM MAL-NUTRITION;
DON'T WORRY THO' – THE REST ARE KEEPING WELL,
BUT IF THE QUESTIONS NOT TOO BOLD
DON'T YOU THINK THE COLONEL MIGHT BE TOLD?
FOR THE CARCASES HAVE A QUITE A RANCID SMELL!

WE'RE GRATEFUL TOO FOR BITS OF INFORMATION,
WE KNOW YOU WOULDN'T LIE, YOU NEVER COULD.
WHEN YOU SAY WITH KIND ENDEAVOUR
THAT IT CANNOT LAST FOR EVER;
WE ARE HAPPY – 'CAUSE WE ALWAYS THOUGHT IT WOULD!

WHEN YOU TELL US THAT THE WHOLE OF EUROPE'S STARVING,
THAT CIVILIAN RATIONS HAVE BEEN FOUR TIMES HALVED.
WHEN YOU SAY THAT WE'RE WELL OFF,
ON OUR LITTLE BIT OF SCOFF,
WE ARE HAPPY TO HAVE LIVED – AND TO HAVE STARVED!

THERE HAS BEEN MENTION OF TOOTH EXTRACTION,
AND OF FALSE ONES TO REPLACE THOSE THAT HAVE GONE
BUT THE QUESTION WON'T ARISE,
IF YOU'LL ONLY REALISE
THAT THERE'S NOTHING HERE THAT WE COULD USE THEM ON!

WE CAN VISUALISE JUST HOW YOU GUARD OUR INTERESTS;
THE SLEEPLESS DAYS YOU SPENT ON OUR AFFAIRS;
THE HEADACHES DURING NIGHTS;
WHEN YOU'RE PONDERING ON OUR RIGHTS,
AND DIVIDING UP THE "SECONDS" IN EQUAL SHARES!

SO DON'T YOU DARE TO WRITE ABOUT US TO GENEVA;
DON'T YOU DARE TO GO COMPLAINING UP AT BERNE;
DON'T YOU WORRY YOUR POOR HEAD
ABOUT THE TRIFLING THINGS WE'VE SAID
FOR WE'RE SO WELL TREATED HERE, WE WON'T RETURN!

SO DON'T YOU WASTE YOUR TIME ON FUTURE VISITS,
TAKE OUR ADVICE - LET CONSCIENCE BE YOUR GUIDE
FOR IF IT'S GOOD YOU WANT TO DO,
AND ALL THE THINGS YOU SAY ARE TRUE,
THEN PASS US BY AND VISIT THOSE OUTSIDE!

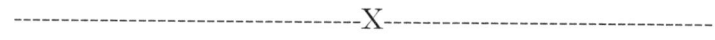

"CHARACTER"

Live your life while you have it. Life is a splendid gift. There is nothing small in it for the greatest things grow by God's law out of the smallest. But to live your life you must discipline it, you must not fritter it away in "Fair purpose, erring act, unconstant will", but must make your thoughts, your words, your acts, all work to the same end and that end not SELF but GOD. That is what we call Character.

Florence Nightingale

"REPUTATION"

Reputation? – that's man's idol set up against God, The maker of all laws, who hath commanded us we shall not kill, and yet we say we must, for reputation! What honest man can either fear his own, or else will hurt another's reputation? Hear to do base unworthy things is valour; if they are done to us, to suffer them is valour too.

Ben Johnson

FROM "THE COMPOUND CADS" ACT OF CONCERT OF 30/9/44

WE'VE COME HERE TO-NIGHT TO GIVE YOU A CHAT,
CONCERNING THIS LUFT CAMP - OUR LIFE - AND ALL THAT.
T'WAS RATHER A BOTHER, IN FACT, QUITE A FAG,
BUT WE REALLY ARE GOOD, THO' WE DON'T WANT TO BRAG.

WE WERE CAUGHT IN ITALY JUST THREE YEARS AGO,
WE'RE GETTING QUITE USED TO IT NOW, DON'T YOU KNOW.
SO IT CAME AS A SHOCK, WHEN ONE OF YOU DOGS,
SAID THOSE TWO AT THE PIANO ARE A COUPLE OF SPROGS.

IT TOOK US THREE YEARS BEFORE WE BOTH KNEW,
JUST HOW TO MAKE TEA AND THE BEST WAY TO BREW;
WE USED TO USE CARDBOARD, A METHOD MUCH SLOWER
COULD HARDLY BE THOUGHT OF – BUT NOW WE'VE A BLOWER!

MY WIFE WROTE AND TOLD ME SHE'D SENT ME SOME FAGS,
TWO HUNDRED A WEEK – I SHOULD HAVE HAD BAGS.
BUT ALL I'VE RECEIVED - IT'S A CURIOUS THING –
WAS THE BOX THEY WERE WRAPPPED IN, SOME PAPER AND STRING.

I HAD AN EX-MUCKER - CLAUDE WAS HIS NAME,
HE'S BACK NOW IN "BLIGHTY" – NOT PLAYING THE GAME.
HE BRIBED HIS WAYHOME WITH A COUPLE OF SLABS
OF CHOCOLATE, SOME COFFEE AND TWENTY-FIVE FAGS.

MY WIFE OFTEN SAYS IT WON'T BE LONG NOW
BUT STRANGELY ENOUGH, I DON'T TRUST HER SOMEHOW;
SHE'S A SWEET LITTLE GIRL, AND ALL THAT DON'T YOU KNOW,
BUT SHE GAVE ME THAT DUFF GEN JUST THREE YEARS AGO!

WE FIND TEST MATCHES HERE – CRICKET DON'T YOU KNOW,
A REALLY RIPPING GAME - PERHAPS A TRIFLE SLOW;
THE BATSMANS STIRLING EFFORT SHOULD BE GREETED WITH A CLAP,

BUT SOME YOUNG CANADIAN SAID "HAY, HAY, HAY –
FRIGHTFUL CHAP".

MODERN AIR FORCE LANGUAGE REALLY DOES AMAZE,
WITH "BODDS", "PRANGS" AND "SKIP" IN EACH PHRASE.
BUT FOR OUR SPECIAL BENEFIT, THEY'RE STARTING A CLASS,
TO TEACH US THIS NEW LANGUAGE – "PER ARDUA AD AS".

LIFE HERE IS NOT SO BAD, FOR BESIDES OUR BREAD
WE GET POTATOES DAILY, SO MANY PER HEAD.
THEN TO ASSIST US – WHILE SEATED ON THE POLE,
EVERY THURSDAY EVENING – LO! - A TOILET ROLL!

OF THE MODERN YOUNG AIRMAN A GREAT FUSS IS MADE,
SUCH AS SILK UNDIES AND "COOKIES" TO TAKE ON A RAID.
TO GO ON LEAVE IS REAL MILK AND HONEY
FOR BESIDES EXTRA PAY – THERE'S THE NUFFIELD MONEY!

SOON WE ARE GOING TO THE CAMP DOWN BELOW
A REAL PRIME PLACE – DON'T YOU KNOW.
REAL LIGHTS IN EVERY ROOM – AND A FIRE,
BUT THERE'S STILL TOO MUCH OF THIS DAMNED BARBED
WIRE.

AND NOW WE'VE COME TO THE END OF OUR TETHER;
WE COULD GO ON FOR ANY REASON WHATEVER.
IF SOMEONE DECLARED IT'S THE END OF THE WAR,
WE'D BE FAR TOO EXHAUSTED TO SAY ANY MORE.

HEARD FREQUENTLY!
OLD GEFANG TO NEW ARRIVAL: "WHAT ARE YOU DOING
HERE?" (!!!)

IF I HAD A MILLION
IF I HAD A MILLION
IT WOULD BUY ME A PERFECT ISLAND HOME,
SWEET SET IN A SOUTHERN SEA
AND THERE I WOULD BUILD ME A PARADISE,
FOR THE HEART O MY LOVE AND ME.

I WOULD PLANT ME A PERFECT GARDEN THERE
THE ONE THAT MY DREAM SOUL KNOWS
AND THE YEARS WOULD FLOW, AS THE PETALS GROW
THAT FLAME TO A PERFECT HOME.

I WOULD BUILD ME A PERFECT TEMPLE THERE
A SHRINE WHERE MY CHRIST MIGHT DWELL
AND THEN WOULD I WAIT TO BEHOLD MY SOUL
DAMNED DEEP IN A PERFECT HELL.

<u>BOXING RESULTS</u>   4/9/44

<u>3 – 2 MINS ROUNDS</u>
1. <u>FLYWEIGHT</u>
   SGT SMART, BROMLEY DREW WITH SGT O'LEARY, AUSTRALIA
2. <u>LIGHT-HEAVY WEIGHT</u>
   SGT PARY-JONES (ALLIED SERVICES CHAMPION) BEAT SGT GRUBB, ISLEWORTH, ON POINTS THE FINAL GOING STOPPED IT FROM BEING A TECHNICAL K.O.
3. <u>LIGHTWEIGHT</u>
   SGT FARRINGTON, BIRMINGHAM BEAT SGT LATCHFORD, SALFORD, ON POINTS.
4. <u>WELTER-WEIGHT</u>
   SGT YARDLEY, CAMBUSLANG BEAT SGT. MANTLES, HEATON ACADEMEICALS, ON POINTS. VERY ONE-SIDED, FOR SGT MANTLES TOOK SOME PUNISHMENT.
5. <u>LIGHTWEIGHT</u>
   SGT WRAY (R.A.F. NORTHERN AREA CHAMPION) BEAT SGT BREWER, BATTERSEA ON POINTS.
6. MILLING CONTESTS (ONE 1MIN ROUND)
   SGT McGRAW BEAT SGT ROWAN ON POINTS
   SGT CLARKE DREW WITH SGT McBURNEY
   SGT PHILPOT DREW WITH SGT NEILS
   SGT LYNCH BEAT F/S STURGESS ON POINTS.

25/8/44   ENGLAND v AUSTRALIA   2ND TEST

1ST INNINGS ENGLAND
SMITH CAUGHT FEATHERS b KIRWIN	22
BADHAM BOWLED EVANS	5
FARRINGTON BOWLED EVANS	8
PARKER CAUGHT PURNELL b KIRWIN	0
WARREN BOWLED KIRWIN	0
EAST CAUGHT FEATHERS b KIRWIN	14
MILLINGTON BOWLED EVANS	5
NICKLIN BOWLED EVANS	1
LANE BOWLED MARTIN	0
HORN NOT OUT	0
CLEAVE BOWLED EVANS	0
EXTRAS	16
	64

KIRWIN 34 RUNS FOR 4 WKTS. EVANS 24 FOR 5 MARTIN 0 FOR 1

2ND INNINGS
SMITH BOWLED MARTIN	24
BADHAM BOWLED KIRWIN	4
FARRINGTON CAUGHT TRANENT b KIRWIN	27
PARKER CAUGHT HALLIGAN b MARTIN	2
WARREN CAUGHT MARTIN B PURNELL	7
EAST BOWLED PURNELL	4
MILLINGTON CAUGHT KIRWIN b MARTIN	0
NICKLIN NOT OUT	6
LANE BOWLED PURNELL	2
HORN BOWLED HALLIGAN	9
CLEAVE BOLWED HALLIGAN	0
EXTRAS	16
	101

KIRWIN 26 RUNS FOR 2 WKTS. EVANS 26 FOR 0. MARTIN 17 FOR 3. PURNELL 14 FOR 3 COLLEDGE 3 FOR 0 HALLIGAN 1 FOR 2.

1ST INNINGS   AUSTRALIA
LYLL CAUGHT LANE b HORN	28
OLSON BOWLED MILLIGAN	1
TRANENT CAUGHT NICKLIN b CLEAVE	5
FEATHERS CAUGHT FARRINGTON b MILLINGTON	25
MARTIN BOWLED HORN	0

HALLIGAN BOWLED HORN	0
COLLEDGE BOWLED HORN	0
KIRWIN CAUGHT NICKLIN b HORN	2
SHEEL BOWLED MILLIGAN	16
PURNELL CAUGHT MILLINGTON b HORN	2
EVANS NOT OUT	1
EXTRAS	<u>2</u>
	<u>82</u>

<u>MILLINGTIN</u> 27 RUNS FOR 3 WKTS <u>CLEAVE</u> 29 FOR 1 <u>NICKLIN</u> 7 FOR 1 <u>HORN</u> 17 FOR 5

2ND INNINGS

LYLL CAUGHT FARINGOTN b NICKLIN	2
OLSON BOWLED HORN	2
TRANENT BOWLED HORN	0
FEATHERS L.B.W. HORN	3
MARTIN (CAPT) BOWLED NICKLIN	0
HALLIGAN CAUGHT NICKLIN b MILLINGTON	18
COLLEDGE BOWLED NICKLIN	0
KIRWIN CAUGHT PARKER b MILLINGTON	39
SHEEL CAUGHT EAST b NUCKLIN	1
PURNELL NOT OUT	1
EVANS CAUGHT BADHAM b NICKLIN	0
EXTRAS	<u>5</u>
	<u>71</u>

<u>NICKLIN</u> 23 RUNS FOR 5 WKTS <u>HORN</u> 30 FOR 3 <u>MILLINGTON</u> 13 FOR 2

7/8/44   ENGALND v AUSTRALIA   1ST TEST

1st INNINGS ENGALND

FARRINGTON CAUGHT & BOWLED EVANS	4
SMITH L.B.W	0
PARKER CAUGHT LYALL b EVANS	5
WARREN BOWLED EVANS	0
KIERLE CAUGHT TAIT b THOMAS	0
LANE CAUGHT LYALL b EVANS	2
EAST BOWLED BETHEL	36
MILLINGTON(CAPT) CAUGHT THOMAS b COLLEDGE	6
NICKLIN CAUGHT KIRWIN b COLLEDGE	4
HALLETT NOT OUT	0

CLEAVE CAUGHT BETHEL b COLLEDGE	2
BYES	<u>6</u>
	<u>65</u>

EVANS 6 RUNS – 4WKTS   <u>KIRWIN</u> 5 FOR 1 <u>THOAMS</u> 23 FOR 1 <u>THOMSON</u> 15 FOR 0 <u>COLLEDGE</u> 5 FOR 3 <u>BETHEL</u> 5 FOR 1

<u>2ND INNINGS</u>

FARRINGTON CAUGHT & BOWLED EVANS	3
SMITH CAUGHT OLSON b COLLEDGE	22
PARKER BOWLED EVANS	0
WARREN CAUGHT KIRWIN b COLLEDGE	17
KIERLE BOWLED KIRWIN	9
LANE BOWLED MARTIN	4
EAST CAUGHT & BOWLED KIRWIN	40
MILLINGTON CAUGHT EVANS b KIRWIN	2
NICKLIN BOWLED KIRWIN	0
HALLETT CAUGHT LYALL b EVANS	3
CLEAVE NOT OUT	2
BYES	<u>9</u>
	<u>111</u>

<u>KIRWIN</u> 40 FOR 4 <u>EVANS</u> 19 FOR 3 <u>BETHEL</u> 10 FOR 0 <u>COLLEDGE</u> 14 FOR 2 <u>MARTIN</u> 20 FOR 1

<u>1st INNINGS</u>   AUSTRALIA

OLSON BOWLED CLEAVE	5
COLLEDGE CAUGHT HALLETT b MILLINGTON	11
THOMAS BOWLED CLEAVE	5
KIRWIN L.B.W. CLEAVE	0
MARTIN(CAPT) CAUGHT WARREN b MILLINGOTN	3
HALLINGTON BOWLED CLEAVE	16
THOSON BOWLED MILLINGTON	4
EVANS BOWLED CLEAVE	6
LYALL NOT OUT	3
TAIT BOWLED CLEAVE	0
BETHEL BOWLED CLEAVE	<u>13</u>
	<u>68</u>

<u>MILLINGTON</u> 19 RUNS 3 WKTS <u>CLEAVE</u> 23 FOR 7 <u>NICKLIN</u> 7 FOR 0 <u>HALLETT</u> 6 FOR 0

2nd INNINGS

OLSON	BOWLED	NICKLIN	15
LYALL	BOWLED	HALLETT	23
THOMAS	BLOWED	NICKLIN	0
HALLIGAN	BOWLED	NICKLIN	1
COLLEDGE	BOWLED	NICKLIN	1
MARTIN	CAUGHT LANE b HALLETT		0
KIRWIN	BOWLED	HALLETT	0
EVANS	BOWLED	NICKLIN	0
THOMSON	CAUGHT HALLETT b NICKLIN		1
BETHEL	BOWLED	HALLETT	11
TAIT	NOT OUT		2
BYES			8
			62

MILLINGTON 9 FOR 0 CLEAVE 15 FOR 0 NICKLIN 12 FOR 6
HALLETT 14 FOR 4 EAST 5 FOR 0

SPORTS DAY   LABOUR DAY 4/9/44

LIST OF EVENTS
100 YDS   (HEATS)   SPORTS RESULTS
SACK RACE   (INC HEATS)   DIVISION 6…33
220YDS   (HEATS)   "   1….27
SKIPPING RACE   "   3….21
THROWING THE RUGBY BALL   "   2….18
LONG JUMP   "   4….12½
THREE-LEGGED RACE   "   7….9
½ MILE RACE   "   5….4½
½ MILE RELAY (INTER-DIV)
SOFT BALL RACE
440 YDS
HIGH JUMP
            …………………..DINNER……………………..

1 MILE WALK   WINNER 3 PTS
STANDING JUMP   SECOND 2 PTS
OBSTACLE RACE   THIRD 1 PT
KICKING THE RUGBY BALL
1 MILE

100 YDS FINAL
220 YDS FINAL
WHEELBARROW RACE
1 MILE RELAY (INTER-DIV)

................TEA........................

BOXING

MY SCHOOL PROGRAMME

	9.30-10.30	10.30-11.30	11.30-12.30	2.00-3.00	3.00-4.00	6.00-7.00	7.00-8.00
MON	FRENCH	ECONOMICS	COMMERCE 70		STATISTICS		BOOK KEEPING 2
TUES			BK KP 1	ECONOMICS		REVISED IN NEW CAMP BK KG 2	AUTO-ENG
WED		LAW GROUP	MUSIC				AUTO-ENG
THUR							
FRI	FRENCH 70			BK-KG 1	COMMERCE 70		STATS 65
SAT					BK KG 2		
SUNDAY							AUTO ENG

COMMENCES   MONDAY 14/8/44

COMMENCED IN NEW CAMP 16/10/44
Started new beginners classes in several subjects. Lights now, so classes go on until 9.00
<u>8 periods a day</u>
9.30 – 12.30   2.00 – 4.00   6.00 – 9.00
Take Book-Keeping stage 1 & 2. Needless to say I've learnt as much as the pupils for it was all practical work that I had done!! When I started I know some knew more than I did.

SOME OF OUR DIFFICULTIES
1)   NO CHALK
2)   NO EXERCISE BOOKS – ONLY LOOSE PAPER
3)   TEXT BOOKS FOR INSTRUCTORS ONLY
4)   FATIGUES
5)   ONLY TWO HUTS
6)   OTHER ATTRACTIONS
7)   'JERRY'! (WORST ONE)

BRIDGE CONTEST
GLENN & ELLIS v

OPPONENTS	POINTS FOR	AGAINST
SCOPES & SMITH 92	5050	-
DAVIDSON & TAYLOR 35	-	410
MUCHA & FRANZAK 146	-	-
BARNET & EDWARS 129	-	2440
MARTIN & CARMICHAEL 34	-	-
NOT COMPLETED		

FOOTBALL TEAMS

ASTON VILLA (A)	LEAGUE CHAMPIONSHIP
BANKAU RANGERS	THE CITY (DIV 1)
ARSENAL	KNOCK-OUT WINNERS
PRESTON N.E	THE CITY (DIV 1)
STALAG UNITED	
HEARTS	
STALAG OPTIMISTS	TEAMS IN NEW CAMP
BARNSLEY	ASTON VILLA (1 DIV)
GEFANGS UNITED	SUNDERLAND (5 DIV)
STALAG ROVERS	MIDDLESBORO (4 DIV)
CATERPILLAR UNITED	PRESTON N.E.(7 DIV)
CATERPILLAR COUNTY	RANGERS (3 DIV)
CARDIFF	ARSENAL (2 DIV)
ASTON VILLA (B)	CHELSEA (6 DIV)
STALAG RANGERS	DERBY CO. (8 DIV)
DONCASTER	
THE CITY	

AUCTION BRIDGE SCORING

POINTS PER TRICK:- TRICKS

	1	2	3	4	5	6	7
CLUBS	12	24	36	48	60	72	84
DIAMONDS	14	28	42	56	70	84	98
HEARTS	16	32	48	64	80	96	112
SPADES	18	36	54	72	90	108	126
NO TRUMPS	20	40	60	80	100	120	140

HONOURS:-

	CLUBS	DIAMONDS	HEARTS	SPADES
SIMPLE	12	14	16	18
FOUR HONOURS	24	28	32	36
FOUR HONOURS IN ONE HAND	48	56	64	72
FIVE HONOURS	60	70	80	90
FIVE HONOURS IN ONE HAND	84	98	112	126

NO TRUMP HONOURS:-

THREE ACES	30 PTS
FOUR ACES	40 PTS
FIVE ACES	100 PTS

SLAMS

SMALL	50 PTS
GRAND	100 PTS

UNDER TRICKS

BID	50 PTS PER TRICK
DOUBLED	100 PTS PER TRICK
RE-DOUBLED	200 PTS PER TRICK

RUBBER   250 PTS

CONTRACT BRIDGE SCORING

	NOT VULNERABLE			VULNERABLE		
	NOT DOUBLED	DOUBLED	RE-DOUBLED	NOT DOUBLED	DOUBLED	RE-DOUBLED
POINTS FOR A GAME						
POINTS PER TRICK:-						
DIAMONDS & CLUBS	20	40	80	20	40	80
SPADES & HEARTS	30	60	120	30	60	120
NO TRUMPS						
FIRST	30	60	120	30	60	120
SECOND	40	80	160	40	80	160
EACH SUB.	30	60	120	30	60	120

OVERTRICKS	TRICK VALUE	100	200	TRICK VALUE	200	400
SMALL SLAM	500	500	500	750	750	750
GRAND SLAM	1000	1000	1000	1500	1500	1500
UNDER-TRICKS:-						
ONE	50	100	200	100	200	400
TWO	100	300	600	200	500	1000
THREE	150	500	1000	300	800	1600
FOUR	200	700	1400	400	1100	2200
FIVE	250	900	1800	500	1400	2800
SIX	300	1100	2200	600	1700	3400
SEVEN	350	1300	2600	700	2000	4000

HONOURS IN ONE HAND:-
ALL HOMOURS   150 PTS
FOUR TRUMP HONOURS   100 PTS
FOUR ACES IN NO TRUMP HAND   150 PTS

REVOKES:-
FIRST OFFENCE   2 TRICKS
EACH SUBSEQUENT   1 TRICK

RUBBER;- TWO GAME 700 PTS: THREE GAME 500PTS.

BRIDGE CONTEST – CLOSED 31/7/44

GLENN & ELLIS v

OPPONENTS	RUBBERS		POINTS	
	FOR	AGST	FOR	AGST
SMITH & STEPHENSON	1	2	-	910
HERRICK & YOUNG	3	0	3310	-
LYALL & RODGERS	2	1	120	-

SCOPES & SMITH	1	2	1870	-
NORRIS & GREEN	2	1	-	700
WRIGHT & WILSON	2	1	1550	-
McCONNELL & VIDDLER	2	1	1330	-
LEANEY & GOODMAN	2	1	2000	-
TOTAL	15	9	10,180	1610

PRIZES
    30 CIGARETTES FOR TEAM WITH MOST POINTS
    30 CIGARETTES FOR TEAM WITH MOST RUBBERS

WINNERS
@ ON POINTS   F/S STURGESS & SGT LYNCH
@ ON RUBBER   F/S STURGESS & SGT LYNCH

N.E FOOTBALL CLUB FIXTURES AND RESULTS

GAME	DATE	VERSUS	FOR	AGAINST
FRIENDLY	16/9/44	LONDON CLUB	0	1
FRIENDLY	22/9/44	LANCS & DIST CLUB	2	1
FRIENDLY	12/10/44	MIDLANDS CLUB	2	0
FRIENDLY	3/12/44	MIDLANDS CLUB	0	6

N.E CLUB SOCCER TEAM (FIRST TEAM)

GLENN

WELSH   FINLAY
                  (V-CAPT)

OATES   STEWART
         CUMBERLIDGE
           (CAPT)
CLARKE   HUTCHINSON

DELAYEN   HUNTER   BELSHAW

RESULTS OF INTERNATIONA MATCHES (SOCCER)

18/8/44	ENGLAND	2	SCOTLAND	2
20/9/44	AUSTRALIA	2	CANADA	0

12/10/44	CANADA	5	AUSTRALIA	1
2/12/44	ENGLAND	0	SCOTLAND	0
11/12/44	ENGLAND	6	CANADA	0
26/12/44	CANADA } SOUTH AFRICA}	0	AUSTRALIA} FRANCE }	2

RESULTS OF CLUB MATCHES

N.E.CLUB	0	LONDON CLUB	1
LANCS & DIST	1	N.E.CLUB	2
N.E.CLUB	2	MIDLANDS	0
N.E.CLUB	0	MIDLANDS CLUB	6

THE POST CARD THAT WASN'T SENT!

APRIL 20TH 1945
MY DEAREST MA, PA, JOAN, MICKEY & PETER. EVERYTHING STILL GOING WELL WITH ME, MUM, SO PLEASE DON'T WORRY. THE WEATHER IS PRETTY GOOD HERE NOW,- LYING IN SUN AS I WRITE. SINCERELY HOPING YOU ARE ALL FIT AND WELL, AS I AM. TAKE GOOD CARE OF YOURSELVES, WON'T YOU? WE WILL SOON BE TOGETHER AGAIN. I AM ALWAYS THINKING OF YOU ALL AND WONDERING ABOUT YOU. STILL HAVE NOT HEARD SINCE DECEMBER FROM ANYONE. CHEERIO ONCE MORE. LOTS OF LOVE ALL. TOMMY

STALAGLUFT 7 DANCE SONGS. COMPOSED HERE

WE'LL SHARE

WE'LL SHARE A CORNER TABLE WHEN WE'RE OUT TO DINE
THE SOFT LIGHTS AND SWEET MUSIC, WILL BE YOURS AND MINE
THE SAME TUNES FOR DANCING - THE SAME SONGS TO SING
THE SAME WEDDING PREACHER – THE SAME BELLS WILL RING
WE'LL SHARE THE SAME TWO-SEATER WHEN WE BOTH LEAVE TOWN
WE'LL SHARE THE SAME UMBRELLA WHEN THE RAIN COMES DOWN.

KEEP THE SAME HOME FIRES BURING - TROUBLES VANISH SOON
WHEN WE TURN THE SAME SIXPENCE TO THE SAME NEW MOON
WE'LL SHARE THE SAME WHITE ROOM, THERE'S NO DOUBT AT ALL
WE'LL SHARE THE SAME SWEET DREAMS WHEN NIGHT MUST FALL.

SING ME TO SLEEP WITH A SWING SONG

MY LITTLE LAD IS THE IMAGE OF HIS DAD,
HE IS HIS MOTHER'S PRIDE AND JOY.
EACH NIGHT HE GOES UPSTAIRS, I HEAR HIM SAY HIS PRAYERS,
PLEASE GOD MAKE ME A GOOD LITTLE BOY.
THEN I SING HIM SONGS THAT MY MOTHER USED TO SING
BUT HE SHAKES HIS LITLE HEAD AND SINGS "I MUST HAVE SWING".

SO
SING ME TO SLEEP WITH A SWING SONG
AND I'LL BE A GOOD LITTLE BOY.
YOU MAY NOT BE "BING", BUT YOU MUST GIVE ME SWING
THAT'S THE ONLY RYTHM I ENJOY.
YOU GIVE ME GRAY HAIRS, WITH YOUR THREE TEDDY BEARS
AND THE SILLY LITTLE PIGS THAT WENT TO MARKET
BUT I AIN'T GOT A YEN, FOR THOSE TEN NIGGER MEN
SO SING ME TO SLEEP WITH A SWING SONG.

REMEMBER ME

I'M WRITING YOU THIS LETTER TO SAY I'LL NE'ER FORGET
THE HOURS WE SPENT TOGETHER, DARLING, SINCE THE DAY WE MET,
I HOPE YOU WILL REMEMBER, ALTHOUGH WE'RE FAR APART
AND KEEP THIS LOVING MEMORY, DEAR, FOREVER IN YOUR HEART.

REMEMBER ME, ALTHOUGH I'M FAR AWAY
REMEMBER THAT I LOVE YOU MORE EACH DAY

REMEMBER SOON, WE'LL BE TOGETHER AGAIN
IN SUNSHINE OR IN RAIN NEVER TO PART AGAIN.
A MILLION YEARS IT SEEMS THAT WE'VE BEEN APART
BUT YOUR LOVLEY SMILE STILL LINGERS HERE IN MY HEART
SO DRY YOUR TEARS, AND QUIET YOUR FEARS
TILL WE MEET THAT HAPPY DAY
REMEMBER THOUGH I'M FAR AWAY.

A XMAS MESSAGE
FROM "THE CAMP" – DECEMBER 1944

THOSE CHRISTMAS BELLS RING ONCE AGAIN;
THEIR CHIMES, THEY CROSS THE SEA
AND REACH THE HEARTS OF MANY MEN
WHO BEAR CAPTIVITY.
THEIR ECHOES BRING THIS MESSAGE FROM
YOUR LOVED ONES O'ER THE FOAM;
"MAY SOON GOD TURN YOUR FOOTSTEPS TO
YOUR LIFE, AND LOVE AND HOME".

IS IT I? BY WARWICK S PRICE

WHERE IS THE MAN WHO HAS NOT SAID
AT EVENING, WHEN HE WENT TO BED,
"I'LL WAKEN WITH THE CROWING COCK,
AND GET TO WORK BY SIX O'CLOCK"

WHERE IS THE MAN WHO, RATHER LATE,
CRAWLS OUT OF BED AT HALF-PAST EIGHT,
THAT HAS NOT THOUGHT, WITH FOND REGARD,
"IT'S BETTER NOT TO WORK TOO HARD"

---X------------------------------------

MY WORTH ON APRIL 26TH 1945

Saved prior to being shot down	123=0=0
Left on station (credited to my a/c)	8=0=0
Remitted home from my credits	100=0=0
Allotment home	43=15=0
Pay less remittance and allotment	83=10=0
6d a day post war credit	27=15=0

Additional 1/6d for 3 yrs service (not confirmed)   2=0=0
Income tax refund due (not confirmed)   33=10=0
                                                      £422=0=0

ON LIBERATION WE EITHER SCROUNGED OR BOUGHT OR TRADED TO RECEIVE THE FOLLOWING:-

		Extras before
Onions	sugar	Steak
Rhubarb	German Dried Milk	Bread
Eggs	coffee	eggs
Margarine	peas	coffee
German Sausage	Bread	flour
German cheese	dehydrated onions	onions
Potatoes	German "bully"	tinned meat paste
Cabbage		
Flour		
Oatmeal		

Sold Fountain Pen (20)
(20) Belt
(40) Small cigarette case
(50) Large cigarette case
(60) Kit bag
(80) Food box (Big one)

CONTENTS OF CANADIAN RED CROSS PARCEL (OLD TYPE)

1LB POWDERED MILK	11-14 LARGE BISCUITS
1LB CREAMERY BUTTER	1 BAR SOAP
1/4LB MAPLE LEAF CHEESE	1 TIN SPAM
6OZ CHOCOLATE	1 TIN CORN BEEF
1/2LB SUGAR (PKT)	1 TIN MARMALADE
PKT CANADIAN COFFEE	1 PKT PRUNES
1 TIN SARDINES	1 PKT RAISINS
1 TIN SALMON	

NOTES CONCERNING MARCH

19/1/45	FRIDAY	5.00AM TO 5.00PM	32KMS
20/1/45	SAT.	6.00AM TO 12.00PM	12 "
20/1/45	SAT	9.00PM TO 9.39 AM SUNDAY	42 "
21/1/45			
22/1/45	MON	3.00AM TO 2.00PM	23 "
23/1/45	TUES.	RESTING	
24/1/45	WED.	5.00AM TO 3.00PM	30 "
25/1/45	THURS	11.00AM TO 6.00PM	24 "
26/1/45	FRI	RESTING	
27/1/45	SAT.	6.00AM TO 1.00PM	21 "
28/1/45	SUN	5.30AM TO 1.00PM	22 "
29/1/45	MON	5.30PM TO 4.30AM TUES	29 "
30/1/45	TUES.	RESTING REMAINDER OF DAY	
31/1/45	WED.	RESTING	
1/2/45	THUR.	8.00AM TO 12.00	14 "
2/2/45	FRI	}Crowded in barn near	
3/2/45	SAT	}Goldberg awaiting	
4/2/45	SUN.	}transport	
5/2/45	MON	6.30AM TO 9.00 Entrained in Cattle trucks – 56 in our truck	9 "
6/2/45	TUES.	In train. Mon. night at Sagan}	3 "
7/2/45	WED.	No rations }	
8/2/45	THURS.	Arrived at camp about 12.00 mid-day	
9/2/45	FRI.	Rations at last. 2/5 Loaf & little dripping	
10/2/45	SAT.	STALAG 111 A, LUCKENWALKE.	

Rations very scarce, Bread, soup, spuds, sugar.

             163 miles!!   **261 KMS**

TOTAL RATIONS PER MAN (21 DAYS)
FOR THE WHOLE TRIP

3⅓ LOAVES OF BREAD	24½ RYE BISCUITS
13/30 TIN OF MEAT	1/8 PKT OF HONEY
2 KILOS OF POTATOES(8LBS)	4 LITRES OF SOUP (8PINTS)
7/8 MARGARINE (PKT)	

The map shows some WW2 POW camps. The line illustrates the journey of 163 miles that 1,500 prisoners, including Tom, travelled from Stalag Luft 7, Bankau to Stalag 3A, Luckenwalde.

TEXT of P.C. TO:- (SENT 16/11/44)
        The Director of Forces request Programme
        British Broadcasting Corporation
        B.B.C. House
        London
        England

Dear Sir

We, the two undermentioned Ps.O.W. in Germany, request you to include in your next request programme two of our families favourite songs. "Just the way you look to-night" for Mrs Glenn, 2 Lansdowne Gardens, Jesmond, Newcastle upon Tyne 2 and "The mountains of Mourn" for Mrs Mate of 17, Auburn Gardens, Fenham, Newcastle upon Tyne, along with the confident hope that the New Year will bring us together once more.

                                        Yours Sincerely
                                        Harry Mate
                                        Thomas Glenn

ELBERT HUBBARD (IN HIS MOST VITRIOLIC STYLE!)
"AN AUDITOR"

"The typical auditor is a man past middle-age, spare, wrinkled, intelligent, cold, passive, non-committal, with eyes like a codfish; polite in contact but at the same time unresponsive, calm and damnably composed as a concrete post or a plaster of Paris cast; a petrifaction with a heart of feldspar and without charm of the friendly germ, minus bowels, passion, or a sense of humour. Happily they never reproduce and all of them finally go to Hell"

I KEEP SIX HONEST SERVING MEN,
THEY TAUGHT ME ALL I KNEW;
THEIR NAMES ARE WHAT, AND WHY AND WHEN,
AND HOW, AND WHEN AND WHO.
RUDYARD KIPLING.

CONTENTS FO NEW AMERICAN PARCEL RECEIVED AT STALAG 111A (NO 10)

1. 2 BARS SOAP
2. TIN CORN BEEF OR SPAM
3. PKT OF RAISINS OR PRUNES
4. 80-120 CIGARETTES
5. 2 BARS OF CHOCOLATE OR 1 BAR AND PKT SWEETS OR TIN OF COCOA-CHOCOLATE
6. PKT BISCUITS (12) OR PKT OATMEAL (CEREAL)
7. 1LB OLEO MARGARINE
8. TIN CONDENSED CHEESE
9. SMALL TIN OF JAM
10. SMALL TIN MEAT PATE OR PEANUT BUTTER
11. TIN OF FISH (TUNA) (SARDINE)
12. 1/2LB SUGAR
13. TIN MEAT (IRISH STEW, PORK & BEANS, MEAT & VEG)
14. 1 TIN OF POWDERED MILK
15. 1 TIN OF AMERICAN COFFEE

----------------------------------x-------------------------

SAME VALUE TO US AS THE OTHER AMERICAN NO. 10

CONTENTS OF ARGENTINE BULK ISSUE RECEIVED SPREAD OVER CHRISTMAS
RATION BELOW FOR 10 MEN

1. 10LBS ARGENTINE CHEESE
2. 8 TINS OF JAM
3. 2 TINS OF HONEY
4. 10 TINS OF CORN BEEF OR MUTTON
5. 13 TINS OF IRISH STEW OR STEAK & ONIONS
6. 2 TINS OF SAUSAGES
7. 8 TINS OF CONDENSED MILK
8. 100 MEAT BISCUITS
9. 180 OATMEAL BISCUITS
10. 8 BARS CHOCOLATE (6ozs)
11. 1LB BUCK TEA
12. 4LBS LUMP SUGAR
13. 4 PKTS PEA FLOUR

TWO WEEK PERIOD DEC. 16TH TO DEC 31ST.

THE FOLLOWING LETTER WAS RECEIVED WITH THE LOG

Dear Friend,

After the Canadian and American editions of the War-Time Log, here is a special issue for British prisoners of war. Though its format is somewhat different, its purpose is just the same as the others: to bring you greetings from friends and to facilitate your recording some of your experiences during these eventful years.

Not everyone will want to use this book as a diary. If you are a writer, here is space for a short story. If you are an artist, you may want to cover these pages with sketches or your camp, caricatures of its important personalities. If you are a poet, major or minor, confide your lyrics to these pages. If you feel that circumstances cramp your style in correspondence, you may write here letters to be carried with you on your return. This book may serve to list the most striking concoctions of the camp kitchen, the records of camp sports or a selection of the best jokes cracked in camp. One man suggested using the autograph of one of his companions (plus his fingerprints?) to head each page, followed by free and frank remarks about the man himself. You may write a commentary on such photographs as you may have to mount on the special pages for that purpose with mounting-corners in the pocket of the back cover. This pocket may be used for clippings you want to preserve, or, together with the small envelope on the last page, for authentic souvenirs of life in camp.

Your own ingenuity may suggest to you many other ways of using this book, which comes to you with our greetings and good wishes.

Yours very sincerely,

WAR PRISONERS' AID OF THE YMCA.

IN MEMORIAM

"Skipper"
Allan James Neville Hockley d. 25 May 1944 Oosterschelde, Zeeland, Netherlands
Loving son of Walter James Hockley and Minnie Blanche née Hogan

"Ray"
Raymond George Victor Simpson d. 25 May 1944 Oosterschelde, Zeeland, Netherlands
Loving son of John Ewen Simpson and Edith Mary née Wadlow

"Nick"
Enoch Lovatt d. 15 October 1957 South Shields, Co. Durham, England
Loving son of Enoch Lovatt and Eva née Pratt
Loving husband of Elsie née Banks

"Jim"
James Edward McCutchan d. 19 March 1985 Edmonton, Alberta, Canada
Loving son of
Loving husband of Norma

"Bob"
Robert Francis Lloyd-Davies d. 1 September 1992 Sefton South District, Merseyside, England
Loving son of Robert Lloyd Davies and Elizabeth Ellen née O'Neil
Loving husband of Betty née Keeling

"Bob"
Robert Yewen Gundy d. 2 May 1996 Ranfurly War Veterans Home, Auckland, New Zealand
Loving son of Walter Edward Gundy and Violet Jenny née Milligan
Loving husband of Josephine Mae née Newberry

"Tom"
Raoul Trichon Lyall d. 1 June 1999 Coffs Hospital, late of Repton, NSW, Australia
Loving son of Francis Griffin Lyall and Eileen née Trichon
Loving husband of Janet Winning née Sneedon

"Tommy"
Thomas Duke Glenn d. 16 February 2000 Newcastle-upon-Tyne, Northumberland, England
Loving son of Cecil Thomas Glenn and Eva née Duke
Loving husband of Margaret née O'Mahony

Graves 171 and 172, Yerseke Cemetery;
Allan Hockley and Ray Simpson

www.ingramcontent.com/pod-product-compliance
Ingram Content Group UK Ltd.
Pitfield, Milton Keynes, MK11 3LW, UK
UKHW041953230426
12048UKWH00008B/303